PRAISE FOR *THE WORK*

This book identifies the colossal barriers y
and then expertly weaves in the authors'
from the classroom and academic researo
being exceptional'. It is a practicable collecuon or approaches for those of
us at the chalkface who battle day to day for better outcomes for children
living in poverty. This is a vital read for anybody working in schools providing the reader with a greater understanding of the complexities and
difficulties youngsters living in poverty face and the strategies to overcome them. Living in poverty needs to be the tenth protected
characteristic!

Mark Ayers, acting head teacher, Appleton Academy

Excellence in any context is a judicious mix of high intention, sincere effort
and intelligent execution. This is an excellent book: very well referenced,
analytical, packed with stories and providing a commanding compendium
of practical ideas for the classroom. The section on speaking, reading and
writing is as succinct and authoritative as any teacher could wish for.

The experienced authors assert that 'much of this book has been written
in anger … angered at how unequal our society has become'. They channel their anger skilfully in producing a text to support teachers and leaders
who wish to make a particular difference for 'the forgotten third' in our
schools. It is fifty years since I first entered a Brixton primary classroom – it
is inspiring to read Matt Bromley and Andy Griffith's contemporary, compelling narrative about changing children's lives.

Roy Blatchford, chair of ASCL's *The Forgotten Third*
and author of *The A–Z of Great Classrooms*

This book deepens the understanding of the reasons why the odds are
stacked against the working class in education and provides practical
solutions to make a positive difference for these pupils in their classrooms.
It can be a read-all-at-once book or, more usefully for busy school practi-
tioners, it can be dipped in and out of, to find strategies that have already
been identified as making a difference elsewhere.

Sue Bourgade, head teacher

As schools across the country grapple with the impact of both the cost of
living crisis and deepening social inequality, this important book could not
be more timely. It is an educational call to arms which is full of practical
ideas and solutions to close the poverty-related attainment gap and enable all young people to thrive.

Christine Downie, head teacher, St Luke's High School

The Working Classroom is a thought-provoking and challenging read. It unpicks the ways in which working-class students are disadvantaged by an education system designed without them in mind and looks at some practical ways in which we as a profession could be doing more to improve the life chances of the disadvantaged. We all go into teaching in the hope that we can make a difference but Andy and Matt challenge those ideals by suggesting that unless we change what we are doing we are likely to be simply contributing to an educational regime which continues to fail those who start their learning journey in last place. Doing what we've always done perpetuates a system which is designed by the middle class for the middle class and continues to see the gap between the 'haves' and the 'have nots' widening.

Duncan Jacques CBE, CEO, Exceed Academies Trust

A compelling and important read. The justifiable anger that the authors feel about the inequities of our society and education system fizzes through the book. As they say, 'We need to do more; we need to take affirmative action'. And *The Working Classroom* gives the educator scores of practical and inspiring ideas about what they can do to effect change, with uplifting case studies, planning templates, reflective questions and model lesson plans. This book is well-researched, comprehensive, readable and well-timed. A must-read!

Rachel Macfarlane, Lead Adviser for Underserved Learners, HFL Education and author of *Obstetrics for Schools* and *Unity in Diversity*

A book that feels in touch with reality. Based upon sound research, with absolute relevance to schools in challenging areas that serve a unique community.

Lots of strategies to support working-class pupils in making progress and overcoming obstacles to achieving their true potential. Focus on parental engagement and the importance of the curriculum – key highlights.

Tony McGuinness, head teacher, All Saints Catholic High School, Kirky, Liverpool

The Working Classroom should be essential reading for anyone concerned about the disadvantage gap in schools. It is both sensitive and punchy: sensitive in its framing of the considerable disadvantages for many pupils and punchy in its bold, yet workable, suggestions for addressing these.

Mary Myatt, education writer, speaker and curator of Myatt & Co

This ground-breaking book achieves two vitally important objectives. First, it puts the elephant of social class firmly back in the centre of the room by clearly outlining the many reasons we should pay attention to inequalities of social class in education. Second, it tells the reader what we can do, as teachers and educators, to address those inequalities. In *The Working Classroom,* Bromley and Griffith present bold and innovative plans that recognise and address the long-neglected need for affirmative action if we are to tackle the extensive class discrimination in education.

Professor Diane Reay, University of Cambridge

Bromley and Griffith have produced a masterpiece with *The Working Classroom.* The investigation of injustices in our contemporary world, and how it is skewed against working-class people, has a depressing whiff of familiarity, but to offer practical solutions for educators to start to deliver social justice from within is a stroke of genius from the authors. The balance of championing working-class culture in the classroom against the very real risk of thereby encouraging classism, is beautifully done. Read the book. Then be angry. Then, well, then let's change the world.

Ant Sutcliffe, Associate Director, Higher Horizons, Keele University

This book gives an excellent account of the role that social class plays in schools, the inequalities it causes, and ways that those in the education system can support students in reducing the inequalities they may face.

The book is laid out in easy-to-read sections that are filled with anecdotes, ideas to improve practice and questions to allow for practitioner self-reflection. Whether you are looking to teach your students about social classes, start an extra-curricular club, become a more adaptive educator or enhance your current curriculum, this book contains all the ideas to help level the playing field and mitigate some of the effects of classism faced by your students.

Everybody working in an education setting who wants to make a difference to their students' lives should read this book.

Laura Tonge, Keele Hub Manager, Higher Horizons

This is a book that is on the side of the group of youngsters for whom the traditional classroom and the learning it offers is difficult to understand. Hard-hitting, poignant, methodical and practical, it helps the teacher look through the eyes of the people they teach and see how they could make the way they work enticing for the pupils and more enjoyable for themselves.

Persuasive insights are supported with analysis of research and well structured advice ... a must for every staffroom and teachers who really care.

Mick Waters, educationalist and author

THE
WORKING
CLASSROOM

How to make school work for working-class students

Matt Bromley and Andy Griffith

Crown House Publishing Limited
www.crownhouse.co.uk

First published by

Crown House Publishing
Crown Buildings, Bancyfelin, Carmarthen, Wales, SA33 5ND, UK
www.crownhouse.co.uk

and

Crown House Publishing Company LLC
PO Box 2223, Williston, VT 05495, USA
www.crownhousepublishing.com

British Library Cataloguing-in-Publication Data
A catalogue entry for this book is available
from the British Library.

Print ISBN 978-178583698-5
Mobi ISBN 978-178583702-9
ePub ISBN 978-178583703-6
ePDF ISBN 978-178583704-3

LCCN 2023939999

Printed and bound in the UK by
CPi, Antony Rowe, Chippenham, Wiltshire

FOREWORD

It has been more than a decade since I appeared on Channel 4's fly-on-the-wall documentary *Educating Essex*, but its legacy means I am privileged to be asked to appear on TV news reports and to review colleagues' books. Being a busy school principal means I usually say no to such offers, but when Matt Bromley and Andy Griffith asked me to contribute the foreword to this book, I read an early draft and simply couldn't refuse. It was too important. As you will soon discover for yourselves, Matt and Andy's backgrounds, which are not dissimilar to my own, have been a driving force in its conception. Their passion for improving the lives of young people springs from the page.

The class system in the UK is a trigger for much anger and frustration. I know that I am not unusual in being a teacher from a working-class background. But when I started teaching thirty years ago, I was convinced that I was going to be a lone voice – the maverick teacher who alone believed in what working-class students could achieve. My armour and white horse were both at the ready.

The experience of leading a school during COVID-19 demonstrated the massive class divide that still exists in our society – and the complete lack of insight of many of our political leaders who are blinded by their privilege. Politicians expected schools to move seamlessly to online learning almost overnight. Lord Adonis, for example, was vociferous in telling schools that hadn't moved online that they were failing their communities. The fact that over 600 students at my school, Passmores, didn't have a suitable device or access to Wi-Fi, and that many lived in accommodation where finding a quiet place to learn was difficult, didn't cross his mind. When I explained to my local MP that staff were creating packs with a month's worth of work, which we were posting home with all the resources required to complete it, along with a stamped addressed envelope, you could see the error 404 message flashing across his face.

Class privilege is so ingrained that we are somehow comforted by the fact that most of our MPs sound more like Jacob Rees-Mogg than Angela Rayner. However, our governments would be so much better if they were populated by people who saw their £86,000 annual salary as sufficient motivation to do a good job and not simply as a stepping stone to the higher paid corporate gig that follows.

When you read *The Working Classroom*, you may feel angry, perhaps even powerless. Wanting to make a difference isn't the same as making a difference. Despite millions of pounds and millions of hours being thrown at the attainment gap, it has barely narrowed.

Matt and Andy argue that our 'education system is rigged in favour of the privileged', so you might be forgiven for thinking there is no point in reading a book like this one if inequality is systemic. This is logical only if you ignore the huge societal changes that have taken place over the last three or four decades regarding same-sex marriage and gender identity. Society and its norms can change, but it requires a collective effort.

In September 2023, the National Centre for Social Research published its fortieth annual British Social Attitudes survey, exploring people's social, political and moral attitudes.[1] What was clear from the results was that the concept of social class has far from disappeared. In fact, the report's authors argue that the propensity to identify as middle class or working class is much the same now as forty years ago. What's more, people who identify as working class are more inclined than ever to accept the view that it is very difficult, if not impossible, to move between classes.

The inequality of opportunity that is inherent in our class system remains a driving force for my work as a teacher. The research highlighted by Matt and Andy in this book shows that 50% of people would be defined as working class, so until half of our MPs and business leaders come from working-class backgrounds, there is much work to be done.

The Working Classroom is in three parts. Part I is full of evidence that classism is real, which left me feeling incredibly frustrated. If you find it hard to read too, be reassured that the remainder of the text motivated and reinvigorated me to keep doing what I can. As Matt and Andy explain, their advice is focused on the aspects of our world that we do have influence and control over as educators.

If you are convinced that classism remains an issue in our society and in our schools, then you will also be convinced that we must continue to do all we can to lessen the damage it causes. This book is a good place to start. Take the ideas in it today and start making a real difference tomorrow.

Vic Goddard

Principal, Passmores Academy

---

1   See https://natcen.ac.uk/british-social-attitudes.

ACKNOWLEDGEMENTS

MATT

The book you are reading carries two names on its cover: those of the authors. But you would not be holding this text were it not for the countless other people who have helped to inspire us and shape our thinking, and who have supported us along the way, including by providing a soft landing for my head as it hurtled towards the wall in frustration! This list is by no means exhaustive, but I would like to think that all the people in my life – whether in a personal or professional capacity – already know what they mean to me and know that I am grateful for all they do.

Firstly, I would like to thank my co-author, Andy Griffith, without whom this book would not exist. We met several years ago in South London at the end of a long day's training and, over a pint (which Andy still reminds me I owe him), discovered a shared history and a shared passion. It was Andy who approached me to write a book with him and, being a control freak, I was not without reservations. But his generosity throughout the process – not to mention his forbearance with my ruthless editing of his words – have made the journey both enjoyable and enlightening. Thanks too to the team at Crown House Publishing – David, Karen, Beverley, Emma and Tom, to name but a few – for their endless encouragement and excellent editing.

Secondly, I would like to thank all the people whose ideas have influenced my thinking in this book – I cite them throughout the text so won't do so again here. We have sought to wear our learning lightly but be in no doubt that we have read a lot of books, spoken to countless colleagues and bent the ear of many a big thinker! I would also like to thank all the people I work with in schools and colleges up and down the land every week. They inspire me and, more importantly, humour me when I test new ideas and strategies in their institutions. You are superheroes, every one.

Finally, though in truth my first *and* final thought, my family. I owe it all to my mum and dad. As you will discover in these pages, my family were not materially rich, but I was raised in a home rich in what really matters: love. Talking of love, I could not do what I do without the daily love and support of my soulmate, Kimberley, and our children, Matilda, Amelia and Harriet. As Sophocles said, 'One word frees us of all the weight and pain of life: that word is love.'

ANDY

I'd like to acknowledge and thank the following people who have supported me with ideas, resources and suggestions:

Mark Ayres, Chris Bayes, Craig Billington, Brian Bradley, Carel Buxton, David Buxton, Paul Dearing, Alex Dunedin, Dr Maureen Farrell, Anna Griffith, Clair Griffith, Joe Griffith, Victoria Hewitt, Duncan Jacques, Laura Johnson, Sarah Lamb, Claire Lamontagne, Francis Lawell, Dr Lucy Maynard, Tony McGuinness, Dr Sandra Mornington-Abrathat, Chris Nolan, Christina Owen, Paul Quinn, Tim Roe, Andy Ryan, Richard Seymour, Dr Peter Shukie, Julian Stevens, Dr Kaz Stuart, Ant Sutcliffe, Dan Sutcliffe, Jayne Sweeney, Joe Toko, Gina Tonic, Gaynor Walker, Professor John West-Burnham, David Williams, Hannah Williams and Matt Wood.

Matt, you've been brilliant to work with and I appreciate all of your support.

CONTENTS

INTRODUCTION

WHY SHOULD YOU READ THIS BOOK?

To answer this question, let's pose another: why do you work in education? And don't say it is for the money. Sure, we all need to earn a crust to cover the mortgage and feed the children, but let's be honest: there are easier ways of paying the bills than working in a school. So, why don't you do one of those easier things? Why did you decide to go into teaching? What is your purpose? Your raison d'être?

If, like us, you decided to enter the teaching profession – or work in another role in the education sector – to 'make a difference', then what difference did you hope to make, and why was that important to you? More pointedly, perhaps, do you feel you *have* made a difference?

We will share our personal stories with you shortly and explain our raisons d'être, but, for now, let's assume that all of us went into teaching to help change lives. For some, that might have been by equipping students with a love of your subject as well as good qualification outcomes. For others, it might have been to help the least fortunate in society – the most disadvantaged and vulnerable – to have a fair chance and to ensure that a child's birth doesn't become their destiny.

In whatever way you intended to change lives, has it worked? Do you feel a sense of achievement? There can be no greater feeling, professionally speaking, than knowing you have helped a young person to fulfil their potential and leave school more able to compete and succeed in life than when they started school.

We have experienced this feeling several times in our careers, and it is what continues to drive us now. We both come from working-class backgrounds and were economically disadvantaged as children. That is why our purpose in writing this book has a very personal resonance. It is also why, predominantly, we support schools in deprived areas and help disadvantaged students.

But we also feel certain that we could have done more to help working-class students like us to succeed in school and then in life. Furthermore, we feel that more action is needed now than was the case when we were at school because disadvantage and the causes of disadvantage have got much worse since 'our day'. Far from 'levelling up', successive UK governments since 2010 have made the gaps between rich and poor, privileged and disadvantaged, wider and therefore social mobility more difficult.

Our intention, then, is to help you make more of a difference more of the time. To achieve this, we will draw on the research evidence, although we don't want the text to be a heavy read. Rather, we want it to be practical and easy to dip into when help and advice are needed most. We will also draw on our own experiences of working in and supporting schools in challenging circumstances, including working directly with working-class students and their parents.

Our main argument is this: working-class students are disadvantaged by the education system, not by accident but by design. As such, those of us who work in the education sector must do something – and urgently – to address the situation. We simply cannot stand by and let the class and wealth divide continue to grow. We cannot continue to live in a society and work in schools where wealth and social status, rather than ability and effort, dictate educational attainment and success in later life. It is immoral and indefensible. It angers us *and* inspires us to do more.

We need to be deliberate in how we design our core curriculum, how we plan and target curriculum interventions, how we design curriculum enhancements, and how we train staff and interact with parents and other stakeholders.

We also argue that, while classism exists in society at large, not just in schools, the UK education system is rigged to fail a third of students. We don't think our society can afford for this to continue; it is a waste of resources, and it perpetuates poverty and social exclusion.

While all of this is somewhat depressing, we firmly believe that education can be a powerful tool for change and that schools can help to create a more equitable society. We can and must do something.

The Working Classroom explores some practical ways that schools can mitigate some of the effects of classism and help working-class students to get a better start in life, so that ability and effort, not where you are born and how much money you inherit, dictate success in school and in later life.

WHY HAVE WE WRITTEN THIS BOOK?

We both have very personal reasons for wanting to write this book. Our stories are what drive us, and our histories are what brought us together with a common purpose, not just to say something but to do something.

We would like to start by sharing those stories with you, not as some self-indulgent act of naval gazing, but as a way to explain why the subject matters so much to us, and as a means of exploring some of the issues we intend to address. We discuss the power of story in Lesson 3, so it seems apt to start by telling our own.

MATT'S STORY

I was born and brought up in a depressed northern town in the shadow of dark satanic mills and disappointment. My family and I lived in a terraced house in a row which stuck out from the valley side like needles on a hedgehog's back. And life was just as spiky.

My childhood, although happy, was one of hand-me-downs and making do. And my primary school – in the days before 'serious weaknesses' and 'special measures' had become the de facto vocabulary of educational failure – was what we used to call 'shit'.

When I wasn't pretending to paint while surreptitiously sneaking a peak at the page 3 model on the newsprint laid out to protect the tables, I sat cross-legged on a threadbare carpet while the teacher strummed his guitar and sang 1960s songs. (And yes, dear reader, he closed his eyes when he hit the chorus.)

As a result, when I transferred schools aged 9, I was unable to construct a sentence. It was only thanks to a determined and dedicated Year 5 teacher who inspired a love of reading that I caught up with my peers.

This story, like all good stories, I suppose, was repeated years later when my Year 9 teacher – an inspirational writer and poet who had lived in Peru and taught me how to bet on horses – recognised and nurtured my talent for writing.

This tale was told once more when my A level English literature teacher – a fierce and frightening man, hump-backed like Richard III, but one of extraordinary talent who ignited my love of Shakespeare – set me on a path to university.

You know how the story goes: I was the first in my family to get to university and lucky enough to be awarded a full grant at a time when the state recognised its duty to educate all, not just those born to privilege. But my grant didn't go far, barely covering course fees and accommodation, so I worked round the clock – stuffing envelopes for a bank and being sworn at on a complaints line – to pay for books and stationery and food and drink. Mainly drink.

On the last day of my first year, I was badly injured playing football and had my right foot set in plaster. I was instructed by A&E to keep my leg elevated and rest for three weeks. Had I followed these instructions, I would be able to walk without pain today, nearly thirty years later. But I had no option: I simply had to work if I was going to afford to return to my studies. Consequently, I walked on crutches to and from the bus stop every day that summer. I took as much overtime as I could get, working seven days a week. And I have lived with the consequences every day since; my foot never healed and it causes constant pain, which is slowly getting worse as arthritis sets in.

POVERTY REMOVES AGENCY

You see, poverty forces people to make tough choices. Actually, that isn't true: poverty removes choice; it denies people agency and opportunity.

Writing in *The Guardian* in June 2022, the food writer and poverty campaigner, Jack Monroe, powerfully describes the consequences of poverty:

> Poverty is exhausting. It requires time, effort, energy, organisation, impetus, an internal calculator, and steely mental fortitude. And should it not kill you, in the end, from starvation or cold or mental ill health, should you scrabble somehow to the sunlit uplands of 'just about managing', I'm sorry to tell you that although your bank balance may be in the black one day, so too will your head.[1]

Monroe goes on to explain how 'years of therapy has alleviated some of [the worst effects of living in poverty, such as panic attacks], some of the time, but [their] physical and mental health will probably never make a full recovery'.

Monroe now suffers from 'complex post-traumatic stress disorder, arthritis exacerbated by living in cold homes, respiratory difficulties from the damp, complex trauma, an array of mental health issues, a hoarding problem, and a slow burning addiction brought to an almost fatal head

---

1   J. Monroe, Poverty Leaves Scars for Life – I'm Still Scared of Strangers at the Door and Bills Through the Letterbox, *The Guardian* (16 June 2022). Available at: https://www.theguardian.com/commentisfree/2022/jun/16/poverty-scars-life-impact-cost-of-living-crisis-felt-for-years.

last year'. However, they argue that their story is by no means unique or exceptional because 'short-term exposure to and experience of poverty – whether fuel poverty, food poverty, period poverty, or the root cause of all of them, the insufficient resources with which to meet your most fundamental human needs – has long-term and disproportionate effects for years to come'.

Childhood exposure to poverty falls under the umbrella of adverse childhood experiences (ACEs), which, according to Monroe, are 'on a par with domestic abuse, childhood sexual assault, [the] loss of a parent, parental incarceration, violence and neglect' and increase the risk of trauma later in life, both mentally and physically.

In fact, exposure to ACEs leads to less favourable health outcomes, a negative impact on general well-being, increased likelihood of risky or criminal behaviours, poor educational and academic outcomes and financial difficulties. We know that children who experience food insecurity, even short term, are more likely to fall ill and need hospital admission and have a slower recovery rate.

ACCESS DENIED

Poverty led to me making tough choices that I live with even now. But I know I was lucky; as well as state-funded support that enabled me to go to university, I had good teachers and loving, supportive parents who provided me with a safe and happy home. But it could easily have been so different. As I mentioned, I was the first in my family to go to university – and that was not uncommon in the mid-1990s because access to higher education had begun to widen. I was, as I say, lucky.

Danny Dorling, professor of human geography at the University of Sheffield, says the fact that the majority of additional places at universities were taken up by children living in the poorer half of British neighbourhoods 'may well be seen … as the greatest positive social achievement of the 1997–2010 government' and that it was achieved 'not at the expense of upper- and middle-class children [but because] the education system as a whole expanded [and there were] massive increases in funding per child in state secondary schools'.[2]

Dorling says the lessons of the pre-2010 era are clear: 'Spend more per child and they will gain better GCSE results, they will then go on to attend university in greater numbers.' There are two other factors: firstly, the introduction of the Education Maintenance Allowance (EMA) 'which

---

2   D. Dorling, *Fair Play: A Daniel Dorling Reader on Social Justice* (Bristol: Policy Press, 2012), p. 180.

enabled many young people from poorer areas to be able to afford to stay on at school' and, secondly, government funding of university places, which is 'the ultimate determinant of what young people's chances are'.[3]

Sadly, these improvements in access to higher education for working-class children have not been sustained. Writing in 2012, Dorling said progress would likely be 'reversed following the Comprehensive Spending Review of October 2010'. He was right: EMA was scrapped in 2010 and the spending review cut up to 75% of government funding in higher education. Even before these cuts – made under the auspices of 'austerity' – 'access to good schools, universities and jobs remained far more socially determined by class and place of birth in Britain, than in almost any other affluent nation'.[4]

THE FEAR OF BEING DIFFERENT

When I went to university, for the first time in my life, I found myself living and socialising with people from vastly different social circles. And – despite the fact that my fellow freshers' higher social status, wealth and expensive education had led them to the same university and that I went on to gain a better degree than many of them – they looked down on and ridiculed my hometown, my accent, and my lack of what we might now call 'cultural capital'. They travelled to lectures in cars bought for them by their parents; I walked or cycled on a second-hand bike I had repaired and repainted. They never had to worry about where their next meal was coming from and never had to say no to a night out or stay in halls while those around them partied, because to go out would have meant being unable to afford the books that were essential reading for their courses.

When I left university, having worked on the student newspaper as a sports and features writer – a post I had to fight hard to get because I didn't have the right school tie – I pursued my chosen career in journalism on my hometown paper. Or, rather, I tried to. Internships were awarded to those whose father knew the editor or proprietor. Although, through sheer tenacity and – more crucially – offering my services for free, I was able to get freelance gigs, there was no hope of a salaried job without a postgraduate qualification in journalism – a requirement of joining the National Union of Journalists.

With student debts from my undergraduate course and no possibility of working for free forever, I had no choice but to find paid alternative employment. For months, I tried to balance the two: working nine to five

---

3   Dorling, *Fair Play*, p. 180.
4   Dorling, *Fair Play*, p. 72.

for a telecoms company and then walking to the newsroom to work evenings for free. But, eventually, paid work had to take precedence and the prospect of overtime and paying off my debts won the day. And, thus, my dreams of a career in journalism slowly died. Not because I lacked the talent, but because I didn't have the money and 'secret knowledge' needed to get a foot in the door.

Telecoms wasn't so class driven, thankfully, and I was lucky to get in at the time that mobile phones were becoming mainstream. I quickly proved my worth and climbed the corporate ladder to senior management. The pay was good, as was the lifestyle; I was in my mid-twenties, working hard and playing harder. All seemed right with the world. But it wasn't. Cue existential crisis.

One day, at the dawn of the millennium, I woke up and realised I needed a greater purpose in life. So, it was a brand-new millennium and a new-brand me – I was going to be a teacher and help build the future. Sadly, my epiphany was short-lived. Soon after starting my self-funded PGCE, my dreams of 'O Captain! My Captain!' fell apart at the seams.

It didn't help that I went from earning a decent salary to paying for the privilege of teaching. I had saved enough money in the years prior to scrape through the course, but it was tough living like a student again. Nor did it help that I was several years older than most of my fellow trainees. But the worst of it was my first school placement, and therefore my first foray into the classroom. To be fair, I was warned. My course tutor told me the university had considered taking the school off its books because it was in special measures and they'd had complaints, but because I was older and had leadership experience, they thought I would be able to cope.

The school had been in special measures for a while by the time I arrived, and staff turnover was high. As a result, many post-16 classes were cancelled and other classes were combined, with students often left to watch television in the canteen. Hence, at the end of my first week, my school-based mentor and head of department (who also quit before the end of my placement), said she thought I was ready to go solo rather than waste my time observing her or team-teaching with more seasoned colleagues. And so I found myself, two weeks into my 'training' and after just one week in a school, teaching a full timetable without any help or support.

Student behaviour was 'challenging'. The canteen was like a scene from *Fight Club*. Staff cars were routinely vandalised, and the fire alarm sounded fifteen times a day – not because some cheeky young scamp had smashed the glass to get out of class but because some cheeky young arsonist had set fire to the building. You might say my early teaching experience was a baptism of fire.

It didn't help my mood when winter set in and the nights grew long and dark. Snow fell early and deep that year, meaning weeks of indoor play. All of which made me think of quitting teaching every single day. Pathetic fallacy or just pathetic, I am still not sure.

I remember struggling out of bed at the call of my bedside alarm feeling sick to my stomach, and the lonely commutes home, feeling lost and alone, out of my depth, utterly exhausted. Although I told no one, I deeply regretted my risky change of career and yearned for a return to my cushy corner office and generous expenses account. But I was scared to admit to anyone else that I had got it wrong. And I was still driven by a desire to do what my teachers had done for me: to give disadvantaged students a fair start in life, to reverse society's ills, to mitigate – albeit in some small way – the consequences of poverty and of living in an unequal, unfair society that privileges the privileged and rewards wealth with wealth.

Against all odds, I persevered and survived to the end of my placement and then to the end of my course. My university tutor wrote a glowing report based not, I suspect, on my teaching ability but on the simple fact that I was not dead. The school even offered me a job. Unsurprisingly, I turned them down.

Having passed my initial teacher training year, I got a job in a school in a deprived area of a northern town, and I stayed there for eight happy years, rising from newly qualified teacher to assistant head teacher. I saw in those 'sink estate kids' (not my phrase but one used liberally and insultingly to describe the students I taught) an earlier me reflected back; I saw students set on a path to failure in need of a teacher who could turn disadvantage into advantage. I had found my vocation – and I have never looked back.

I have never considered leaving the profession. Yes, I have changed course – I have moved from teaching to leadership and from leadership to consultancy – but each move I made has been an attempt to do more for disadvantaged children, to increase the size of my classroom and thus the impact of my actions.

This commitment has driven me for over two decades, as a teacher, middle leader, senior leader, head teacher, multi-academy trust director and now school improvement advisor. And this commitment has brought me here to write *The Working Classroom*. I have authored several other books of which I am proud but, to quote the movies, this time it's personal.

And I have found a like-minded co-author in Andy Griffith. To prove it, here is his story.

ANDY'S STORY

I was born in Edmonton, North London, and went to primary school in Tottenham. My real father was a magician: he disappeared when I was 8 years old, and I haven't seen him since. He took out a second mortgage on our family home and gambled it all away. He was working as an insurance agent for a company called Prudential collecting money door to door, as they did in those days, and gambled that away too. I have a memory of him taking me to his office on the day he was sacked from his job; I guess he was trying to use me as a reason for the firm to keep him on. That tells you something of the man's character.

What followed for me, my mum and brother were bailiffs, temporary accommodation, a council flat, a spell in hospital for me with pneumonia and pleurisy, and quite a lot of stress. Well, they do say that moving house is stressful.

Some years later, my mum met a guy who eventually became my stepfather. His name was Emerson Griffith, and he was originally from Barbados in the West Indies. He was part of the Windrush generation. When I went to secondary school, I took my stepdad's surname and, after a few years, began calling him 'dad'. He had a lot of good qualities and valued education. He initially started as a welder for British Oxygen before becoming a lorry driver for the Post Office (or GPO as it was then known). Outside of work, he was a football official. In the 1980s, he became the first Black linesman in the football league and refereed for many years at semi-professional level.

When I wasn't playing football, I went to his games and watched from the stands. We became close, and I guess learning about his life really opened my eyes to how racist people could be. All the way through his life, Emerson had some significant mental health issues to contend with and he also had a problem with gambling. What are the odds on that! When he retired from his job at the GPO, he gambled away his lump sum of over £25,000 in the space of about six months and then proceeded to blame the world and his wife, my mum, for his errors. It is a long story, but he ended up kicking my mum out of the house, and a few months later setting fire to it as a protest against a court ruling, consequently invalidating much of the insurance.

Anyway, I would rather talk about my mum. All through my childhood, my mum was a constant source of encouragement and supported every interest I had. Despite the fact there wasn't much money, she would always bring home magazines such as *Look and Learn* and *World of Wonder*, take us to the local library, and on trips to museums and famous London land-marks, always on the bus or train as we didn't have a car.

My mum, like many working-class children of her generation, had to leave school at 15 before she could take O levels. I have no doubt she would have excelled. As testament, she has got a book at home that she was awarded for winning the prize as the best historian in Peckham School for Girls. Mum had to get paid work in order to support her family. Her mum, my nanny Alice, was disabled and unable to work. She transferred this love of learning, especially history, to her sons; every qualification I have achieved since, I dedicate to her.

IGNITING A SPARK

Every child needs at least one encourager or 'sparker' in their life, some-one who opens up future possibilities and helps them to see what might be possible. Later in the book, we will talk about lucky kids, a metaphor borrowed from early years specialist and author Penny Tassoni.[5] I want to make it clear that, like Matt, I consider myself lucky to have had a mum who read to me, took me places, talked with me and set boundaries for me. But what about kids who don't have someone like that in their lives? Should schools deliberately try to make up for that? My view is, yes, they should.

I went on to a comprehensive secondary school in London where I was pretty well-behaved bar the odd fight here and there. I might have been kicked out of a modern day 'no excuses' school, but I was regarded as an asset: captain of the football team, top sets, high grades and so on, and one of the few students who went on to university.

My school was a true comprehensive: a mix of people from all social back-grounds, religions and races. I had some working-class and some middle-class friends – some whose parents were reasonably wealthy. They are still my friends to this day. We have helped each other over the years, and one friend in particular has helped me through some difficult times. I would be worse off if I had closed myself off from having friends from middle-class backgrounds.

During these years, I also represented my borough, Haringey, at football. Like school, I had to travel to training and matches by bus. This was a gift because I enjoyed travelling and used that time to read. One experience playing for Haringey has really stuck with me. The team went to Holland

5   P. Tassoni, *Reducing Educational Disadvantage: A Strategic Approach in the Early Years* (London: Bloomsbury, 2016).

on a football tour, and I was the only one who didn't go as my family couldn't afford it. All the other lads came back with new kit and shared experiences; I have never felt so left out.

FIRST ENCOUNTERS WITH CLASSISM

It was at Manchester University that I first experienced what I have come to understand as 'classism' – some people treating me as inferior because I was from a working-class household. It is easy to internalise that feeling of being 'less than' because your family cannot pay for branded clothes. I always got my jeans and school trousers from Edmonton market. Even at university, I was still wearing hand-me-down clothes from my cousin – even underwear, and she wasn't even my size! That feeling of being poor never leaves you. Even now, when I have the money to make a major purchase, I still go into a cold sweat of thinking I cannot afford this.

It was at Manchester where I first met people from private school. They seemed to be much more self-confident. It took me over a year to realise that confidence doesn't equate to intelligence. One tutorial stands out for me still. A guy started talking and a bulb lit up in my head. I realised that he wasn't bothered if he was right or wrong – in fact, he was an idiot. Me? I was scared of saying anything that might be incorrect.

Like most working-class students, I had to work while I was at university. Luckily for me, being from London, I could always pick up jobs during the holidays, such as working as a bin man or road-sweeper (I was very good, by the way, and if I had stuck at it, I could have won the prestigious Golden Broom). My jobs didn't affect my studies, but these days working-class students face a very different labour market. They have to work evenings and weekends in bars or supermarkets, which inevitably reduces their study time.

After university, the advantage of coming from a wealthy family really kicks in. Working-class graduates simply don't have the connections and networks to apply for certain career pathways that are dominated by the more affluent. Some do break through into the professions as barristers, doctors and so on, but it is a far tougher path. This lost talent is a massive waste to both the economy and to the well-being of those who could have had a different life path.

When I left university, I went into teaching. From 1989, I taught for twelve years in two different state sector secondary schools. I taught subjects such as economics and business studies to Key Stage 4 and 5 classes; lots of exams and lots of marking. I enjoyed teaching, but I didn't enjoy the restrictive exam syllabuses. It felt like I was training students to pass exams, not to understand the subject. Still, I proved to be pretty good at this. However, with each passing year, my enjoyment of being a teacher 'in the system' went down and down.

In the last few years of my full-time teaching career, I got the break that I was looking for – to work with students on a curriculum of my own design. My school decided to take the opportunity to 'disapply' some students from the national curriculum – that is, to remove certain Year 10 and Year 11 students from lessons such as languages and get them doing something else. These were generally statemented students; many had poor motivation and poor behaviour.

I offered to create a programme for them called Lifeskills, where I taught them for two hours a week over two years. These students learned how to analyse a film, how to revise, how to talk about yourself confidently, how to recognise your own strengths, how to cook at least five different dishes and how to present to an audience. Pedagogically, there wasn't much writing, plenty of discussion and lots of one-to-one work (the students created career portfolios and scrapbooks); nearly all the students gained in terms of confidence, and they gathered a few certificates too.

In 2001, I left full-time teaching and became self-employed. This was during the New Labour years when it felt like there was more money in education. The experience of creating the Lifeskills course was something I wanted more of. Initially, I started training teachers in areas such as careers education and citizenship (I was on the Qualifications and Curriculum Authority (QCA) writing team for citizenship). I created numerous different training courses, and eventually ended up creating a course that thousands of teachers attended called Outstanding Teaching. Its sister course, Embedding Outstanding Teaching, aimed at school leaders, was also very popular. Both have subsequently been turned into modular school programmes involving the video analysis of teachers and strategies for leaders to get the best out of staff.

Being on the training circuit has been an interesting experience. There are lots of talented people out there, but it is surprising that some of those most respected in education are actually snobs. Some have real disdain for working-class people and working-class places. You will have to buy me a pint or two for me to reveal more.

I am now in the autumn of my career. My shampoo is called Back and Shoulders, and it is taking me longer and longer to wash my face every morning. I am now working in places like Kirkby in Merseyside, Bradford in Yorkshire, Newham in London and Fleetwood in Lancashire. I seriously love my working life. I work with great colleagues who are motivated by social justice every day. I decided a few years ago to only work in certain places and only with certain people. I have made a commitment to these communities. In each case, I am just an extra resource, a friend of the school. The core work is done by the leaders, teachers and support staff, but I hope my training and coaching with adults and young people adds something too.

There are some great individuals working in and across schools. They are motivated by fairness, justice and compassion. They are continually trying to close gaps and take daily action to support disadvantaged families. To be around them is inspiring – and you won't get that from most other career paths.

If you are at all motivated by issues such as fairness and justice, I hope you get something from this book. I am sure you are already helping many people in your career, but my hope is that this book will influence you to help even more. Maybe you are a bit worn down by the system or the school you are in? In that case, I hope it will reinvigorate you for a few more years.

Although Matt and I were both touched by poverty in our early lives, we have written *The Working Classroom* to inspire everyone involved in education and from every social background. Indeed, for us, it is even more impressive when education professionals from middle-class backgrounds involve themselves in this work. In many ways, they 'get it' much more than some working-class people who have, by their own reckoning, progressed into being middle class and consider this was purely through their own merits.

OTHER STORIES

Those are our stories, but there are other stories too. This book is peppered with the stories of individuals we have met along the way. We have changed some of their names to protect their anonymity, but their accounts are real.

These 'other stories' are more important than ours because they represent some of the people whom this book hopes to support. There will be tales of struggle, success, enlightenment and more.

HOW HAVE WE WRITTEN THIS BOOK?

As we have mentioned, we firmly believe the education system is rigged in favour of the privileged. Working-class students are disadvantaged from day one: all too often their birth is their destiny; they start at a disadvantage and end at a disadvantage.

The only way to truly fix inequality is, of course, by reducing inequality. As Imran Tahir, a research economist at the Institute for Fiscal Studies (IFS), says: 'Instead of being an engine for social mobility, the UK's education system allows inequalities at home to turn into differences in school achievement. This means that all too often, today's education inequalities become tomorrow's income inequalities.'[6]

While we acknowledge that, because inequality is systemic, to truly tackle it society at large must change, we will focus on actions that school leaders and teachers can take to help working-class students compete equitably at school and in later life.

We will focus on three strands of support that schools can offer to help counter the classism that is inherent in the education system:

---

6   I. Tahir, The UK Education System Preserves Inequality, *Institute for Fiscal Studies* (13 September 2022). Available at: https://ifs.org.uk/inequality/the-uk-education-system-preserves-inequality.

EQUALITY, EQUITY AND EXTENSION

1   Equality through the core curriculum and extra-curricular activities.

2   Equity through curriculum adaptations and interventions.

3   Extension through curriculum extras and enhancements.

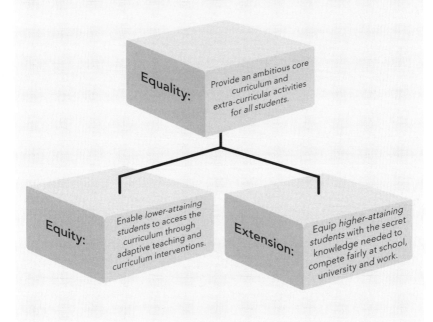

1. EQUALITY THROUGH THE CORE CURRICULUM AND EXTRA-CURRICULAR ACTIVITIES

The core curriculum is made up of the programmes of study that all students are taught, usually in subject disciplines via timetabled lessons. They are traditionally academic in nature and include, as a minimum, the foundation subjects stipulated in the national curriculum.

Extra-curricular activities, meanwhile, are the activities that some students participate in outside of the academic timetable. These are typically voluntary and may include sports, the arts, music or theatre groups, community service projects and so on. Participation in extra-curricular activities provides students with opportunities to develop new skills, make new friends and build self-confidence; they can also help students to become well-rounded individuals and widen their experiences and knowledge of the world. We regard the purpose of extra-curricular activities as being threefold: meeting new people, exploring new places and doing new things.

Together, the core curriculum and extra-curricular activities are the first strand of support we can use to counter classism in education because when we get these things right all students benefit, and there is less need for additional interventions and support later on. As they (whoever 'they' may be) are wont to say, a rising tide lifts all ships.

2. EQUITY THROUGH CURRICULUM ADAPTATIONS AND INTERVENTIONS

Curriculum adaptations and interventions are inclusive teaching approaches and additional support strategies, including but not limited to one-to-one and small group tuition, designed to help lower-attaining working-class students access the same experiences as their peers by converting the causes of disadvantage into tangible classroom consequences, so these barriers may be overcome. The most effective curriculum interventions are short-term, intensive, tailored and focused.

Curriculum adaptations and interventions are the second strand of support because, while a rising tide may indeed lift all ships, some students' survival at sea is rigged because they sail boats full of holes. Interventions, when thoughtfully and strategically designed, can plug the gaps in the hulls of these vessels.

3. EXTENSION THROUGH CURRICULUM EXTRAS AND ENHANCEMENTS

Curriculum enhancements are carefully designed enrichment activities specifically targeted at high-attaining working-class students. They provide long-term opportunities for them to acquire the secret knowledge and skills otherwise denied them because of their position in society, as well as to develop behaviours, attitudes and values that allow them to compete with their more advantaged peers.

This is the third strand of support because, while a rising tide lifts all ships and interventions can plug the holes in the hulls of some students' vessels, others are left frantically swimming against the tide because they didn't inherit a boat at birth. Curriculum enhancements provide the life raft needed to survive a storm.

In Part II, we will explore each of these three strands in detail. In Part III, we will offer some lessons that you can teach your students in order to turn the theory into practice. But first, in Part I, we want to examine the ways in which secondary schools are classist.

ICONS USED THROUGHOUT THE BOOK

At the start of each chapter, we will pose key questions which we will attempt to answer in the pages that follow. You can use these questions to provoke discussions in your school.

 **IDEAS**

We want this book to be practical, to arm you with the tools you need to make a genuine difference to the working-class students in your charge.

Accordingly, wherever you see the 'ideas' icon, you'll find a list of suggestions you can put into immediate practice in your school.

 KEY QUESTIONS

At the start of each chapter, we will pose key questions which we will attempt to answer in the pages that follow. You can use these questions to provoke discussions in your school.

 REFLECTIVE QUESTIONS

In writing this book, we don't just want to *say* something, we want to *do* something. We want *The Working Classroom* to lead to real change. Wherever you see this icon, you'll find some self-evaluative questions to help you assess your current practices and identify your next steps.

 STORY

As we say above, this book will be full of stories. Look for this icon to read case studies and reflections from all those people who've inspired us or helped us write this book.

 TEMPLATE

Another way in which we want this book to be practical is by providing you with planning templates to help you design and deliver effective interventions and enhancements. We provide more templates on our website at www.theworkingclassroom.co.uk.

PART I

WHY ISN'T SECONDARY SCHOOL WORKING FOR WORKING-CLASS STUDENTS?

CHAPTER I

WHO ARE THE WORKING CLASS AND WHY DO THEY UNDERACHIEVE?

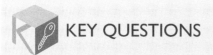

KEY QUESTIONS

In this chapter we will answer the following questions:

- How is the working class defined, and what are the causes of their educational disadvantage?

- What is classism, and how does it contribute to working-class underachievement?

- Why is reducing the effects of classism in all our best interests?

WHO ARE THE WORKING CLASS?

There are many different constructions of class, and many schemas and labels exist to determine who falls into which social category.

For thousands of years, people have been ranked or divided into their place in society – for example, religions produced rankings not dissimilar to social classes. Each person's place within the hierarchy was due to the will of God. Individuals were expected to defer to those above them and command those under them. The English poet Robert Southey wrote: 'That appointed chain, / Which when in just cohesion it unites / Order to order, rank to rank, / In mutual benefit'.[1]

Meanwhile, revolutionaries like Thomas Paine, not to mention Karl Marx, saw society in dichotomous terms: two classes, us and them. Paine wrote:

---

1   R. Southey, *The Complete Poetical Works of Robert Southey* (New York: D. Appleton & Company, 1851), p. 212.

'there are two distinct classes of men in the nation, those who pay taxes, and those who receive and live upon the taxes'.[2] For Marx, it was the bourgeoisie and the proletariat.

The two most common social classifications of people today are a tripartite system of upper, middle and lower classes, and a system of five categories based on occupation from A to E. Let's explore the latter.

Sociologists tend to classify people according to five categories (one of which is subdivided): A, B, C1, C2, D and E. Indeed, this is the system used every ten years for UK Census data, which defines 16–64-year-olds based on employment status, qualification, tenure and whether they work full-time or part-time.[3] ABC1 and C2DE are often used as shorthand to refer to the middle classes and working classes respectively.

In 2013, the BBC's Great British Class Calculator divided society into seven categories: elite (6%), established middle class (25%), technical middle class (6%), new affluent workers (15%), traditional working class (14%), emergent service workers (19%) and the precariat (15%).[4] The survey rejected the usual occupational labels that can indicate a person's social position. Instead, the authors placed a much greater emphasis on social capital – the occupations of your social acquaintances or network.

Even more confusingly, your social class can be affective. People can define themselves as working class if they *feel* working class, even if they are in occupations that sociologists would describe as middle class. Katie Beswick, in a paper entitled, 'Feeling Working Class: Affective Class Identification and its Implications for Overcoming Inequality', says that 'care and nuance in our methods for understanding class and labelling class inequality [are] important'.[5]

We have turned to Professor Danny Dorling for some help in defining the working-class students we seek to assist. In 2013, he said: 'Two statistics will broadly suffice to work out what class you are in: your household income and your family wealth. Often your postcode can reveal a great deal about these.'[6]

2   T. Paine, Letter Addressed to the Addressers, on the Late Proclamation (London: H. D. Symonds and T. C. Rickman, 1792). Available at: https://www.gutenberg.org/files/31270/31270-h/31270-h.htm.

3   See https://www.ons.gov.uk/methodology/classificationsandstandards/otherclassifications/thenationalstatisticssocioeconomicclassificationnssecrebasedonsoc2010.

4   P. Kerley, What is Your 21st Century Social Class?, BBC Magazine (7 December 2015). Available at: https://www.bbc.co.uk/news/magazine-34766169.

5   K. Beswick, Feeling Working Class: Affective Class Identification and its Implications for Overcoming Inequality, Studies in Theatre and Performance, 40 (2020), 265–274 at 265.

6   D. Dorling, How Social Mobility Got Stuck, New Statesman (16 May 2013). Available at: https://www.newstatesman.com/business/economics/2013/05/how-social-mobility-got-stuck.

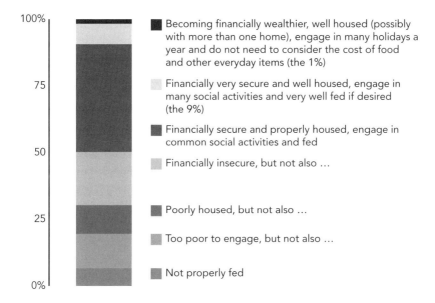

Social divisions of poverty and wealth among
people in Britain by status (2013)

In this book, we will define the working class as anyone who is from a household in the last four categories in the graph above. This roughly corresponds to 50% of the population, which loosely maps to the social class category of C2DE. We feel that this description of social class better enables us to focus on a person's current economic circumstances.

Note: this definition may make you, the reader, feel that you aren't part of the working class. However, like us, you could have working-class origins that make you sympathetic to the issues of underachievement and disaffection. Or your origins might be from a social class such as A or B, but you live by a value system that makes you care about unfairness in society. Or you could be someone reading this who right now is worried about where the next meal or rent payment is coming from. You are all welcome to come on this journey with us.

Now that we have shared our definition of working class, let's move on and explore the notion of class inequality.

WHY ISN'T SECONDARY SCHOOL WORKING?

Class inequality relates to injustices throughout society where people from the so-called 'lower classes' are discriminated against. This leads to underachievement and under-representation. Class inequality is intersectional; its impact is entwined with other social injustices such as racism and sexism. For example, the class pay gap is worse for women, ethnic minorities and people with disabilities. The Labour Force Survey found that women from working-class backgrounds earn on average £19,000 a year less in elite occupations than men from privileged backgrounds. The figure is even higher for non-white women.[7]

Statistics show us that working-class people are less likely to have a degree, go to a Russell Group institution, work in professional employment or be an academic compared to those from more elite backgrounds. For their book, *The Class Ceiling: Why It Pays to Be Privileged*, Sam Friedman and Daniel Laurison conducted almost 200 interviews across a range of elite occupations. Their conclusion: working-class employees not only find it much harder to gain access to these careers, but once there, they fail to progress as fast as their more privileged peers, earning, on average, 16% less.[8]

Evidence of working-class underachievement is vast, and we will only scratch the surface in this book, but let's start with underachievement in the education system itself before we turn to other areas, such as the workplace.

EDUCATIONAL UNDERACHIEVEMENT

Working-class students (particularly boys) are among the lowest performers in our schools, and the link between household income and attainment is multiracial. If you are a high-ability student from a low social class, you aren't going to do as well in school and in later life as a low-ability student from a high social class. To put it another way, it is social class and wealth – not ability – that define a student's educational outcomes and their future life chances.

---

7   See S. Friedman and D. Laurison, The Class Pay Gap: Why It Pays to Be Privileged, *The Guardian* (7 February 2019). Available at: https://www.theguardian.com/society/2019/feb/07/the-class-pay-gap-why-it-pays-to-be-privileged.

8   S. Friedman and D. Laurison, *The Class Ceiling: Why It Pays to Be Privileged* (Bristol: Policy Press, 2019).

For proof of this, look at the recent research carried out for the IFS entitled the Deaton Review of Inequalities.[9] The review concludes that disadvantaged students: 'start school behind their better-off peers, and the education system isn't succeeding in closing these gaps. Educational inequalities result in substantial differences in life chances, leaving millions disadvantaged throughout their lifetime.' The report finds that:

those who have not been successful at school are left behind by an education system that doesn't offer the right opportunities for further education.

It finds inequalities, such as the disadvantage gap at GCSE, have barely changed over the last twenty years and are likely to increase following the COVID-19 pandemic, which looks to have hit the attainment of poorer primary school children twice as hard as their peers'.

Key findings from the report show that today's education inequalities are tomorrow's income inequalities:

- Inequalities by family background emerge well before school starts. Just *57% of English pupils eligible for free school meals reached a good level of development at the end of Reception in 2019*, compared with 74% of their better-off peers. These inequalities persist throughout primary school. [Whether or not you regard eligibility for free school meals as a suitable proxy for being economically disadvantaged or not, these children are all from working-class households.]

- Children from disadvantaged backgrounds also make slower progress through secondary school. Fewer than half of disadvantaged children reach expected levels of attainment at the end of primary school, versus nearly 70% of their better-off peers. And of those who do achieve at the expected level, *just 40% of disadvantaged pupils go on to earn good GCSEs in English and maths versus 60% of the better-off students.*

- The relationship between family background and attainment isn't limited to the poorest pupils: *at every step up the family income distribution, educational performance improves.* For example, while just over 10% of young people in middle-earning families (and fewer than 5% of those in the poorest families) earned at least one A or A* grade at GCSE, over a third of pupils from the richest tenth of families earned at least one top grade.

- Ten years after GCSEs, *over 70% of those who went to private school have graduated from university* compared with just under

9   See https://ifs.org.uk/inequality.

half of those from the richest fifth of families at state schools and *fewer than 20% of those from the poorest fifth of families.*[10]

CAREER UNDERACHIEVEMENT

The Deaton Review also highlighted that:

educational inequalities translate into large future earnings differences. By the age of 40, the average UK employee with a degree earns twice as much as someone qualified to GCSE level or below. In part, this reflects very slow earnings growth for the low-educated: *the most common annual salary for 45- to 50-year-olds with at most GCSEs is between £15,000 and £20,000,* which is exactly the same as for 25- to 30-year-olds with these qualifications.[11]

Despite only 7% of students going to private schools, this cohort are disproportionately overrepresented in many professions. These findings were presented in *Elitist Britain 2019*, a report by the Sutton Trust and Social Mobility Commission.[12] The report charts the educational backgrounds of leading figures across nine areas: politics, business, the media, Whitehall, public bodies, public servants, local government, the creative industries and sport.

In a press release, the Social Mobility Commission states that 'power rests with a narrow section of the population – the 7% who attend private schools and 1% who graduate from Oxford and Cambridge. The report reveals a "pipeline" from fee-paying schools through to Oxbridge and into top jobs.' Private school alumni dominate many public bodies such as senior judges (65%) and civil service permanent secretaries (59%). In politics, at the time of writing, 57% of those currently sitting in the House of Lords and 29% of MPs in the House of Commons were privately educated.

---

10   C. Farquharson, S. McNally and I. Tahir, Lack of Progress on Closing Educational Inequalities Disadvantaging Millions Throughout Life, *Institute for Fiscal Studies* [press release] (16 August 2022) (original emphasis). Available at: https://ifs.org.uk/inequality/press-release/lack-of-progress-on-closing-educational-inequalities-disadvantaging-millions-throughout-life.

11   Farquharson et al., Lack of Progress on Closing Educational Inequalities (original emphasis).

12   Social Mobility Commission, *Elitist Britain 2019: The Educational Backgrounds of Britain's Leading People* (24 June 2019). Available at: https://www.gov.uk/government/publications/elitist-britain-2019/elitist-britain-2019-the-educational-backgrounds-of-britains-leading-people.

The media also has some of the highest proportions of privately educated people of any employment sector. 'Of the 100 most influential news editors and broadcasters, 43% went to fee-paying schools. Similarly, 44% of newspaper columnists were privately educated, with a third – 33% – attending both an independent school and Oxbridge.'

In the TV, film and music industries, 'a substantial number – 38% – attended independent schools with our bestselling pop stars at 30% and top actors at 44%'.

In sport, '37% of international rugby players and 43% of England's cricket team' went to private schools.

Across the thirty-seven categories of the nine broad areas surveyed in the report, it was only among men and women footballers that the privately educated were under-represented.[13]

Your social background helps you in almost every sector of employment. According to the Office for National Statistics, only 10% of those from working-class backgrounds reach Britain's higher managerial, professional or cultural occupations. You are seventeen times more likely to go into law if your parents are lawyers, while the children of those in film and television are twelve times more likely to enter these fields.[14]

One reason for this is unpaid internships. The Sutton Trust report, *Pay As You Go?* found that 'the highest proportions of unpaid internships were in retail (89%), the arts (86%) and the media (83%)',[15] meaning they can only be afforded by those whose inherited personal wealth (or that of their parents) can fund this. And yet these internships are a gateway into paid employment. Another reason for this is personal connections. Most internships aren't advertised, so awareness of their very existence is dependent on connections and inside knowledge.

---

13   Social Mobility Commission, Elitism in Britain, 2019 [press release] (24 June 2019). Available at: https://www.gov.uk/government/news/elitism-in-britain-2019.

14   See https://www.ons.gov.uk/methodology/classificationsandstandards/ otherclassifications/thenationalstatisticssocioeconomicclassification nssecrebasedonsoc2010.

15   *BBC News*, 'Most' Internships Unpaid in Retailing and the Arts (21 November 2018). Available at: https://www.bbc.co.uk/news/business-46315035. See also: C. Cullinane and R. Montacute, *Pay As You Go? Internship Pay, Quality and Access in the Graduate Jobs Market* (London: Sutton Trust, 2018). Available at: https://www. suttontrust.com/our-research/internships-pay-as-you-go.

WHAT ARE THE CAUSES OF
WORKING-CLASS INEQUALITY?

Who is to blame for working-class underachievement and under-representation? Some argue it is the working class themselves.

Michael B. Katz, writing about American history, argues that socio-economically deprived people are viewed as 'undeserving of sympathy' because they caused their own poverty through 'laziness and immorality' or being 'culturally or mentally deficient'. In other words, poverty is the result of a personal failure. It is caused by the deficiencies of the individual. The notion of the undeserving poor:

> stretches from the late eighteenth century through to the present. Poverty, in this view, results from personal failure and inferiority. The historical record shows this idea in the past to have been scientifically dubious, ethically suspect, politically harmful, and, at its worst, lethal. That is why we should pay close attention to its current resurgence.[16]

The 'individual versus society' argument is also strong in the UK, where we are based.

There is, of course, an endless list of possible causes for working-class underachievement. This would include poor parenting, genetics, decline of pride in being working class, poor teaching, an inappropriate curriculum, undiagnosed special educational needs, low aspirations, low motivation, fear of failure, low impulse control – the list goes on.

Our contention is that, of all these possible causes and any more you wish to cite, we educators must focus on what is within our control and discount causes that arise from dubious evidence.

16   M. B. Katz, *The Undeserving Poor: America's Enduring Confrontation with Poverty* (New York: Oxford University Press, 2013 [1989]), p. 1.

REFLECTIVE QUESTIONS

At this juncture, as well as at various points throughout the book, we would like you to reflect on the following questions:

- What do you consider to be the main causes of working-class underachievement?

- Do your views clash with those of your colleagues?

- What do you suspect your colleagues' views are?

WHY ARE THE WORKING CLASS UNDERVALUED?

Working-class underachievement and under-representation are a long-standing problem. Writing as long ago as 1958, Michael Young argued that students from poorer areas often had to work much harder than upper-class youngsters to get into university.[17] Over sixty years later, this is still the case. At least in the 1970s, 1980s and early 1990s, working-class students were supported by the state in the form of free university education, grants and bus passes, as well as through the benefit system.

Sadly, as we discovered in Matt's story in the Introduction, these improvements in access to higher education for working-class children haven't been sustained. Slowly and steadily, we have seen the removal of free education, grants and free travel passes.

Also note that during this period changes in the economy have left some parts of the UK behind. Fewer people now work in jobs that were thought of as traditional working-class occupations, such as miners, dockers, steel-makers and so on. Those jobs were often dangerous and dirty, but they also gave working-class people a great sense of pride. Workers knew that they were doing something of great economic and symbolic value to the country. The wages derived from those jobs were increased through

---

17   M. Young, *The Rise of the Meritocracy* (New Brunswick, NJ and London: Transaction Publishers, 1994 [1958]).

being part of a strong trade union. People also spent a large percentage of their wages within their community.

As the jobs went, the local income went with it. Many of these left-behind areas are located in the outer-urban neighbourhoods of Northern England and South Wales and in our coastal towns. The money that was drained from these areas has never been replaced. What were once proud communities are now hollowed out; what were once thriving neighbourhoods are now places of misery.

Within all these communities are local heroes who work tirelessly to support others who, without intervention, will literally die. From running food banks and boxing gyms to sports teams and social clubs, local people are being supported by their neighbours in these difficult times but neglected by their elected representatives.

We digress but, as educators, it is important to know some basic history and economics. This should be taught on every teacher training course. Some of our students come from households that feel devalued by society, and some are made to feel ashamed. It is hard not to internalise that narrative.

And inequality is getting worse. Nearly one in three children in the UK (31%) grows up in poverty, and it is on the increase. According to government figures, there were 4.2 million children living in poverty in 2019. During the pandemic, this rose to over five million and is now rising even further due to the cost-of-living crisis.[18]

So, what, if anything, can be done to help? Commenting on the IFS Deaton Review we cited earlier, the former Department for Education advisor Sam Freedman has said that 'Politicians, from all parties, love the idea that education is the answer to inequality,'[19] but we can only truly tackle inequality by providing financial support to those who need it.

We agree with Freedman, but we are also of the view that we can take some action within the current system before or alongside the systemic changes that desperately need to happen. We simply cannot afford to wait for society to change. To wit: upcoming chapters in this book will consider how we can redesign the core curriculum and extra-curricular activities, utilise adaptive teaching approaches, design and deliver curriculum interventions, and develop innovative curriculum enhancements which make a difference.

---

18 See https://cpag.org.uk/child-poverty/child-poverty-facts-and-figures and Children's Commissioner, Fact Checking Claims About Child Poverty (22 June 2020). Available at: https://www.childrenscommissioner.gov.uk/2020/06/22/fact-checking-claims-about-child-poverty.

19 S. Freedman, The Truth Is That Schools Do Little to Reduce Inequality, Financial Times (22 August 2022). Available at: https://www.ft.com/content/da6ba133-a2ec-40f3-8f81-260c582cb22e.

The problem of working-class underachievement is too big for us to tackle alone. But just because the causes are societal and systemic, and just because the challenge is vast, it doesn't mean that as educators we shouldn't try to do more to help, albeit in a small way.

There are lots of matters outside our control, but by zooming in on one possible cause of working-class underachievement we might make our schools more equitable places. In this book, we will focus on classism.

WHAT IS CLASSISM?

Classism or class discrimination is bias, discrimination, prejudice or oppression directed towards a person or group of people based on social class or socio-economic status. This form of discrimination isn't covered by the Equality Act 2010, which provides employees with protection against discrimination and harassment in respect of nine protected characteristics, including sex, race and disability.[20] It is the forgotten prejudice.

Despite class discrimination being unprotected by law, research shows that 'a staggering 67% of Brits think social class is an issue for people when it comes to securing a job; with one in three (29.3%) feeling discriminated against during their job search because of their class'.[21]

According to the Social Mobility Commission's 2019 poll, 77% of people feel there is a large gap between the social classes in Britain today.[22] However, there are no provisions for class or socio-economic status despite 60% of the British population identifying as working class. It is therefore technically legal to discriminate against candidates due to their accent or home address, and for individuals to perpetuate negative stereotypes of working-class people with disparaging and offensive comments.

Earlier, we argued that the system fails working-class students by design rather than by accident. You may be dubious. You may think that everyone has our best interests at heart and that no one would want to fail working-class students. But you would be wrong. Just as some acts of racism are

---

20   See https://www.legislation.gov.uk/ukpga/2010/15/contents.
21   CV Library, Brits Believe Class Is an Issue When Securing a New Job (28 January 2020). Available at: https://www.cv-library.co.uk/recruitment-insight/class-issue-securing-new-job.
22   Social Mobility Commission, Social Mobility Barometer: Public Attitudes to Social Mobility in the UK, 2019 to 2020 (21 January 2020). Available at: https://www.gov.uk/government/publications/social-mobility-barometer-poll-results-2019/social-mobility-barometer-public-attitudes-to-social-mobility-in-the-uk-2019-to-2020.

deliberate while others are accidental, some forms of classism are deliberate, not accidental. Some classism is intentional – and some of it exists in your school.

William Ming Liu identified four forms of classism: downward, upward, lateral and internalised.[23] The concepts most relevant to this book are that of downward classism and internalised classism.

Downward classism occurs when people in higher social class groups discriminate against or marginalise people whom they perceive to be in a lower social group. Downward classist behaviours and attitudes often take the form of micro-aggressions – that is, everyday interactions that intentionally or unintentionally degrade, insult or diminish the humanity, customs or values of people in non-dominant groups.

Internalised classism is the acceptance and justification of classism by working-class people themselves. Examples include feeling inferior around higher-class people, deference to the values of higher-class people or shame about your family background or heritage.

REFLECTIVE QUESTIONS

Once again, we would like you to reflect on the following questions before continuing:

- Do you have any personal experience of classism?

- Do you agree that society seems to undervalue working-class people? If so, how?

- Is there any evidence that there is some bias against working-class families in your organisation? If so, how does that bias show itself?

---

23   W. M. Lui, *Social Class and Classism in the Helping Professions: Research, Theory, and Practice* (Thousand Oaks, CA: SAGE, 2011).

WHERE IS THE EVIDENCE OF CLASSISM IN EDUCATION?

We believe that classism is embedded in all aspects of education. For example, many universities remain the preserve of middle- and upper-class students and aren't representative of modern society. By way of illustration, think of the lack of working-class representation on courses such as medicine. In 2016, the King's Fund found that only 4% of doctors in the UK come from working-class backgrounds.[24] As the occupational figures we cited earlier show, it is no accident that the elites have the best opportunities, jobs and incomes.

Classism most rears its head when elites fear that their territory is being threatened by interlopers from the lower social classes. From passive-aggressive behaviour to downright bullying, many (but by no means all) of the more privileged will put barriers in the way of those who aren't like them. They will make certain spaces unwelcome. Classism as a deliberate strategy is something we will return to later. We think that educators cannot undo all aspects of classism, but we can be similarly deliberate in the way we respond to it.

In this book, we will tackle the classism inherent in the secondary school context. In the next chapter, we will focus on three areas within the control of school leaders and teachers, but first let's drag the elephant into the middle of the room.

One reason why the classroom isn't working for working-class students is money. According to Professor Diane Reay's research, working-class students do less well simply because less money is spent on them.[25] Reay and others highlight that the funding deficiencies suffered by state schools have led to a marked decline in art, drama, dance and music provision. Less affluent families cannot afford to pay for their children to experience these activities outside of school.

There has been a funding crisis in the state sector for many years. Head teachers like Vic Goddard have campaigned tirelessly for more funding and to help the general public understand the extent of the problem. His school in Harlow, Essex cannot afford to buy textbooks for their

---

24 A. Heller, Diversity in the Medical Workforce: Are We Making Progress?, *The King's Fund* (3 February 2020). Available at: https://www.kingsfund.org.uk/blog/2020/02/diversity-medical-workforce-progress.

25 D. Ferguson, 'Working-Class Children Get Less of Everything in Education – Including Respect' [interview with Diane Reay], *The Guardian* (21 November 2017). Available at: https://www.theguardian.com/education/2017/nov/21/english-class-system-shaped-in-schools?

students.[26] We want to give readers of this book ideas for what we will call 'the extra and the different' for working-class students in your school community but, as Goddard explains, many schools cannot even afford the basics, let alone the extras.

Every government makes economic choices. Policies such as austerity have clearly led to schools being underfunded. Meanwhile, in the private sector, fee-paying schools continue to be exempt from paying VAT due to their dubious charitable status.

Earlier, we defined the working classes according to the social class category of C2DE. In doing so, it is important to note that the category is broad and that the working class aren't therefore synonymous with those living in poverty. Many working-class people don't, in fact, live in poverty.

But it is equally important to note that all those who do live in poverty are, by definition, working class because the class system is based not solely on the type of work you do but on relative affluence; to be middle class you must be more affluent than the working classes. In addition, a high proportion of those in poverty are also in work.

At the time of writing, more than one in five of the UK population are classed as living in poverty, which equates to a staggering 13.4 million people. Of these, 8.1 million are working-age adults, 4.3 million are children and 2.1 million are pensioners. Child poverty continues to rise with almost one in three children in the UK (31%) living in poverty. To put that into context, that's an average of nine students out of a class of thirty. Some 75% of children in poverty live in a household where at least one person works.[27]

According to the charity Child Poverty Action Group (CPAG), 'pupils experiencing poverty in England are financially excluded from full participation in a wide range of school subjects and activities, including PE, music, swimming and art and design'. In addition, 'Day-to-day practices in England's schools often unintentionally draw attention to family incomes and make children feel embarrassed and different. These include expensive uniform policies, non-uniform days and requests from school to bring in material possessions like pencil cases.'[28] Some schools' food policies mean that children living in poverty are not afforded the same lunch options as their peers.

---

26 C. Jones, Essex School Cannot Afford Textbooks Due to Cost of Living Crisis, *BBC News* (8 September 2022). Available at: https://www.bbc.co.uk/news/uk-england-essex-62828555.
27 See https://endchildpoverty.org.uk/key-facts.
28 Child Poverty Action Group, *The Cost of the School Day in England: Pupils' Perspectives* (March 2022), p. 5. Available at: https://cpag.org.uk/policy-and-campaigns/briefing/cost-school-day-england-pupils-perspectives.

We agree with Professor Diane Reay's claims that, 'If you're a working-class child, you're starting the race halfway round the track [because] less afflu-ent children […] get a more restrictive educational offer' and are denied an education in art, drama or dance because 'their parents can't afford to pay for them to do those activities out of school'.[29]

To help working-class students catch up in the race, we therefore need to offer them more than their more affluent peers.

WHY IS IT IN ALL OUR BEST INTERESTS TO CHALLENGE CLASSISM?

There are two main arguments for tackling classism. Firstly, there is the *mutuality* argument. A 2014 report from the Private Equity Foundation Impetus says that the high number of NEETs (not in education, employ-ment or training) costs the UK economy 'in excess of £77 billion a year'.[30] This figure is arrived at through calculating lost taxes and additional asso-ciated costs that come from youth crime and poor health.

In a briefing for the Centre for Economic Performance, the authors of *What Do We Know and What Should We Do About Social Mobility?*, Lee Elliot Major and Stephen Machin, argue that 'Greater social mobility would mean less talent unfulfilled, more representative elites and a boost to the national economy.' The authors go on to say that 'if levels in Britain were improved to those in Canada, it … would lead to an annual increase in the country's GDP of around 4.4%'.[31] In other words, it is in all our mutual interests to tackle classism because we will all reap the economic benefits.

Secondly, there is the *justice* argument. An elderly woman Andy used to know when he was growing up in London had a big influence on him. Her name was Bess Calvert. Over a cup of tea in a crowded cafe, Bess passed on some wisdom: 'Listen to people and don't judge them.' Bess's sage advice echoes that of cognitive behaviour therapy expert Dr Paul Hauck who has written a self-help book called *Hold Your Head Up High*.[32] The book offers a three-step approach to feeling better about yourself: (1)

---

29   D. Ferguson, 'Working-Class Children Get Less of Everything in Education'.
30   Impetus, *Make NEETs History in 2014* (London: Impetus, 2014), p. 4. Available at: https://www.impetus.org.uk/assets/publications/Report/Make-NEETs-History-Report_ImpetusPEF_January-2014.pdf.
31   L. E. Major and S. Machin, *Social Mobility* (Centre for Economic Performance 2019 Election Analysis Series) (November), p. 7. Available at: https://cep.lse.ac.uk/pubs/download/ea045.pdf.
32   P. Hauck, *Hold Your Head Up High* (London: Hachette UK, 1991).

never rate yourself and others, (2) develop performance confidence and (3) make people respect you.

To put a working-class spin on this advice, you should aim to become a nicer, happier person by trying to excel at something in life and not judging others too harshly. The advice is a recipe for feeling neither superior nor inferior.

Our contention is that reducing the impact of classism will help society. As Dorling writes:

We live in an increasingly hierarchical society. We talk about some people being way above and others being way below other people. And yet we are not that different from each other. This sham hierarchy has been created by elitism, exclusion, prejudice, and greed. The end result is increasing amounts of despair, not only among the poor, but also among groups like the children of aspirational parents. If we want a content and happy society, we are currently going in the wrong direction.[33]

Of course, not everyone will be happy with this suggestion. There are many with vested interests who will oppose our ideas. It will be a long, hard but exciting road. If you want to make the journey with us, we think you will need to be equipped with a bit more understanding of the main problems that classism causes. Our next chapter seeks to do just that.

---

33 D. Dorling, An Introduction to Injustice: Why Social Inequality Still Persists (2010). Available at: https://www.dannydorling.org/books/injustice/injustice-anintroduction. pdf.

CHAPTER 2

HOW IS THE 'GAME' RIGGED?

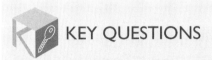 **KEY QUESTIONS**

In this chapter we will answer the following questions:

■ What is the core curriculum, and how might it be rigged against working-class students?

■ How might curriculum assessment – including the content of exams and how much is expected of students outside of school – also be stacked against the working class?

■ What is the hidden curriculum, and how might it be having a negative impact on working-class students' beliefs, as well as denying them access to the secret knowledge needed to succeed?

We will be focusing on three problems in particular – curriculum design, curriculum assessment and the hidden curriculum – but first let's explore the influential writings of Pierre Bourdieu who, along with Jean-Claude Passeron, coined the now-familiar term 'cultural capital'.

Bourdieu first used the term cultural capital in his essay 'Cultural Reproduction and Social Reproduction' (1977), which he expanded on in 'The Forms of Capital' (1986) and *The State Nobility: Elite Schools in the Field of Power* (1996).[1] In 'The Forms of Capital', Bourdieu described embodied cultural capital as a person's education (knowledge and intellectual skills) which provides advantage in achieving a higher social status. Bourdieu used game metaphors in much of his writing about social class

1   P. Bourdieu, Cultural Reproduction and Social Reproduction. In J. Karabel and A. H. Halsey (eds), *Power and Ideology in Education* (New York: Oxford University Press, 1977), pp. 487–511; P. Bourdieu, The Forms of Capital. In J. G. Richardson (ed.), *Handbook of Theory and Research for the Sociology of Education* (Westport, CT: Greenwood, 1986), pp. 241–258; and P. Bourdieu, *The State Nobility: Elite Schools in the Field of Power* (Cambridge: Polity, 1996).

and argued that the 'game' is rigged. The game Bourdieu refers to is, of course, the game of life, of which education is a significant element.

In this book, we are focusing on the secondary education phase, so it is an examination of what we do with the 5,000-plus hours that students spend at school from the age of 11 to 16. We think it is important to lay out these problems clearly, so you can examine the extent to which they exist in your own school.

As we progress through this chapter, we will provide you with reflective questions that might help you to consider how and why your school does what it does. These questions might also encourage you to think about what you can control and influence. Through this process of reflection, you will be able to focus your energies on areas that will make the most difference to working-class students. The questions may also help you consider how much you are personally contributing to the rigged game or – we hope – trying to unrig it.

We will start by looking at *what* schools teach.

SOME CONTEXT

As we saw in Chapter 1, around 7% of students in the UK currently attend private fee-paying schools, 5% attend grammar schools and 88% attend state schools, which are a mixture of comprehensive schools, faith schools, academies and free schools.[2]

The national curriculum is written by the government at Westminster and is a programme of study offered to all students in state schools.[3] It is the formal, planned part of the curriculum and is delivered in lessons usually demarcated as subject disciplines on the timetable. Private schools don't have to follow the national curriculum. Here, we might discern, is our first problem: the system isn't equal. Of course, academies don't have to follow the national curriculum either, but they must demonstrate that they teach something more ambitious and so the vast majority do subscribe to the national curriculum.

To be clear, a school's curriculum is much more than what is prescribed in the national curriculum, but this is as good a place to start as any.

We can trace the evolution of the national curriculum in England back to a speech by the then Labour Prime Minister James Callaghan at Ruskin

---

2   See https://comprehensivefuture.org.uk/facts-figures-and-evidence-about-grammar-schools.
3   Department for Education, National Curriculum (14 October 2013; updated 16 July 2014). Available at: https://www.gov.uk/government/collections/national-curriculum.

College, Oxford, in 1976. Certainly, it signalled the state's intention to assume a greater role in deciding what was taught in its schools, not just funding and facilities. In the so-called 'Great Debate' speech, Callaghan argued that education should 'equip children to the best of their ability for a lively, constructive, place in society, and also to fit them to do a job of work. Not one or the other but both.'[4]

The debate about what children should learn in schools continued into the 1980s. By then, the Conservatives were in power, and the Education Reform Act 1988 made Callaghan's vision a reality with the first national curriculum, which was officially introduced in schools in 1989.

The current iteration of the national curriculum says that 'Every state-funded school must offer a curriculum which is balanced and broadly based, and which promotes the spiritual, moral, cultural, mental and physical development of pupils at the school and of society [and] prepares pupils at the school for the opportunities, responsibilities and experiences of later life.'[5] Furthermore, the national curriculum provides students with 'an introduction to the essential knowledge they need to be educated citizens. It introduces pupils to the best that has been thought and said, and helps engender an appreciation of human creativity and achievement'.[6]

With this last sentence, the national curriculum alludes to Matthew Arnold who, in *Culture and Anarchy*, said that culture is 'a pursuit of our total perfection by means of getting to know, on all the matters which most concern us, the best which has been thought and said in the world'.[7] We will return to Arnold's notion of 'the best' later, for herein lies one of the causes of classism in the core curriculum.

The purpose of the national curriculum, therefore, is to set out the principles, aims and content of the subjects to be studied by students in primary and secondary schools, and to ensure that all students in England encounter the same content and material. As such, the national curriculum isn't the entirety of a school's curriculum; it is only those aspects afforded to all students. Any school is free to teach whatever it wishes in addition to the national curriculum. The real curriculum is created by teachers, every day.

---

4   J. Callaghan, A Rational Debate Based on the Facts. Speech delivered at Ruskin College, Oxford, 18 October 1976. Available at: http://www.educationengland.org.uk/documents/speeches/1976ruskin.html.

5   Department for Education, National Curriculum in England: Framework for Key Stages 1 to 4 (2 December 2014), section 2.1. Available at: https://www.gov.uk/government/publications/national-curriculum-in-england-framework-for-key-stages-1-to-4/the-national-curriculum-in-england-framework-for-key-stages-1-to-4.

6   Department for Education, National Curriculum in England: Framework for Key Stages 1 to 4, section 3.1.

7   M. Arnold, Preface. In *Culture and Anarchy* (New York: Start Publishing, 2017 [1869]), p. vii.

In 2011, the Expert Panel for the National Curriculum Review said: 'Education can thus be seen, at its simplest, as the product of [an] interaction between socially valued knowledge and individual development. It occurs through learner experience of both of these key elements. The *school curriculum* structures these processes.'[8]

The unplanned parts of the curriculum are often referred to as the 'hidden curriculum', a term first coined by Phillip Jackson in 1968.[9] Jackson argued that what is taught in schools is more than just the formal curriculum, and that schooling should be understood as a socialisation process whereby students receive messages through the experience of being in school, not just from what they are explicitly taught in lessons.

The hidden curriculum, therefore, includes learning from other students and learning that arises from an accidental juxtaposition of the school's stated values and its actual practice. More on this later in the chapter.

THREE REASONS WHY THE CLASSROOM DOESN'T WORK FOR WORKING-CLASS STUDENTS

Let's explore why we consider schools to be classist or, more specifically, why we feel the education system disadvantages working-class students.

Firstly, working-class students must work much harder than their peers. Michael Young, writing as long ago as 1950s, asserted that students from poorer areas had to work harder than upper-class youngsters to get to university,[10] and this is still the case over sixty years later. Sadly, improvements in access to higher education for working-class children made during the 1970s, 1980s and 1990s haven't been sustained. Slowly and steadily, we have seen the removal of free education, maintenance grants and free travel passes.

Secondly, so much of what schools do is classist, including the way the curriculum is designed, the way the assessment system works and the impact of the hidden curriculum on students. Let's look at each of these in turn.

---

8   Department for Education, *The Framework for the National Curriculum: A Report by the Expert Panel for the National Curriculum Review* (2011), p. 11 (original emphasis). Available at: https://www.gov.uk/government/publications/framework-for-the-national-curriculum-a-report-by-the-expert-panel-for-the-national-curriculum-review.
9   P. Jackson, *Life in Classrooms* (New York: Teachers College Press, 1968).
10 Young, *The Rise of the Meritocracy*.

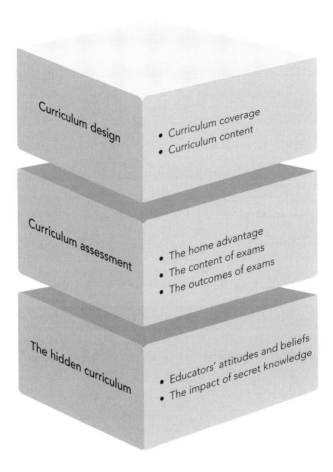

PROBLEM 1: CURRICULUM DESIGN

The stated aim of the national curriculum is to ensure that all students in England encounter the same content and material. The curriculum should provide students with 'an introduction to the essential knowledge that they need to be educated citizens'.[11] There are, we think, two problems with this.

Firstly, curriculum coverage – one size doesn't fit all. Providing all students with the same curriculum further disadvantages those who are already disadvantaged. We hope you agree that we shouldn't reduce the curriculum for working-class students. To do so is to deepen their existing

---

11   Department for Education, *The National Curriculum in England: Key Stages 1 and 2 Framework Document* (September 2013), p. 6. Available at: https://assets. publishing.service.gov.uk/government/uploads/system/uploads/attachment_data/ file/425601/PRIMARY_national_curriculum.pdf.

disadvantage and deny them the opportunities afforded to their more affluent peers. We must offer the same ambitious curriculum to every student, irrespective of their background, additional and different needs, and starting points. But we should offer more, not less – but, crucially, not the same – to our working-class students. We must broaden the curriculum for working-class students to ensure *equity* as opposed to *equality*.

According to the Equality and Human Rights Commission, equality is about 'ensuring that every individual has an equal opportunity to make the most of their lives and talents',[12] whereas equity is about giving more to those who need it. Equity isn't the same as equality, and nor, crucially, is it the same as inequality; it is simply giving more to those who need it proportionate to their own circumstances to ensure that everyone has the same opportunities.

Therefore, we need to provide the same ambitious curriculum to all, and *then* complement it with additional opportunities for those whose starting points are lower or for whom opportunities are more limited.

The aim of equity in education should not be *social mobility*. Social mobility implies lifting students out of the working classes and leaving behind all that they are and identify with. Rather, the aim of equity in education is to celebrate and embrace students' working-class roots, while simultaneously ensuring those roots don't take a stranglehold of their life chances. We want to widen horizons and remove barriers to success; we don't want the sun to set on working-class students' rich and proud ancestry. As such, the aim of equity in education is *social justice*. 'Social mobility says your mum and dad are shit … Social mobility says, provided a few boats rise, the tide does not have to change. Social mobility says the structures that separate rich from poor are right and just.'[13]

So, the first problem to counter with classism in schools is the belief that we feed every student the same diet; that we offer equality of opportunity rather than equity. The way to counter classism in schools is to provide equality and *then* equity; to offer the same ambitious curriculum to all and ensure fair access to the same extra-curricular activities, and *then* do more for those who start with less.

Secondly, curriculum content – definitions of core knowledge are classist. In other words, definitions are based on the notion that wealth and social status confer taste and discernment, and the selection of knowledge is made by those of a higher social standing rather than by a representative group of people from across the social strata.

---

12   See https://www.equalityhumanrights.com/en/secondary-education-resources/useful-information/understanding-equality.

13   P. Beadle, *The Fascist Painting: What Is Cultural Capital?* (Woodbridge: John Catt Educational, 2020), pp.228–229.

Since 2019, Ofsted have inspected the way that schools develop students' cultural capital. Controversially, perhaps, they describe cultural capital as 'the best that has been thought and said',[14] but who decides what constitutes the 'best'? Notions of best are, by definition, subjective value choices. Sadly, all too often, these choices are made by politicians from middle-class backgrounds. Every school's curriculum should celebrate working-class culture alongside culture from the dominant classes. Working-class students tend to be denied the experiences their middle-class peers are afforded, such as reading books at home, visiting museums and art galleries, taking part in educational trips, enjoying foreign holidays and so on.

We aren't arguing against the teaching of knowledge; we are simply suggesting that we need to think more carefully – nationally and locally – about who decides what knowledge is taught, when and why. We should also think more carefully about how representative that knowledge is of our school communities, how effectively it talks to students' lived experiences and to their family traditions and cultures. Once we have selected knowledge that does reflect our school community, we need to identify curriculum content that celebrates diversity beyond our community so we can broaden our students' horizons.

PROBLEM 2: CURRICULUM ASSESSMENT

Our current assessment system could also be regarded as classist. Firstly, there is the home advantage. Students are expected to complete schoolwork at home, whether that is homework, coursework or revision. Those who don't have a home life that is conducive to independent study are therefore placed at a disadvantage, which is compounded for those who don't have parents or carers with the capacity to support them – whether in terms of time, ability or money (e.g. buying learning resources such as a computer, books, pens and paper).

And then there is private tuition. Sir Peter Lampl, chair of the Sutton Trust, told *The Guardian* in 2016 that 'Private tuition is widespread and increasingly so … [but] many cannot afford to benefit from this extra support.'[15]

However much a working-class student may want to learn and grow, the lack of a suitable place to study is a serious handicap. Spending cuts have

---

14   Ofsted, School Inspection Handbook (2019, updated 13 September 2023), para. 226. Available at: https://www.gov.uk/government/publications/school-inspection-handbook-eif.

15   S. Weale, Sharp Rise in Children Receiving Private Tuition, *The Guardian* (8 September 2016). Available at: https://www.theguardian.com/education/2016/sep/08/sharp-rise-in-children-receiving-private-tuition.

led to a steep decline in the number of libraries in the UK and cuts to the opening hours of those libraries that remain standing: 'Spending on libraries in 2009 was at £1 billion, but by 2019 it had fallen by a quarter. The same decade saw 773 libraries close – that's one fifth of libraries in the UK.'[16] Libraries can be warm, quiet spaces for students to study. Their demise has hit working-class people especially hard.

Secondly, there is the content of exams, which tend to have a middle-class bias, such as requiring students to have personal experience of foreign travel and theatre visits.[17]

Thirdly, there is the outcome of exams. The assessment system is designed to fail a third of students every year – and it is the working classes who suffer the most. The Association of School and College Leaders (ASCL)'s 2018 independent Commission of Inquiry explored ways of improving the prospects of what they called the 'forgotten third' – 'the students who do not achieve at least a grade 4 standard pass in GCSE English and maths at the end of 12 years of schooling'.

The ASCL argues that:

the fact that this represents around a third of 16-year-olds year in year out is not an accident but the product of the system of comparable outcomes whereby the spread of GCSE grades is pegged to what cohorts of similar ability achieved in the past. Young people who fall below this bar pay a high price in terms of reduced prospects in progression to further and higher education and to careers.[18]

16   A. Walton, The Quiet Disappearance of Britain's Public Libraries, *Tribune* (17 January 2021). Available at: https://tribunemag.co.uk/2021/01/the-quiet-disappearance-of-britains-public-libraries.
17   For some examples, see C. Lough, New Crackdown on GCSE Questions with Middle-Class Bias, *The Independent* (12 May 2022). Available at: https://www.independent.co.uk/news/uk/aqa-maths-england-english-ofqual-b2077543.html.
18   Association of School and College Leaders, *The Forgotten Third: Final Report of the Commission of Inquiry* (September 2019), p. 6. Available at: https://www.ascl.org.uk/ASCL/media/ASCL/Our%20view/Campaigns/The-Forgotten-Third_full-report.pdf.

PROBLEM 3: THE HIDDEN CURRICULUM

All schools have a hidden curriculum. It exists in a school's rules and routines; in its behaviour policies, rewards and sanctions systems; in its physical environment, social environment and learning environment; and in the way all the adults who work in the school interact with each other and with the students.

Students in private schools have an extra hidden curriculum – albeit hidden in plain sight. Private school students are taught that they are part of the elite and their place in society is to rule over others. It is their destiny and their birthright because that is the way we do things in this country. And it works.

Working-class students in state schools might be told that we live in a meritocracy – that with hard work and the right mindset anyone can achieve anything. But they soon realise that merit is all smoke and mirrors. It is harder to have a growth mindset if you live in a cold, damp and overcrowded rented flat. It is harder to attend an after-school drama club if you are expected to collect a younger sibling from primary school. And it is harder to do well in exams if you have nowhere to study and no access to the internet or a computer.

The very idea of meritocracy – that no matter your social background, you compete on the same level playing field – is deeply flawed. In his ground-breaking book, *The Tyranny of Merit*, Michael Sandel argues that the 'meritocratic conviction that people deserve whatever riches the market bestows on their talents makes solidarity an almost impossible project'.[19]

It is much harder for working-class people to get in and get on in various professions. Alongside the costs of entry to the professions and the advantages that accrue from having connections and work experience in the relevant field, a person's intelligence and ability are often conflated with their cultural tastes, mannerisms and confidence. These are all signals of social class but not necessarily of aptitude. Describing someone as the 'right fit' for a job is a statement laden with class assumption and prejudice.

---

19 M. Sandel, *The Tyranny of Merit: What's Become of the Common Good?* (London: Penguin Random House, 2020), p. 227.

PART II

WHAT CAN WE DO TO MAKE SECONDARY SCHOOL WORK BETTER FOR WORKING-CLASS STUDENTS?

Problem 1:
Curriculum design
Curriculum coverage
Curriculum content

Solution 1:
Equality
... through the core curriculum
and extra-curricular activities

Problem 2:
Curriculum assessment
The home advantage
The content of exams
The outcome of exams

Solution 2:
Equity
... through curriculum
adaptations and interventions

Problem 3:
The hidden curriculum
Educators' attitudes and beliefs
The impact of secret
knowledge

Solution 3:
Extension
... through curriculum
enhancements

CHAPTER 3

WHAT CAN WE DO ABOUT CLASSISM?

 **KEY QUESTIONS**

In this chapter we will answer the following questions:

- What secret knowledge do students from elite backgrounds tend to possess which puts them at an advantage over working-class students, and how can we close this advantage gap?

- How can we build working-class students' cultural and social capital by embedding four knowledge domains?

- How might adopting a three-step process of equality, equity and extension counter the impact of classism and better prepare working-class students for future success?

In Part I, we set out the problems with classism in education. That was important because many of those problems are hidden. We believe that the first step towards countering classism is to acknowledge that it exists both in society and in schools, and then to unpack the causes and consequences of classism in order to identify the solutions.

Now that we have explained what we think are the main issues, it is time to roll our sleeves up and get our hands dirty uncovering the solutions.

A reminder: we think that we can counter classism in the classroom by improving the core curriculum and extra-curricular activities, making more effective curriculum adaptations and interventions, and instigating curriculum enhancements.

All of this is underpinned by a framework we call the *four knowledge domains*. Before we share this framework with you, we want to explore something that we call 'secret knowledge'.

SECRET KNOWLEDGE

Google the term 'secret knowledge' and you will be directed to a host of conspiracy theory websites. Swerve the conspiracies; in this book, secret knowledge refers to the knowledge favoured by the privileged. With this knowledge, the elite feel born to rule.

It is no secret why a parent would want to send their child to a private school. After all, in doing so they are guaranteed smaller classes and therefore more attention and feedback. The quality of teaching is likely to be similar to that in a state school, but private schools tend to be better resourced and have their own swimming pools, cricket pitches, music equipment and so on. In addition, parents hope that their children will mix with more of the 'right kind of people'.

Private schools also have access to a large alumni who support them with direct funding and provide opportunities through their knowledge and connections. Private education is an expensive undertaking, so parents will want value for their investment.

We want to make it clear that we are envious of private schools. Yes, we said it. We envy their smaller class sizes, their excellent resources and the way they prepare their students for their future roles in the world. On their own terms, private schools are very successful. What we don't like is the fact that a student's birth dictates their access to such opportunities. We would love it if everyone in society had equal access, not just those lucky enough to be born into wealth and social status. Note our use of the word 'lucky' again here; it is pure luck, not merit, that determines a child's educational success and success in later life.

We cannot change the system and we cannot increase funding for schools, but we can better understand what beliefs, skills and attributes private schools teach their students, which are often denied to working-class children, and then find ways of including them in the state school curriculum. We have the power to drag this secret knowledge out of the shadows and into the light.

We believe that one way to do this is by embedding four knowledge domains in the curriculum.

FOUR KNOWLEDGE DOMAINS

Our preferred definition of social justice, which we have adopted throughout this book, comes from Laura Chapman and the late Professor John West-Burnham, who argue that social justice 'requires deliberate and specific intervention to secure equality and equity'.[1]

The comedian Frankie Boyle once wrote that 'one of the reasons evil people triumph is that good people have such fuller diaries'.[2] We know that educators are already overworked, and this is likely to be one reason why we don't do more to help working-class students.

We don't want to add to your workload. Rather, we hope to persuade you (or, if you are already a convert, help you to persuade those around you) to redirect some of your existing work time towards practical measures that will help you and your institution to be more effective in delivering social justice. Social injustice isn't an inevitability; it can be reduced by intelligent action.

One way we can do this is by thinking about the types of knowledge we develop in our students. We advise embedding four knowledge domains throughout the curriculum, which can act as an antidote to the secret knowledge outlined above: disciplinary, personal, cultural and social.

1   L. Chapman and J. West-Burnham, *Social Justice in Education: Achieving Wellbeing for All* (London: Continuum, 2008), p. 26.
2   F. Boyle, *The Future of British Politics* (London: Unbound, 2020), p. 33.

DISCIPLINARY KNOWLEDGE

Disciplinary knowledge is the ability to speak, read and write in ways that befit each subject discipline – for example, being able to speak, read and write like a mathematician, a historian, an artist, a scientist and so on. The development of disciplinary knowledge dominates the secondary school curriculum, and rightly so, because a lack of disciplinary knowledge holds back students from lower socio-economic backgrounds.

PERSONAL KNOWLEDGE

Building personal knowledge is about wisdom and well-being. What you learn in your school years helps you to get the best out of yourself. Personal knowledge encompasses developing an empowering self-concept through the story you tell yourself about who you are and who you might become. It is also about self-motivation, time management, realising strengths and managing emotions, especially negative ones such as anger and anxiety that could derail you from taking a successful path.

We believe that growing personal knowledge is a key indicator of future success. In practice, it involves:

- Developing metacognitive knowledge and self-regulation skills, which are thought to be key ingredients of academic success.

- Learning about emotions (such as anxiety, anger and sadness) and understanding the reasons for their existence and the best way to process them.

- Understanding notions of 'self' and the power of the stories you tell yourself about who you are, the beliefs you hold and how you can alter your own personal stories or scripts.

- Realising personal strengths and interests that can unlock future career and leisure paths.

Key to understanding self is understanding 'story'. The stories we tell ourselves derive in large part from our conditioning, perceptions and lived experiences. Our view is that understanding our own stories can help us to choose a better script to live by. When people realise that they can change their narrative, especially when the current one is self-defeating, and do so, extraordinary things can happen.

CULTURAL KNOWLEDGE

When you hear the word 'culture' what do you think of? Art? History? Music? How people's tastes and traditions differ? Do you think of the words beauty, grace or elegance?

Every secondary school faces the dilemma of deciding, within the 5,000 or so hours available to them, what types of cultural knowledge they will try to impart. In her book, *Obstetrics for Schools*, Rachel Macfarlane walks us through some of the dilemmas that staff faced at the Isaac Newton Academy when trying to decide what students should be taught in terms of culture:

> We had a clear vision and rationale because we had spent time discussing (and, at times, arguing about!) what we meant by cultural education and what cultural activities we believed it was essential for all our students to experience. We had the debate with our staff about who gets to determine what type of experiences are non-negotiables and whether a cultural education should comprise skills that the students are interested in – for example, gaming or beat-boxing – or be made up of activities that we, with our adult perspective, might believe that they should experience – such as capoeira or cricket. There is a danger than cultural education programmes can acquire a middle-class, paternalistic whiff: 'It's important that everyone can read Latin and appreciate opera.' However, if the range of cultural activities is limited to students' requests, it won't expand horizons or build self-esteem in the same way. Inevitably, we sought to strike a happy medium.[3]

Cultural education at Isaac Newton Academy involves building a cultural passport – a set of guarantees or entitlements for all students. We like this idea and will return to it later.

We think a school's cultural curriculum should stress two other elements. Firstly, that the dominant class uses their knowledge of culture as a tool to exclude others. As such, cultural knowledge should involve learning about so-called 'high art' and art (which we believe can also be 'high') created by the working classes. Secondly, that no matter your social class, anyone can enjoy any form of art or culture. People should enjoy what they enjoy, and not allow others to decide that a particular form of culture isn't for them.

---

3   R. Macfarlane, *Obstetrics for Schools: A Guide to Eliminating Failure and Ensuring the Safe Delivery of All Learners* (Carmarthen: Crown House Publishing, 2021), p. 149.

Comedian Mark Thomas, when interviewed about his stage show *Bravo Figaro!*, paid tribute to his father's love of opera.[4] His dad was a self-employed builder who, much to the annoyance of the other workers on his building site, enjoyed opera music, even during the latter stages of his life when he suffered from dementia. A high trust setting, which we hope all schools strive to be, should be a place where staff and students can comfortably reveal their cultural likes and dislikes. Some of what other people like or love can surprise us. It can also teach us. This passion and knowledge for a form of culture can become ours.

Remember that a student's school years might be the last time someone tries to introduce them to an aspect of culture they might never otherwise encounter.

SOCIAL KNOWLEDGE

The fourth and final knowledge domain that should be embedded across the school curriculum is social knowledge. This refers to the way in which society is organised and in whose interests it operates.

We think it is a pity that few schools now teach sociology or social sciences; it is no accident that business studies has become its replacement in most instances. Learning about the writings of sociologists such as Pierre Bourdieu can be very instructive to young people, especially if they are from a working-class background.

Bourdieu's work can be taught as part of the core curriculum. His work on *field*, *doxa* and *habitus* may be complex, but it is also highly instructive. According to Bourdieu, society is structured through a series of hierarchically organised fields (e.g. family, religion, education), each with its own set of rules – or what Bourdieu calls doxa – which are often unstated and involuntary but mutually recognised by individuals (or agents) within a field. Habitus, meanwhile, refers to the deeply ingrained habits, beliefs and tastes we have internalised due to our life experiences.

Each decision about which movie to watch or which leisure pursuit to follow – and, indeed, which occupation to try and enter – is shaped by our habitus. In the right situation, our habitus allows us to successfully navigate certain fields and feel like a fish in water or that we can play this game well. However, the same set of skills and dispositions may prove useless in other fields, and we may feel like a fish out of water or that there is no point in even trying to play the game because we are bound to lose.

---

4   See https://www.youtube.com/watch?v=b_rsOj2bkys.

Schools talk a lot about 'mindset', often derived from the work of Professor Carol Dweck,[5] but they rarely, if ever, consider habitus. Teaching about social knowledge requires helping students to recognise that some professions or fields are hard to access if you are from a working-class background and to appreciate how society is rigged in favour of the dominant classes.

The development of students' social knowledge inevitably involves raising their political awareness. Done well, young people will leave school with a greater understanding of why things are as they are. For example: why do we have so many food banks? Why do refugees want to come to the UK? Why do we have a House of Lords? Why do some companies have more power than nations? Of course, the best questions will come from the students themselves, and by teaching them about society and the agents within it, they can play their own roles with more understanding and empathy.

WHY THESE KNOWLEDGE DOMAINS, AND WHY ONLY FOUR?

We have deliberately chosen the knowledge domains set out in our framework to counteract some of the secret knowledge we outlined earlier.

We think that trying to develop too many domains could be a mistake. It is tempting to come up with a long list of hopes or desirables for any student's school journey, but experience has taught us to be concise about what we are trying to achieve. A tighter set of standards or domains is also easier to communicate to staff and other stakeholders involved in its delivery, and it is easier to monitor too.

Let's be clear: we aren't saying that each domain should have an equal share of curriculum time, despite the way they are represented in our graphic. Disciplinary knowledge is by far the most important facet of this framework because it will have the most impact on attainment and open doors to students' future successes. Nevertheless, the other three facets are important and need more time devoted to them.

The aim of embedding these four knowledge domains in our core curriculum is to ensure that all students – including those from working class backgrounds – are supported to form well-rounded relationships with people from all walks of life and to feel comfortable in a range of social situations.

5   C. S. Dweck, *Mindset: Changing the Way You Think to Fulfil Your Potential*, updated edn (London: Robinson, 2017).

We want students to be knowledgeable about and proud of their heritage – their family history, their hometown, their place in the world. We want them to be able to express themselves with confidence. We want them to be able to spot when someone is lying to them or trying to shame them.

 REFLECTIVE QUESTIONS

■ Does your school use an overarching framework to try and address cultural capital and social capital? If so, what is it and how is it shared?

■ What is the balance, in terms of time and status, between the development of these four knowledge domains in your school? Do you feel you have got the balance right? If not, how would you change it?

■ How much time is given to you and other staff to help you consider your curriculum choices and analyse how they match the values your school wants to foster in its students?

EQUALITY, EQUITY AND EXTENSION

To recap: we think schools are classist, and there are three lines of attack that we, as educators, can mount to counter these problems. We are now going to tackle each aspect in turn and provide some practical solutions.

It might help to think of this in terms of a three-point plan:

In the next two chapters, we will start, logically enough, with step 1.

CHAPTER 4

EQUALITY THROUGH THE CORE CURRICULUM

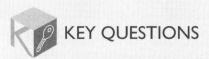

KEY QUESTIONS

In this chapter we will answer the following questions:

- How can we ensure equality for working-class students through ambitious curriculum design?

- How might following a six-step process ensure that all students can access that ambitious curriculum?

- How might different subject disciplines contribute to building students' schemas and help build cultural and social capital?

In the previous chapter we posited a three-point plan of equality, equity and extension. Let's explore the first solution in some detail.

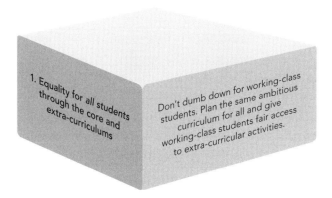

1. Equality for all students through the core and extra-curriculums

Don't dumb down for working-class students. Plan the same ambitious curriculum for all and give working-class students fair access to extra-curricular activities.

But first an explanation. This book is about helping working-class students compete more fairly with their better-off peers. It is about turning disadvantage into advantage. Most of what we suggest here is aimed at doing more for those who start with less – the extra and the different. But the first step on our three-point plan to counter classism is about levelling the playing field; it is about ensuring that all students are taught the same ambitious curriculum and have access to the same extra-curricular activities.

This might sound contradictory, but it is not. We will argue in favour of giving equal access to all students – irrespective of their backgrounds, their starting points and their additional and different needs – to an ambitious, broad and balanced, and planned and sequenced curriculum with excellence at its heart, and to have access to the same extra-curricular activities. Why? Because to do otherwise is to perpetuate existing disadvantage and double-down on difference.

In short, equality is an antidote to dumbing down or reducing the curriculum for some students. To offer less is to say that a child's birth will be their destiny; it is to deny them the chance to compete fairly.

So, equality is about giving all students access to the same curriculum. It is also about embedding the four knowledge domains throughout the curriculum and using the curriculum as a means of giving students access to the secret knowledge that will help them get on in life.

If, as you read this chapter, you think we have steered away from our mission to help working-class students, be under no illusion: this is only the first step. Once we have given all students equal access to the same ambitious curriculum, *then* we need to do more for working-class students to help them access this curriculum and achieve. Doing more might take the form of adaptive teaching or interventions, or it might take the form of curriculum enhancements, or it might be all of the above. We will explore each strategy in turn and let you decide what is best for your students.

A SIX-STEP PROCESS OF CURRICULUM DESIGN

The regulatory standards for independent schools provide a useful way of thinking about curriculum coverage. The standards require schools to provide a curriculum that gives students experience in the following areas: 'linguistic, mathematical, scientific, technological, human and social, physical and aesthetic and creative education', so that it promotes spiritual, moral, social and cultural development.[1]

---

1   Department for Education, *The Independent School Standards: Guidance for Independent Schools* (April 2019), p. 7. Available at: https://www.gov.uk/government/publications/regulating-independent-schools. See also Part 1, section 2(a) of the Education (Independent School Standards) Regulations 2014: https://www.legislation.gov.uk/uksi/2014/3283/schedule/made.

A broad curriculum, therefore, might be regarded as one in which there are enough subjects on a student's timetable to cover all these experiences. Narrowing the curriculum for working-class students clearly runs counter to this definition of breadth. A broad curriculum offers all students a wide range of subjects for as long as possible.

A balanced curriculum, meanwhile, might be regarded as one in which each subject isn't only taught to all students but is afforded sufficient space on the timetable to deliver its distinct contribution. The danger here is that some subjects, such as art, music and languages, are squeezed out of the timetable by English, maths and science. It isn't uncommon for English to have five or more lessons on the timetable per week and art just one, or for the arts to operate on a carousel whereby design technology is only taught for one term of the year.

In Matt's 2019 book, *School and College Curriculum Design 1: Intent,* he articulated a six-step process for designing an ambitious, broad and balanced, and planned and sequenced curriculum to which all students are afforded equal access.[2] The six steps are as follows:

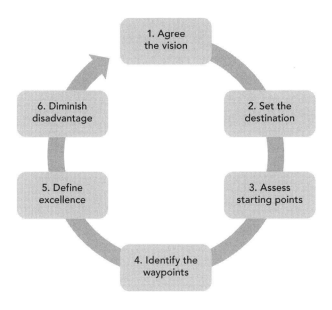

Let's walk through each step in turn.

---

2   M. Bromley, *School and College Curriculum Design 1: Intent* (Hinckley: Spark Education Books, 2019).

STEP 1: AGREE THE VISION

The first step requires each school to consult on and communicate a shared definition of what is meant by the word 'curriculum', as well as a working definition of what that curriculum encompasses in practice within the context of that school. This working definition might include, where relevant, aspects of the national, basic, local and hidden curriculums.

Agreeing a curriculum vision is also about deciding on and articulating the purpose of education within that school (e.g. Why do we exist? What is our hope for all students?).

STEP 2: SET THE DESTINATION

The second step is to identify what we want all students to know and be able to do at the end of their curriculum journeys – whether that is the end of a module or topic, the end of a year or key stage or phase, the end of their school studies or, indeed, in ten years' time.

This stage begins by developing a shared understanding of the importance of knowledge – especially the four knowledge domains we articulated earlier – and then agreeing, within the subject disciplines, what knowledge matters most to our students' future successes.

Part of the process of setting the destination is identifying the key concepts that must be taught – and learned – in each subject discipline. These 'foundational' concepts – a combination of knowledge and skills – provide the end points towards which all students are headed.

STEP 3: ASSESS THE STARTING POINTS

Broadly speaking, the starting points take two forms: the taught curriculum and the learned curriculum.

The *taught curriculum* is what is written down in curriculum plans (national curriculum documents, awarding body specifications, schemes of work, etc.) and taught by teachers. The *learned curriculum* is what each student has acquired – what they know and can do, including their misconceptions and misunderstandings.

In terms of the taught curriculum, it is important to know the end points of the previous curriculum – that is, what students are expected to know and be able to do by the time they begin studying your curriculum. As far as possible, you need to ensure that there is curriculum continuity, that each stage of education flows smoothly and naturally into the next, and that each new year, key stage and phase of education consolidates and builds on what has gone before rather than needlessly repeating prior content. This can be achieved, in part, by ensuring that transition arrangements are improved, and that teachers and subject leaders in each phase work more closely with their counterparts in the preceding and succeeding phases to share data and engage in joint professional development and curriculum planning.

In terms of the *learned curriculum*, it is essential to understand what each student knows and can do and what they do not yet know and cannot yet do. We can accomplish this through better data-sharing but also by using ongoing assessments – such as class discussions, hinge questions, multiple-choice quizzes and exit tickets – to ascertain each student's 'struggle zone', as well as to activate their prior learning.

STEP 4: IDENTIFY THE WAYPOINTS

Once the destination and the starting points are known, the curriculum must carve a path between the two, which must grow ever steeper as students near the end. The curriculum needs to be increasingly complex and challenging as they travel through it, and it must also help them to develop as independent learners. One way to do this is to isolate the threshold concepts that students must acquire at each stage – the checkpoints through which they must pass on the way to their destination. These thresholds concepts can also act as a source of meaningful assessment – a progression model – that measures students' progress.

STEP 5: DEFINE EXCELLENCE

Defining excellence is partly about developing a growth mindset – believing that every student is capable of achieving excellence, no matter their starting points and backgrounds. But it is also about 'teaching to the top' for all students and not dumbing down or reducing the curriculum offer for working-class students. Defining excellence is also about having high expectations for every student and about explicitly teaching them the study and research skills – including how to take notes and revise – they need to succeed.

Delivering excellence requires the curriculum – and teachers – to pitch learning at an appropriate level, which is to say hard but achievable; if the work is too easy or too difficult then the students simply won't learn.

STEP 6: DIMINISH DISADVANTAGE

The sixth and final step towards designing an ambitious curriculum involves accepting that not all students start from the same point, and some will require more support and more time to reach their destination.

We will go deeper into this sixth step in the next chapter when we explore equity but, suffice to say for now, we can help to diminish disadvantage by better understanding the root causes. One such cause – though by no means the only cause – is a lack of knowledge and cultural capital. One of the most tangible forms that cultural capital takes is vocabulary, and so our curriculum should be a means of explicitly teaching vocabulary – the language *of* and *for* learning – in order to equip students with the tools they need to access the curriculum and achieve.

Providing equal access to the same ambitious curriculum by using these six steps is about teaching to the top and embodying high expectations for all. It is a key principle of this book and a way to help working-class students because:

- Every student gets the same entitlement to seeing and experiencing excellence.

- Every student is treated as though they can incorporate elements of excellence into their own work.

- It helps all students to improve on their previous best work.

- It helps students to realise that all improvement comes from an iterative process of comparing their current work to the excellent models that have been deconstructed for them.

How might you build the four knowledge domains across the whole school? Let's start with disciplinary knowledge.

BUILDING DISCIPLINARY KNOWLEDGE

A reminder: disciplinary knowledge is about improving students' abilities to speak, read and write in ways that befit each subject discipline.

As well as approaching each element – speaking, reading and writing – separately, and doing so in domain-specific ways to highlight the way that language is used differently in each subject discipline, it is important that we make connections between them and between different subject disciplines. Students need to develop their thought processes and understanding – as well as their ability to recall, select and analyse ideas and information – which calls for them to communicate in a coherent, considered and convincing way both in speech and in writing.

In practice, we believe this means that students should be encouraged to:

- Make extended, independent contributions that develop ideas in depth.
- Make purposeful presentations that allow them to speak with authority on significant subjects.
- Engage with texts that challenge preconceptions and develop understanding beyond the personal and immediate.
- Experiment with language and explore different ways of discovering and shaping their own meanings.
- Use writing as a means of reflecting on and exploring a range of views and perspectives on the world.

SPEAK LIKE A …

Learning to speak in ways that befit each subject discipline is about developing the ability to:

- Listen and respond to others (adding to or arguing against).
- Speak and present (with increasing formality).
- Participate in group discussion and interaction.
- Engage in drama, role play and performance (where relevant).

We have already seen that, by teaching rhetoric, private schools explicitly develop the above skills.

Reading ability in children cannot exceed their listening ability. Dorothy Latham asserts that 'spoken language forms a constraint, a ceiling not only on the ability to comprehend, but also on the ability to write, beyond which literacy cannot progress'.[3] Classroom talk is an important part of disciplinary knowledge because comprehension derives not just from writing and creating but also from talking. Moreover, communication and understanding improve with practice.

---

3   D. Latham, *How Children Learn to Write: Supporting and Developing Children's Writing in Schools* (London: Paul Chapman, 2002), quoted in D. Myhill and S. Fisher, *Informing Practice in English* (London: Ofsted, 2005), p. 4. Available at: https://dera. ioe.ac.uk/id/eprint/5475.

Providing students with opportunities to talk in the classroom is vital if they are to develop their understanding. Talking also helps to build students' vocabulary knowledge – a process that continues across all years and all levels of schooling and which isn't, therefore, solely in the domain of early years teachers or English teachers. Indeed, every teacher in the secondary phase has a duty to help students develop their spoken language, and they should continue to help them become more articulate and sophisticated users of the English language.

In addition, we should ensure that the development of spoken language permeates the school day. After all, we use spoken language all day, every day, so we should take advantage of this and build oral language activities into daily routines, such as during tutor time (e.g. ask each student a question that they must answer in a sentence), when handing out materials, when students enter and leave the classroom, and when giving instructions.

We should also make sure that students have regular opportunities to speak. The teacher tends to dominate most classroom discussion – and it is right that teachers talk a lot because they are the experts in the room and in possession of the knowledge and experience the students need. However, it is important that the students get a chance to interact with the teacher and with each other, and to do so beyond responding to closed questions.

What is more, we should plan opportunities for one-to-one discussion. Spoken language develops best through paired conversation, especially when one of the pair has a better developed vocabulary. Therefore, it is worth investigating ways of pairing up students with someone with more sophisticated language skills, perhaps an older student, parent or volunteer.

This could be a case of volunteers reading a book with a student or simply engaging in conversation. One-to-one conversation also enables young people to develop conversational skills such as turn-taking, intonation and eye contact.

 IDEAS

Wherever you see this icon, we will share our top five takeaway tips for putting the theory outlined above into practice. So, here are our top five tips for helping students to speak like a subject specialist.

1   **Classroom debates and discussions:** Encourage students to participate in classroom debates and discussions where they can practise speaking about topics related to different subject disciplines. This will help them to develop their critical thinking and communication skills as well as their ability to articulate complex ideas.

2   **Role-playing activities:** Design role-playing tasks where students take on the role of experts in a particular field, such as scientists, historians or economists. This will lead to a deeper understanding of the subject matter and help students to talk with greater confidence and authority.

3   **Presentations:** Ask students to create presentations about different subjects, requiring them to research the topic thoroughly and organise their thoughts into a coherent, persuasive argument. Encourage them to use visual aids, such as charts or graphs, to support their points and to help them to speak more confidently.

4   **Group projects:** Assign group projects that require students to work together to solve a problem or complete a task related to a particular subject discipline. This will help them to develop their collaboration and communication skills as well as their ability to speak about the subject matter in a clear and concise manner.

5   **Peer-to-peer feedback:** Encourage students to provide feedback to their peers on their presentations, debates and other speaking assignments to develop their ability to evaluate and critique the work of others, as well as to receive constructive criticism and feedback on their own work.

In sum, teaching students to speak like a subject specialist is achieved when we:

- Provide opportunities for them to talk in extended, structured ways (e.g. allow more wait time).

- Model the clear and correct use of spoken language.

- Regularly check for understanding.

- Use simple, direct language (e.g. start instructions with verbs).

- Teach active listening skills and note-taking.

- Elaborate on answers and extend contributions with questions.

READ LIKE A …

Reading is about developing the ability to:

■ Decode increasingly complex and challenging words in each subject discipline.

■ Read for meaning using reading strategies such as prediction, skimming, scanning, inference, summarising and so on.

■ Understand a writer's craft by analysing the effect of the use of features of form, structure and language.

■ Read and engage with a wide variety of texts.

■ Research for a wide range of purposes.

One of the key aspects of teaching disciplinary reading skills is the use of subject-specific vocabulary. For students to be able to understand and use with accuracy words with which they are unfamiliar, we need to introduce them to those words in a careful sequence.

For example, we could begin by reading aloud a sentence in which the new word appears. Then we could show students the word written down and ask them to say it aloud several times. Next, we could debate possible meanings with the class and point out any parts of the word that might help with meaning – for example, a prefix or Greek or Latin root.

After this, we could reread the sentence to see if there are any contextual clues and explicitly explain the meaning of the word through simple definition and the use of synonyms. We could provide several examples of the word being used in context and ask questions to determine whether students have understood the word.

We could also present some sentences and ask the students to judge whether or not the word is used correctly and get them to write their own sentences using the word. Finally, once we have introduced and reinforced the word in the lesson, we could explicitly use the word during the next few days to emphasise its meaning. One of the advantages of this sequence is that it ensures the students are exposed to new vocabulary several times and get to see, hear and use new words in context.

Once new subject-specific words have been introduced, we need to help students to read these words quickly and accurately, adopting the appropriate intonation. This is called fluency. Fluency requires a background knowledge of words and a text, as well as rapid retrieval of the requisite vocabulary. It also requires a knowledge of syntax and grammar to predict the words that are likely to appear next.

The ability to adapt our vocabulary and intonation according to the syntax and grammar of a text, as well as the ability to read ahead, assists with both speed and accuracy. Experienced readers integrate these processes so that reading becomes automatic, which allows them to focus their cognitive energy on the task of discerning meaning.

A useful analogy is learning to tie your shoelaces. When you first learn to tie your laces, you must dedicate all your attention to it because it is unfamiliar. However, once you have mastered the art of lace-tying – through repeated exposure to it – you begin to do it automatically, without having to think about it, and can do so while holding a conversation.

There is a strong correlation between fluency and reading comprehension; indeed, it is such a strong link that fluency and comprehension can be regarded as interdependent. After all, fluency only occurs when a reader understands the text; if reading is hesitant and disjointed, then meaning is lost.

It is impossible to be a fluent reader if you have to keep stopping to decipher an unfamiliar word. To be fluent, you must move beyond the decoding stage to accurately read whole words. Therefore, one of the first skills to teach to achieve fluency is accuracy.

A fluent reader has ready access to a vast bank of words which they can apply in different contexts. The words to which a reader has immediate access are called their 'sight vocabulary'. Even complex words that originally had to be decoded (like 'originally' and 'decoded' rather than monosyllabic function words like 'that' and 'had'), but which can now be recognised on sight, become part of the fluent reader's lexicon.

But recognition isn't enough for fluency. As well as being in the reader's sight vocabulary, words are also stored in their 'receptive vocabulary' – that is to say, words the reader knows the meaning of. The larger the bank of words that are both recognised and understood on sight, the broader the range of texts that are accessible. For this reason, developing students' sight vocabularies and receptive vocabularies are the most effective ways of developing both fluency and reading comprehension.

Once you have developed accuracy, you need to develop speed, thereby increasing the rate at which your students can access texts. Reading speed isn't the same as reading fast. People who read too quickly – and therefore show little regard for punctuation, intonation or comprehension – aren't fluent readers. Reading speed is about being able to process texts quickly while also understanding the text, taking account of punctuation and adopting an appropriate intonation. In short, improving students' reading speed is important, but it must not be at the expense of comprehension.

After accuracy and speed, the third component of reading fluently is prosody – that is, reading with expression. Prosody is more difficult to achieve than accuracy and speed because it involves developing stress, pitch and rhythm. However, prosody is essential in rendering reading aloud meaningful. Poor prosody can cause confusion and impacts on a reader's interest and motivation to read. By contrast, good prosody makes reading aloud come alive and reflects the author's message more accurately and more meaningfully.

Understanding what a text means is about much more than decoding or word recognition. The depth of understanding differentiates the weak reader from the strong. Comprehension is an active process, which is heavily dependent on the reader's spoken language skills as well as their understanding of word meanings and the syntactic and semantic relationships between words. Comprehension is the ability to engage with a text at a deep level.

Active engagement with a text depends not only on the skill of the reader but also on the nature of the text. Broadly speaking, we can divide texts into three levels of comprehension: independent, instructional and frustration. It is important to know which kind of text to give to students in which situations.

1   **Texts at the independent level.** The reader can read most or all of the text with fluency, finding no more than about one word out of every twenty challenging. We should give students texts that are at their independent level for self-directed reading activities. By reading fluently, students will be able to engage with the material and take meaning from it. They may need strategies to decode the odd unfamiliar word, but they should be able to do so independently and without losing their thread.

2   **Texts at the instructional level.** The reader finds the text challenging (with one word in ten proving difficult) but manageable and can read it with support. Support enables students who are reading at this more difficult level to access additional sophisticated vocabulary and sentence structures.

3   **Texts at the frustration level.** The reader has difficulty with more than one word in ten, and thus finds the text frustrating to read. Ideally, we should not ask students to read texts at this level – even with support – because interrupting the text every time they struggle with a word means they become exasperated and so lose their motivation and enthusiasm.

When working independently, we should give students texts to read that fall within their independent level. When involved in guided reading aimed at developing their vocabulary, we should give them texts that fall within their instructional level. We can still use texts pitched at a student's frustration level in class – this helps to expose them to more sophisticated vocabulary and syntax – but only if the teacher reads them to the students.

IDEAS

Here are our top five tips for helping students to read like a subject specialist.

1   **Close reading:** Teach the students how to read closely by emphasising the importance of paying attention to the details, structure and language used in the text. Encourage them to take notes and annotate the text as they read to help them identify key themes and arguments.

2   **Reading strategies:** Teach students different reading strategies that are specific to each subject discipline. For example, in science, they might need to focus on understanding technical language and diagrams, while in history, they might need to focus on understanding different perspectives and primary sources.

3   **Contextualisation:** Help the students to understand how the text they are reading fits into the broader context of the subject discipline. For example, in literature, they might need to understand the historical and cultural context in which the text was written, while in science, they might need to understand how a particular discovery fits into the larger body of scientific knowledge.

4   **Vocabulary building:** Encourage the students to build their vocabulary by focusing on the key terms and concepts used in the subject discipline. This will help them to better understand the text and to speak more confidently about the subject matter.

5   **Practice and feedback:** Provide the students with regular opportunities to practise their reading skills and to receive feedback on their progress. For example, you might assign reading quizzes or comprehension exercises, or you might ask students to work in small groups to discuss and analyse a particular text. Provide feedback on their work, highlighting areas where they are doing well and where they can improve.

In sum, teaching students to read like a subject specialist is achieved when we:

◼ Introduce a new word carefully: provide repeated exposure to it, say it and write it, define it and exemplify it.

◼ Develop fluency: speed, accuracy and prosody.

◼ Teach comprehension skills.

◼ Use texts at the appropriate difficulty level.

WRITE LIKE A …

Writing in a way that befits each subject discipline is about developing the ability to:

◼ Generate, plan and draft ideas for composition.

◼ Select, shape and construct language for expression and effect in composition.

◼ Proofread and redraft written work, drawing on conventions and structures.

◼ Use accurate grammar, punctuation and spelling.

Writing has traditionally been one of the weakest areas of literacy teaching because, all too often, teachers assume that imparting knowledge – making sure students know stuff – is enough. In reality, of course, the most common and effective means by which most knowledge is demonstrated and assessed – whether in exams, controlled assessments, coursework, classwork and homework – is through students' writing.

Writing, therefore, needs to be taught by every teacher who uses writing as a means of demonstrating and assessing learning. This isn't a case of asking teachers to do anything technical or beyond their comfort zones. It is simply about helping students to write like a designer, artist, musician, historian, mathematician or scientist and so on.

The quality of students' writing is usually better when it emerges from reading other people's writing. However, that doesn't mean simply displaying a good model of a text on the board; rather, it involves:

◼ Modelling: sharing information about a text.

◼ Joint construction: working with students to create a text collaboratively.

- Independent construction: students constructing a text in a new genre independently of others, albeit with support.
- Actively teaching vocabulary and sentence structures.

If we simply show writing exemplars on the board, we are in danger of giving students the mistaken impression that writing is a product rather than a process. Students need to see that writing involves making decisions and making mistakes. Students need to see their teacher – and that means their teachers in all subjects – writing. This might involve some of the following approaches.

- **Contemplating the 'what' and the 'how' of a text:** What is its purpose? Who is its intended audience? The answers to these questions will affect how the text is written, both in terms of its language and its presentation.

- **Examining the conventions of a text:** Again, this is in terms of both language (formality, style, sentence structure, etc.) and presentation (paragraphs, sequence, bullet points, images, etc.).

- **Demonstrating how the text might be written:** This involves students observing the teacher as they 'think aloud' and explain the decisions they make. For example, thinking aloud might sound like this: 'I need to write this like a historian would write it. It will need to be in the third person, so "he/she/they" not "I". It will need to be formal, not colloquial, but not too stuffy either – it must be accessible to a wide audience. Now, talk to your partner about what your first sentence might say. Then we'll listen to some of your examples and compare them with what I write down.' This articulation moves from modelling to composition to assessment.

Writing a text while providing a running commentary involves explaining the decisions you are making and how and why you select and reject words.

 IDEAS

Here are our top five tips for helping students to write like a subject specialist.

1   **Analyse and model professional writing:** Provide students with examples of professional writing within the specific subject area that they can analyse and model. This will help them to better understand the writing conventions and language used in the subject area.

2   **Provide writing prompts:** Assign writing prompts that are specific to each subject discipline. For example, in science students might be asked to write a lab report, while in social studies they might be asked to write a research paper.

3   **Develop discipline-specific writing skills:** Teach students specific writing skills that are important in each subject area, such as writing hypotheses in science, developing arguments in social studies or crafting thesis statements in English.

4   **Peer editing and feedback:** Encourage students to share their writing with peers and provide feedback. This will help them to receive constructive criticism and feedback on their writing as well as to learn from the writing of their peers.

5   **Practice and revision:** Provide opportunities for students to practise their writing skills and revise their work. This could include drafting and revising multiple versions of a writing assignment, peer review sessions or teacher feedback on written assignments. By practising and revising their writing, students can improve their writing skills and become more confident writers in different subject disciplines.

In sum, teaching students to write like a subject specialist is achieved when we:

■ Explain the who (audience), what (purpose), how (technique) and the conventions of a subject-specific text.

■ Model disciplinary writing while thinking aloud.

■ Co-construct disciplinary texts with the class.

■ Allow class time for independent practice and feedback.

■ Actively teach vocabulary and sentence structure.

As we have observed, the building of disciplinary knowledge will likely take up a large part of core curriculum time. And rightly so – it is how students' overall attainment at secondary school is measured.

But, as we also remarked, the other three knowledge domains require some serious consideration too. We will explore these shortly, but first, time to pause and reflect on your own practice.

REFLECTIVE QUESTIONS

■ How does the way we have outlined the teaching of disciplinary knowledge compare to the methods currently being used in your school?

■ How successful is each subject team in your school at teaching disciplinary knowledge? Where is the evidence of this success?

■ How does each subject team look outwards and consider what other schools do in teaching this knowledge domain?

■ How do subject teams share their approaches to teaching disciplinary knowledge with each other?

FURTHER QUESTIONS

Now, using steps 3–6 of the six-step curriculum design model we outlined earlier in this chapter, how does each subject team:

■ Assess students' starting points in speaking, reading and writing at each key stage and for each unit of work (step 3)?

■ Ensure that the knowledge and skills associated with speaking, reading and writing build progressively over time (step 4)?

■ Ensure all topics/units have clear examples of excellence embedded within them (step 5)?

■ Ensure all topics/units have a range of appropriate support materials available to students, and that teachers, teaching assistants and students are trained in their use (step 6)?

BUILDING PERSONAL KNOWLEDGE

Personal knowledge is taught at various points in a school's curriculum. Sadly, because it isn't yet formally assessed at age 16, this knowledge domain has a low status in many schools. Whether we can or should measure the growth in a student's personal knowledge is perhaps a moot point anyway. Not every aspect of a student's progress can or should be assessed, but growing personal knowledge should be valued.

Ofsted already judges schools based on how well they develop students' personal development. According to the inspection framework, as well as helping students to become 'responsible, respectful and active citizens', schools are required to show how they are developing each student's 'character', 'confidence' and 'resilience'.[4]

Ofsted strongly advise schools that the development of these qualities isn't limited to personal, social, health and economic (PSHE) education lessons and tutor time; rather, curriculum subjects should also contribute to students' personal development. This means not just helping them to understand how to become better thinkers and learners in their subject disciplines, but also helping them to develop skills, attitudes and habits that support their well-being.

Students from working-class backgrounds, especially the most disadvantaged, will need more support from all the adults in the school community to develop their personal knowledge. One example of where class position is likely to play a factor is knowledge of potential career paths. High-quality careers information and guidance is especially important for students whose parents have little knowledge of careers outside of their own social networks. Alongside this, students need to become more aware of their own strengths, so they can make career choices that are potentially fulfilling.

We believe that to build personal knowledge students should learn to:

■ Take control of their own personal story and realise how this affects their self-concept.

---

4 Ofsted, School Inspection Handbook, para. 293.

- Acquire a deeper appreciation of the forces behind motivation, or the lack of it – physiological, psychological and social.

- Be increasingly aware of their personal strengths and talents and how they can best contribute to their community.

- Appreciate how their interests and strengths might align with their future careers.

- Develop better emotional regulation to support their current and future lives.

In this chapter, we have made some suggestions to help students develop their self-concept, motivation and emotional regulation. These ideas can be taught in a number of places within the curriculum. Ideally, students shouldn't encounter them just once. Instead, we should consistently reinforce these messages in lessons, assemblies, tutor time, one-to-one reviews, parents' evenings, drop-down days and so on.

So, with this in mind, how can we develop students' personal knowledge?

Well-being should have a central place in your school for both students and staff. We like this definition of well-being: 'feeling good and functioning well'.[5] Note: boosting well-being is something that many of the world's top companies invest in every year as they strive to recruit and retain the best employees. We think every organisation should focus on developing the well-being of their people.

Andy's last book, *The Learning Imperative*, made the link between well-being and relational trust: when relational trust is high, organisations do better.[6] In schools, the level of relational trust has a strong correlation with better educational outcomes. Megan Tschannen-Moran and Christopher Gareis argue that 'Few other variables examined by educational researchers come close to the level of predictive power of trust on student achievement.'[7]

The best schools, quite rightly, have high expectations for their students, but with this comes pressure. Students must learn to manage their mental health at school as they juggle studying with navigating relationships, social media, physical changes and much more.

---

5   J. Aked, N. Marks, C. Cordon and S. Thompson, *Five Ways to Wellbeing: A Report Presented to the Foresight Project on Communicating the Evidence Base for Improving People's Well-Being* (London: New Economics Foundation, 2008), p. 1. Available at: https://neweconomics.org/uploads/files/five-ways-to-wellbeing-1.pdf.

6   M. Burns and A. Griffith, *The Learning Imperative: Raising Performance in Organisations by Improving Learning* (Carmarthen: Crown House Publishing, 2019).

7   M. Tschannen-Moran and C. R. Gareis, Principals, Trust, and Cultivating Vibrant Schools, *Societies*, 5 (2015), 256–276 at 258. Available at: https://www.researchgate.net/publication/315364994_Principals_Trust_and_Cultivating_Vibrant_Schools.

We are all aware of the 'knowing–doing gap'. We know that we should eat at least five pieces of fresh fruit and vegetables a day, exercise and get a good night's sleep, but how many of us adopt this universal wisdom for ourselves? Alongside teaching knowledge, schools with strong pastoral systems work tirelessly with students and their parents or carers to find suitable strategies to enhance well-being.

We recommend that both students and parents are regularly surveyed about well-being and how it can be enhanced. We also believe that schools should teach time management strategies. (We have shared some ideas for teaching time management in Lesson 7.)

A high-status PSHE curriculum and/or drop-down days (where a whole year group or even a whole school go off timetable) is a great way of help-ing students to gain knowledge about personal well-being. On a drop-down day, school staff and external agencies tend to run activities on a carousel. This can include learning a new sport or martial art that isn't included within the PE curriculum, meditation, journalling, horticulture, animal husbandry, playing a musical instrument, creative writing, com-puter programming and so on.

Enjoyment of these activities can lead to a student joining an after-school club or signing up to a local organisation. It is good for young people to encounter new and different faces in this context, and many might have their interests sparked (there is more on sparking in Chapter 5).

 **IDEAS**

Here are our top five tips for developing students' personal knowledge.

1   **Portfolio-building:** Many professionals build portfolios. From nurses to architects, having a physical (and increasingly digital) record of the quality of your work can help with career advancement. Universities are embracing this too. Alongside their academic studies, students build portfolios using software from companies such as PebblePad to support their post-degree employability.[8]

2   **Examining beliefs:** When someone says they know something, what they are really saying is that they believe it very strongly. We think it is important for students, and indeed adults, to frequently

8   See https://www.pebblepad.co.uk.

evaluate their beliefs. Are they rational or irrational? Could they be wrong? Such questions can be explored through philosophy. Setting up a philosophy club and/or teaching through Philosophy for Children (P4C) can be a powerful tool for helping students to expand their self-knowledge. Many of the principles of P4C can be applied in most subject disciplines, so it would be useful for staff to undertake some training in this area.[9]

3   **Story writing:** One project that is great for teaching students about story is the White Water Writers project with Higher Horizon, which is part of their widening participation provision.[10] This project gives groups of young people the opportunity to collaboratively write and publish a novel in just one week. A facilitator at the camp guides them through the process of ideas generation and character development. As the week progresses, the facilitator gradually steps back, giving the group greater ownership of the story and its editing. The development of characters gives the students an opportunity to explore future possible selves. Work like this enables young people to find their voice. Helping others to find their voice, especially if they feel marginalised, is another way of building a sense of agency. (We have some stories to share about this below.)

4   **Learning about motivation:** Wouldn't it be great if more students, from whatever social background, emerged from school with a deeper understanding of what motivates them? When students learn about motivation it can be insightful and empowering. Understanding the impact of things like nutrition, sleep, beliefs, self-narratives, personal habits and emotional disturbances should regularly be revisited in the school curriculum.

5   **How we communicate success and well-being:** Psychologists tell us that if we want to find happiness, we should learn to measure success in our own terms. They exhort us to 'run in your own lane' and not to compare ourselves with others. Unfortunately, we live at a time when individualists seem to have gained the upper hand. The media and the current norms of society often lead people to follow metrics that ultimately cause unhappiness. At a school and system level, we also need to examine our own metrics and see whether they are fit for purpose. What does it say about us as a school when we communicate 'success' solely

---

9   You can access free training resources at https://www.sapere.org.uk.
10   See https://whitewaterwriters.com.

in terms of how well someone does in written exams? Listening up is important. Regular dialogue with parents and students about what they want from education can provide insights into other people's lives – and what was hidden becomes unhidden.

 STORY

Richard Seymour of Keele University shared the following stories with us about students who have taken part in the White Water Writers project:

OTHER STORIES: RICHARD

One Year 9 student I remember well. She didn't have a uniform, and she was clearly a bit of a handful for the teachers. But she had a big personality, which can be great if channelled. By the middle of the week, she was just quietly writing and causing no trouble at all. Teachers were coming in to have conversations with her that didn't involve shouting. I found out that a few weeks after I left, the same student was going into local primary schools to lead creative writing workshops. There were no books in her house as neither of her parents could read, yet there she was, helping those younger than her to write creatively.

Another Year 9 girl had a very successful writing week. She was clearly the smartest in the room, and she very quietly ran the group, keeping the boys, especially, under creative control. At the end of the week, when the writers were all celebrating, I noticed she was in tears. She told me that while everyone else in the writing group would be okay, she knew that every time she cleared a barrier, another would appear in front of her. She told me a little about her life. She wasn't stupid. She knew exactly what life was going to be like for her. I couldn't tell her everything would be all right, but I did tell her that after what I had seen of her that week, she'd be all right. That was a few years ago, and I have since found out she did well in her GCSEs and went on to excel at college.

I had a group of Year 9 boys. I didn't know anything about them, which is the way I prefer it. They were as good as gold. Teachers popped in several times to ask how their behaviour was, but I never had any complaints. I learned later that the boys were all in danger of exclusion and that the school were working hard with them. This makes it all the more remarkable that they took to the project so well. A few weeks after the project, the boys led an assembly, reading from their book and, according to the school, each of them turned their school careers around.

REFLECTIVE QUESTIONS

- How does the way we have outlined the teaching of personal knowledge compare to the methods currently being used in your school?

- How much time is allocated to personal reflective processes where students consider the impact of what they are learning on their current or future life?

- Where is story taught within your school? How are the students encouraged to take control of their own story and find their voice?

- How and where do you listen up? How do you gather information about individual students to better understand the barriers they may be facing?

FURTHER QUESTIONS

Now, using steps 3–6 of the six-step curriculum design model we outlined earlier in this chapter, ask yourself: how does each subject team:

- Consider each student's starting point in terms of how we have defined personal knowledge, especially their perceived strengths and weaknesses (step 3)?

- Ensure that the knowledge and skills associated with an empowering self-narrative and emotional regulation build progressively over time (step 4)?

- Ensure all topics/units have clear advice on how students can manage their time and emotions as they tackle challenging work (step 5)?

- Ensure all topics/units have a range of appropriate support materials such as schedules to help students (step 6)?

Now, let's turn to the two other knowledge domains: social knowledge and cultural knowledge. Inevitably, there is an overlap between them, but we have tried to make suggestions to fit in with our earlier definitions.

BUILDING SOCIAL KNOWLEDGE

The contention of much of this book is that a large proportion of working-class people in our society are undervalued and under-represented. This is, in part, by design. Elites make the world much more unstable and precarious for working-class people. It is harder for us to enter certain professions, buy our own homes and be in secure employment.

The UK is the currently the second most unequal country in the G7,[11] and poverty is on the increase, as the number of food banks and warm banks attest. The biggest cause of death for men under 50 is suicide. From 2011 to 2015, 'males working in the lowest-skilled occupations had a 44% higher risk of suicide than the male national average; the risk among males in skilled trades was 35% higher'.[12]

As educators, we think that we have a responsibility to prepare students for their life beyond school. It seems obvious to us that lots of what is happening in our society is unjust. The question is: how much of this do we present to young people? For affluent students and their parents, these injustices work in their favour, so they may not want these social issues raised, let alone studied.

---

11   A. Fitri, The UK is the Second-Most Unequal G7 Country, New Statesman (6 September 2022). Available at: https://www.newstatesman.com/chart-of-the-day/2022/09/uk-second-most-unequal-g7-country.
12   Office for National Statistics, Suicide by Occupation, England: 2011 to 2015 (Data and Analysis from Census 2021). Available at: https://www.ons.gov.uk/peoplepopulationandcommunity/birthsdeathsandmarriages/deaths/articles/suicidebyoccupation/england2011to2015.

We believe that the most ethical approach to building social knowledge is to present information to students and then let them determine what to do with it. In our experience, it is in your late teens and early twenties when you start to properly form political views. Students are likely to be better formed if they are trained to become critical thinkers. This is best done in a domain-specific way through the subject disciplines.

Understanding class and the impact of class is under-addressed by schools. We would like to change this, and we would like you to join us.

Professor Valerie Walkerdine from Cardiff University, a working-class academic, calls for a fresh approach to the study of class so that the impact of classism can be reduced. Walkerdine argues that the working class need to be involved as creators of knowledge: 'Working-class people need to be able to offer their experiences with pride, knowing that doing so increases the sum total of knowledge.'[13]

We agree with this; it is the reason we have suggested that working-class writers, musicians and other artists are worthy of study. It is also why we have counselled schools to undertake audits to ensure that the voice and values of the working class come through to all students.

Of course, we will face opposition from those who think classism doesn't exist, and those who may have fallen prey to the belief that some people in our society are simply underserving of success and are the creators of their own problems. This idea may have formed through what writer Imogen Tyler describes as 'social abjection'. In her excellent book, *Revolting Subjects*, she explains how the right-wing media have deliberately and effectively built anxiety around particular groups of people: refugees, travellers, the young, the poor and the disabled.[14]

Hopefully, by helping students to understand the methods used by the media, examine data and encounter different people in these groups, our students will become informed consumers of information and will stop swallowing the stereotypes.

In *Thrive*, Valerie Hannon and Amelia Peterson 'advocate a new purpose for education in a rapidly changing world' and 'identify four levels of thriving': 'global – our place in the planet, societal – place, communities, economies, interpersonal – our relationships [and] intrapersonal – the self'.[15] Hannon and Peterson assert that all social classes need to reflect on how their behaviour affects others and can be affected by others. The

13 Research Outreach, Classism in Education Still Exists: Here's What to Do About It (5 February 2021). Available at: https://researchoutreach.org/articles/classism-education-exists-heres-what-about.

14 I. Tyler, *Revolting Subjects: Social Abjection and Resistance in Neoliberal Britain* (London and New York: Zed Books, 2013).

15 V. Hannon and A. Peterson, *Thrive: The Purpose of Schools in a Changing World* (Cambridge: Cambridge University Press, 2021), p. xiv.

book draws on the work of economists such as Nobel Prize winners Amartya Sen and Joseph Stiglitz who argue that policymakers 'are like pilots trying to steer a ship without a reliable compass'.[16]

The OECD's Learning Framework 2030 uses the same metaphor of the compass.[17] It describes education's role in helping young people to develop a 'learning compass' for their life's journey. A large part of that journey will involve navigating numerous relationships at all four levels.

Excessive income and wealth inequality is bad for the planet, too, according to the Nobel Prize-winning economist Thomas Piketty, author of *Capital in the Twenty-First Century*.[18] Following an event at the London School of Economics in 2020, he said there was a 'growing awareness that the environmental crisis cannot be solved with current levels of inequality or under the current economic system'.[19]

Helping students to become more prosocial and less individualistic is a challenge. Young people are bombarded with advertising, and we live in a world where, depressingly, influencers such as the Kardashians can become billionaires. What can we do as educators to counteract this? The good news is that humans are by nature social animals. If the COVID-19 lockdowns taught us anything, it is that most of us are altruistic – millions volunteered to support the more vulnerable, after all.

Although schools only have access to students for about 15% of their lives between the ages of 11 and 16, we can do a lot to stimulate social knowledge. We can build it in innovative ways, such as engineering discussions, organising debates, reading, game creation and film analysis.

In practice, we believe that, to build social knowledge, students should learn to:

■ Develop a deeper knowledge of social history and why this side of history is under-represented and undervalued.

■ Foster a deeper understanding of power relationships within society and question whether individualism advances social progress.

16   J. E. Stiglitz, A. Sen and J-P. Fitoussi, *Report by the Commission for the Measurement of Economic Performance and Social Progress* (2009), p. 9. Available at: https://ec.europa.eu/eurostat/documents/8131721/8131772/Stiglitz-Sen-Fitoussi-Commission-report.pdf.
17   Organisation for Economic Co-operation and Development, *The Future of Education and Skills: Education 2030* (Paris: OECD Publishing, 2018), p. 4. Available at: https://www.oecd.org/education/2030/E2030%20Position%20Paper%20 (05.04.2018).pdf.
18   T. Piketty, *Capital in the Twenty-First Century* (Cambridge, MA: Harvard University Press, 2017).
19   T. Piketty: 'The Current Economic System Is Not Working When It Comes to Solving Inequality', *London School of Economics and Political Science* (21 February 2020). Available at: https://blogs.lse.ac.uk/europpblog/2020/02/21/thomas-piketty-the-current-economic-system-is-not-working-when-it-comes-to-solving-inequality.

- Express solidarity and empathy with fellow working-class people.
- Critique and analyse the media they consume.

 IDEAS

Here are our top five tips for helping students to develop their social knowledge.

1   **Debating:** Debating helps students to develop social knowledge as they become clearer about social issues and how different people's values contrast with their own. Teaching students how to debate, either through a debating club and/or within subjects, can get them accustomed to presenting their opinions and seeing the difference between weak and strong arguments. The Economist Educational Foundation has some good resources for running debates.[20] Choose topics that have a class or political component, such as: 'Should social class become a protected characteristic under employment law?', 'Does the media fairly reflect the working class?', 'Is our society fairer than it was fifty years ago?', 'Should nature have the same rights as people?', 'Does our culture prime us to feel envy?' or 'Is justice blind when it comes to social class?' All topics up for debate will require the students to do some research. We can use debating frames, like writing and oracy frames, to help students form arguments and develop counterarguments. We need to ensure that different students get to debate and that weaker orators get their chance too. We could use a points system to stimulate competition and engage students in the process.

2   **Discussion of events:** Talking about major political events that have had a disproportionate effect on working-class people is also important. For students to leave secondary school not knowing about them seems remiss. Events might include the Hillsborough disaster – how it was covered by the media, especially the *Sun* newspaper, and the subsequent fight for justice by the families; the 2008 financial crash – the fraudulent bank practices that led to years of austerity; and the Grenfell Tower fire – the slow, painful pace of the British justice system for the victims and their families. Surely, if your school curriculum is

---

20   See https://economistfoundation.org.

going to show that it truly values its working-class students, then it should help them to understand how society has treated them in recent years. Assemblies, PSHE and subjects such as history and geography are good places for this.

3   **Interviewing successful working-class adults:** Successful working-class adults provide real case studies and can be role models to current students. Interviews can be done in person or via video calls. In this way, students can gain vital career knowledge and become informed of likely obstacles they might face based on the interviewees' experiences. There are many examples of working-class people entering professions such as the law, medicine and academia. Learning about their careers and embracing their wisdom can help students from non-traditional backgrounds to get in and get on. For now, we need to assure students that aspirations are important, but advise them that they are more likely to succeed if they are fully aware of the challenges ahead rather than naively thinking their journey will be an easy one. We also need to reassure them that we – and others within the school community – are there to support them along the way.

4   **Film and TV education:** Film education can be a wonderful way of building social knowledge, especially when the films are expertly studied and debriefed. Subjects like media studies are great for this, but if you don't have media studies on the curriculum, there is still space to include some of these films, or at least sections of them, in subjects such as English, history, geography, business studies, PSHE and RE. Here are some suggestions of films that have a strong class component and explore social inequality: *An Inspector Calls* (1954), *The Admirable Crichton* (1957), *A Taste of Honey* (1961), *Kes* (1969), *Trading Places* (1983), *Matewan* (1987), *Life Is Sweet* (1990), *Brassed Off* (1996), *Trainspotting* (1996), *Office Space* (1999), *Billy Elliot* (2000), *Bowling for Columbine* (2002), *This is England* (2006), *Snowpiercer* (2013), *Elysium* (2013), *Pride* (2014), *The Big Short* (2015), *I, Daniel Blake* (2016), *Sorry to Bother You* (2018), *Burning* (2018), *Parasite* (2019), *Us* (2019) and *Life and Death in a Warehouse* (2022). There are also a great range of award-winning television series that focus on issues around society, oppression and inequality. Here are some shows that we recommend: *The Century of the Self* (2002) written by Adam Curtis, *The Wire* (2002–2008) written by David Simon, *Shameless* written by Paul Abbott (2004–2013), *Black Mirror* (2011–) written by Charlie Brooker, *Broken* (2017) written by Jimmy McGovern, *In My Skin*

(2018–2021) written by Kayleigh Llewellyn and *Anne* (2022) written by Kevin Sampson.

5 **Books and music education:** We would also like to share a list of books that explore class and social issues which could be studied in their entirety or as extracts: Elizabeth Gaskell – *North and South* (1854); Charles Dickens – *Great Expectations* (1861); George Eliot – *Middlemarch* (1871); Émile Zola – *Germinal* (1885); Thomas Hardy – *Jude the Obscure* (1895); W. H. Davies – *The Autobiography of a Super-Tramp* (1908); E. M. Forster – *Howard's End* (1910); D. H. Lawrence – *Sons and Lovers* (1913); Robert Tressell – *The Ragged Trousered Philanthropists* (1914); George Orwell – *Down and Out in Paris and London* (1933), *The Road to Wigan Pier* (1937), *Nineteen-Eighty Four* (1949) and *The Collected Essays, Journalism and Letters, Volume 1* (1920–1940); Alan Sillitoe – *The Loneliness of the Long-Distance Runner* (1959); Mikhail Bulgakov – *The Master and Margarita* (1967); Alan Garner – *Red Shift* (1973); Sue Townsend – *The Queen and I* (1992); Barry Unsworth – *Sacred Hunger* (1992) and *The Quality of Mercy* (2011); Roddy Doyle – *Paddy Clarke Ha Ha Ha* (1993); Irvine Welsh – *Trainspotting* (1993); James Kelman – *How Late It Was, How Late* (1994); Andrea Ashworth – *Once in a House on Fire* (1998); Zadie Smith – *White Teeth* (2000); Stuart Maconie – *The People's Songs* (2013); and Douglas Stuart – *Shuggie Bain* (2020).

Another valuable resource is *Common People: An Anthology of Working-Class Writers* edited by Kit de Waal.[21] This is a collection of essays, poems and memoir written as a celebration of working-class life. It was published through crowdfunding, highlighting the difficulty that many working-class writers face when approaching publishers. It includes stories from writers such as Malorie Blackman and Stuart Maconie.

The collection closes with an essay by Dr Dave O'Brien highlighting publishing's 'serious class problem, as it is one of the most socially exclusive of creative industries'.[22] O'Brien cites an analysis of the ONS's Labour Force Survey 2014 which claims that almost half of all authors, writers and translators were from the most privileged backgrounds whereas only 10% came from

---

21 K. de Waal (ed.), *Common People: An Anthology of Working-Class Writers* (London: Unbound, 2019).

22 D. O'Brien, Class and Publishing: Who Is Missing from the Numbers? In K. de Waal (ed.), *Common People: An Anthology of Working-Class Writers* (London: Unbound, 2019), pp. 275–280 at p. 278.

working-class origins.[23] In order to develop social knowledge, we think students need to know that these gaps exist and understand why. Building social knowledge is also about developing an appreciation of the positive contributions of the working classes to our shared history; in particular, we need to teach students about acts of resistance and struggle.

Studying classism through music can be a terrific way of educating students about social history. Here is a list of songs and the artists who created them that could be studied. For each one we have written a brief description of the social issue to which the artist is drawing our attention: 'This Land is Your land' by Woody Guthrie (1944) – issue: land rights, 'Coat of Many Colours' by Dolly Parton (1971) – issue: poverty, 'Them Belly Full (But We Hungry)' by Bob Marley and the Wailers (1974) – issue: poverty, 'Career Opportunities' by The Clash (1977) – issue: discrimination in the jobs market, 'Another Brick in the Wall' by Pink Floyd (1979) – issue: how the education system alienates, 'Eton Rifles' by The Jam (1979) – issue: class conflict, 'Redemption Song' by Bob Marley (1980) – issue: the transatlantic slave trade, 'Ghost Town' by The Specials (1981) – issue: mass unemployment and class discrimination, 'The Message' by Grandmaster Flash and the Furious Five (1982) – issue: urban tensions, 'Shipbuilding' by Robert Wyatt (1982) – issue: manufacturing decline and unemployment, 'Between the Wars' by Billy Bragg (1984) – issue: war and what society values, 'The World Turned Upside Down' by Billy Bragg (1984) – issue: the Diggers social movement, 'People Like Us' by Talking Heads (1986) – issue: working-class life, 'Heartland' by The The (1986) – issue: urban decay, government neglect and greed, 'Fast Car' by Tracy Chapman (1988) – issue: expectations of working-class women, 'Fight The Power' by Public Enemy (1989) – issue: class and racism in the United States, 'All Together Now' by The Farm (1990) – issue: First World War, 'Common People' by Pulp (1995) – issue: class snobbery, 'If You Tolerate This Your Children Will Be Next' by the Manic Street Preachers (1998) – issue: the Spanish Civil War, 'Jobseeker' by the Sleaford Mods (2007) – issue: the benefits system, 'The Complete Banker' by the Divine Comedy (2010) – issue: the 2007–2008 financial crisis, 'Let England Shake' by PJ Harvey (2011) – issue: the First World War/Afghanistan

---

23 D. O'Brien, D. Laurison, S. Friedman and A. Miles, Are the Creative Industries Meritocratic? An Analysis of the 2014 British Labour Force Survey, *Cultural Trends*, 25 (2016), 116–131. See also https://www.ilo.org/surveyLib/index.php/catalog/7721.

conflict, 'The Thieves Banquet' by Akala (2013) – issue: global corruption and evil, 'Royals' by Lorde (2013) – issue: opulence and comparison, 'Iron Sky' by Paolo Nutini (2014) – issue: fascism, 'This is America' by Childish Gambino (2018) – issue: police violence in the United States, and 'Blood on My Nikes' by Loyle Carner (2022) – issue: knife violence.

REFLECTIVE QUESTIONS

- How does the way we have outlined the teaching of social knowledge compare to methods currently being used in your school?

- How much time is allocated to the teaching of social knowledge? How is this monitored?

- Where in the curriculum is social knowledge taught in your school? What topics or approaches are having the biggest impact on learning? How do you know this?

- Where are there missed opportunities to teach more social knowledge?

FURTHER QUESTIONS

Now, using steps 3–6 of the six-step curriculum design model we outlined earlier in this chapter, how does each subject team:

- Consider each student's starting points in terms of how we have defined social knowledge (step 3)?

- Ensure that social knowledge builds progressively over time (step 4)?

- Ensure some topics/units have exemplar work to use with students which shows strong understanding of social knowledge (step 5)?

■ Ensure all topics/units have a range of appropriate support materials and that teachers, teaching assistants and students are trained in their use (step 6)?

BUILDING CULTURAL KNOWLEDGE

This section is slightly different from the previous three knowledge domains because it will pose more questions. This is because we want your school to think hard about how it teaches all things cultural.

We know that schools can spark interest in culture in numerous ways. There is a long list of books, films and documentaries that you can encourage students to study, there are hundreds of places to take students on trips that can open up new worlds, and there are scores of organisations/individuals who can come into school and stimulate an interest that wasn't there before.

So, what is your plan for building students' cultural knowledge? What learning about culture will your students come to value when they look back on their school days in later life? What cultural experiences will they be inspired to give their own children?

The key message about culture the students must receive is that, no matter your social class, you can enjoy any form of art or culture. People should enjoy what they enjoy and not allow others to decide that a form of culture is 'not for them'.

Here, it is important to bring back the sociologist Pierre Bourdieu whose reflections on the concept of habitus are particularly worthy of study and analysis. Bourdieu explains how students may 'feel like a fish out of water' in some cultural settings, and this will make many self-exclude from even trying a new experience. Moreover, being made to feel unwelcome is a tactic that is used by elites to preserve their privilege. They want us to feel awkward in certain situations so they can continue to dominate those spheres. We think it is important that we prepare working-class students for such scenarios and train them to question their imposter syndromes.

We are sure you are aware of the adage 'Travel broadens the mind'. It follows that a lack of travel will narrow the mind. Some working-class students will be in poverty, and families in poverty have less funds available for travel, so it is highly likely that these students will have limited cultural experiences. We need to be mindful that the cultural experiences we organise for our students aren't regarded as one-offs: if a student's interest is sparked, we need to consider how we can support them to foster this even further. This might require some creative thinking, but it is likely to involve helping students and families by providing extra information and/or supporting them to seek extra funding or sponsorship. Otherwise, these students won't be able to experience a possible lifelong joy, or even a career, in the arts, which is available to the more affluent.

In practice, we believe that to build cultural knowledge students should learn to:

- Understand notions of habitus and how they affect personal decision-making around cultural choices.

- Appreciate how our habitus can change in order to experience different forms of culture without prejudice.

- Be confident in expressing their opinions around what aspects of culture they enjoy.

- Appreciate how working-class people have fought throughout history to gain access to the arts.

- Appreciate the challenges that working-class people face when trying to pursue a career in the arts.

 IDEAS

Here are our top five tips for developing students' cultural knowledge.

1   **Teach sociology:** In Chapter 2, we wrote about Pierre Bourdieu and his work on habitus. He argued that our habitus will determine the types of culture we consume. Teaching students about habitus and setting up discussions around this concept will help them to like or dislike examples of culture for the right reasons and not just parrot the views around them. The Latin word *habitus* refers to habits, conditions or states, particularly of the body. Bourdieu referred to it as a 'system of acquired dispositions functioning on the practical level as categories of perception and assessment or as classificatory principles as well as being the organizing principles of action'.[24] Understanding habitus can help us explain to students that some aspects of the culture we introduce them to will *feel* wrong, and it can be

24   P. Bourdieu, *In Other Words: Essays Toward a Reflexive Sociology* (Redwood City, CA: Stanford University Press, 1990), pp. 12–13.

difficult to counter this feeling because it has been years in the making. Therefore, we should try to ensure we take account of habitus when we are designing our cultural curriculum. For every cultural experience, we need to make it clear that *everyone* is entitled to enjoy it.

2   **Investigate accentism:** Dr Maureen Farrell from Glasgow University offers some insights on how learning about different accents can help us to counter stereotypes. As she says, 'certain accents are "loaded" with pre-conceived ideas'.[25] Historically, the rich were taught to use Received Pronunciation or RP (which is an elite accent) and Standard English or SE (which is an elite dialect). Being able to code-switch can be a valuable tool for working-class students, but they should not associate RP and SE with intelligence and superiority, and nor should they – or others – associate their own accent and dialect with a lack of intelligence and inferiority. Farrell urges schools to teach students to be 'true to your accent, give consideration to the listener, be prepared to repeat yourself and it's a good thing to have in your repertoire the ability to use the standard form of the language when appropriate'.

3   **Teach about working-class artists and autodidacts:** The working classes have a vibrant history of creating art, music, theatre, literature and so on, which needs to be reflected in the core curriculum. By looking through the lens of race and gender, most schools have a more diverse offering of writers compared with when we both went to school. It is right that more Black voices and more female voices are represented in the school curriculum. Their work opens new insights for readers as well as providing Black and female students with more role models. Similarly, there should be a strong emphasis on the work of working-class artists, no matter the social demographic of the school. Does your school's cultural curriculum offer reflect artists from all social classes?

An autodidact is a self-taught person. History is littered with notable examples of autodidacts, and many of them come from working-class roots because they couldn't afford to pay for their education. We think that students' cultural knowledge will expand if they learn about these people. Among history's most famous self-educators are Nobel Prize winners for literature such as Hermann Hesse and Eugene O'Neill, the ground-breaking

---

25   Dr Maureen Farrell, interview with Andy Griffith, 20 January 2023.

psychologist Melanie Klein, authors such as Charles Dickens and Charlotte Perkins Gilman, artists such as Vincent Van Gogh and Frida Kahlo, musicians such as Janice Joplin and Jimi Hendrix, orators such as the former slave Frederick Douglas, social activists such as Malcolm X, educators such as Booker T. Washington and inventors such as Garrett Morgan. The list goes on. Learning about autodidacts can teach students that where there is a strong desire to learn, we will find a way. Wouldn't it be great if schools harnessed more of this spirit? Perhaps our cultural curriculum offer can do this. We hope that students in your school understand how working-class people yearned for learning and the right to be literate. They believed in mutual improvement, fought for schooling for their children and built libraries within their communities. They were pro-learning and pro-reading.

4 **Explore high and low culture:** Your school's cultural curriculum will also need to say something about the differences between so-called high and low culture and should reflect examples from each. High culture or high art is often associated with ballet, opera, classical music and so on. Does this mean that any other type of culture is low? Students can learn a lot about culture through studying music. There are many advantages to this, as teaching about and through music doesn't carry a lot of financial cost. We saw in the social knowledge section above how studying certain song lyrics can give students insights into social history. Studying genres or even musicians can also be insightful.

5 **Cultural passports:** Does your school have a plan for taking students on a cultural journey? What will they experience in Year 7, 8, 9, and so on? Could you incorporate this journey into a passport of sorts? Many schools, such as Isaac Newton Academy, have created documentation to ensure that each student undertakes varied cultural experiences. This could be a booklet or in a digital format. What cultural entitlements you offer will be determined by factors such as your school's location and budget. A lot of cultural experiences can be delivered 'in-house' in the form of external speakers, films and documentaries or virtual reality. Other cultural experiences will require excursions. In either case, creating a cultural passport helps staff to plan experiences that complement and supplement previous experiences. The very creation of such a document, and different contributions to it, will give you an overview of the breadth of experiences your school offers its students.

REFLECTIVE QUESTIONS

- How does the way we have outlined the teaching of cultural knowledge compare to methods currently being used in your school?

- Does your school have a manifesto or a passport for teaching about culture? What would be the advantages and challenges of moving to this approach?

- Does your school teach about both high and low culture?

- What messages about consuming culture do you think your students get when passing through school?

FURTHER QUESTIONS

Now, using steps 3–6 of the six-step curriculum design model we outlined earlier in this chapter, how does each subject team:

- Consider each student's starting points in terms of how we have defined cultural knowledge (step 3)?

- Ensure that cultural knowledge builds progressively over time (step 4)?

- Ensure some topics/units have exemplar work to use with students which shows strong understanding of cultural knowledge (step 5)?

- Ensure all topics/units have a range of appropriate support materials and that teachers, teaching assistants and students are trained in their use (step 6)?

CHAPTER 5

EQUALITY THROUGH EXTRA-CURRICULAR ACTIVITIES

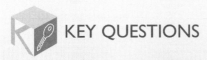 **KEY QUESTIONS**

In this chapter we will answer the following questions:

- How can we ensure fair access for working-class students to extra-curricular provision?

- How might extra-curricular activities help to build working-class students' life experiences and prepare them for future success?

- What kinds of extra-curricular activities can spark students' curiosity most successfully and promote lifelong interest in cultural pursuits?

In Chapter 4, we focused on ensuring equality by providing access to the same ambitious, broad and balanced, and planned and sequenced curriculum for all students – including working-class students. Now let's explore the second part of solution 1: providing fair access to extra-curricular activities for working-class students.

A great way to build the four knowledge domains, particularly cultural knowledge, is through our extra-curricular programme. It is important, therefore, when we talk about equality, that, as well as giving all students equal access to the same ambitious curriculum, we also provide all students with equal access to extra-curricular activities. We can achieve this, in part, through more targeted funding for those who would otherwise be denied these opportunities. We will explore ways to fund activities for working-class students shortly but, first, let's define our terms.

Extra-curricular activities are widely regarded as essential to expanding students' life experiences. For example, a paper by the Social Mobility Commission called *An Unequal Playing Field: Extra-Curricular Activities, Soft Skills and Social Mobility* argues: 'The breadth of extra-curricular activities, spanning the musical, artistic, social and sporting domains, are widely considered valuable life experiences that should be open to all young people, regardless of background or where they happen to live.'[1]

We think that extra-curricular activities have three purposes: meeting new people, exploring new places and doing new things. Here are some suggested activities that exemplify these purposes:

- Manga comics club
- Guitar club
- Singing club/choir
- Drama club
- Dance club
- Knitting club
- Debating club
- Reading club
- Martial arts club
- Horticulture club
- School magazine
- School radio
- Football fanzine club
- Journalism club
- Art club
- Philosophy club
- Baking club
- International cooking club
- Chess club
- Board game club
- Computer game club
- Languages club
- Robotics and F1 club

---

1   M. Donnelly, P. Lažetić, A. Sandoval-Hernandez, K. Kumar and S. Whewall, *An Unequal Playing Field: Extra-Curricular Activities, Soft Skills and Social Mobility* (London: Social Mobility Commission, 2022), p. 2. Available at: https://assets. publishing.service.gov.uk/government/uploads/system/uploads/attachment_data/ file/818679/An_Unequal_Playing_Field_report.pdf.

Apart from the inherent value of extra-curricular activities, the Social Mobility Commission report asserts that 'young people can also develop positive tangible outcomes from these experiences of interacting and working with others … which could benefit them in later life'.[2] However, the authors concluded that access to extra-curricular activities was not yet universal, and the impact of such activities was not yet good enough.

To help further improve the situation, the report sets out four key findings and four recommendations for policy and practice:

1 **'Extra-curricular activities are important to young people and result in a range of positive outcomes.'** Research findings suggest that 'extra-curricular activities are important in developing soft (especially social) skills as well as being associated with a range of other positive outcomes'. Regardless of instrumental outcomes, 'extra-curricular activities [are] hugely valuable to young people themselves in ways that are not quantifiable [because they] boost young people's confidence to interact socially with others; extend their social networks; and provide them with new skills and abilities. Above all, they offer an important space to have fun and relax.'[3]

2 **'Opportunities to take part in extra-curricular activities are unequally distributed.** Wide parts of life experience gained from extra-curricular activities are unavailable for the most marginalised groups in society. Opportunities to participate are driven by household income, school attended, gender, ethnicity and geographic location. Household income is by far the most important factor driving gaps in participation, with children from the poorest households much less likely to take part in all types of extra-curricular activities, but especially music classes and sport.' The report also found that 'independent schools [are] likely to offer an unparalleled breadth and range of activities compared to state schools', thus further impacting social mobility.[4]

3 **'Employers in the UK labour market increasingly demand soft skills [which] could be an important factor in driving intergenerational social mobility.'** The report notes that 'demand exists for soft skills from employers in the UK labour market' and that 'There is evidence of an association between soft skills … and intergenerational social mobility.' Indeed, the researchers 'found a correlation between higher levels of some soft skills (readiness to learn, problem-solving, and

---

2 Donnelly et al., *An Unequal Playing Field*, p. 3.
3 Donnelly et al., *An Unequal Playing Field*, p. 3.
4 Donnelly et al., *An Unequal Playing Field*, p. 3.

planning skills) and upward social mobility defined as an individual having higher educational attainment than their parents'.[5]

4   **'New programmes and initiatives are required to widen opportunities to participate in extra-curricular activities.'** The report proffered four recommendations 'aimed at levelling the playing field and improving access to a breadth of life experience provided by extra-curricular activities'. These 'cover both national-level policy as well as the delivery of activities in practice'. The recommendations are: '(1) Introduce a national extra-curricular bursary scheme. (2) Provide funding to develop and extend third-sector initiatives that successfully facilitate access to extra-curricular activities. (3) Increase the organisational capacity of schools to support their extra-curricular provision and improve information on the availability of activities in local areas. (4) Improve data collection and carry out further research into the nature of soft skills developed and deployed across different settings.'[6]

The government hasn't acted on any of the recommendations in the report. So, as usual, it is up to schools to try and provide rich extra-curricular experiences with limited resources. We are going to suggest how your school can effectively design and deliver these extras.

THE BENEFITS

In its Teaching and Learning Toolkit, the Education Endowment Foundation comments on the effectiveness of arts participation as an extra-curricular activity: 'The average impact of arts participation on other areas of academic learning appears to be positive but moderate, about an additional three months progress.'[7]

Ofsted inspects schools based on their curriculum and, in line with the national curriculum, expects to see that it is both broad and balanced. Indeed, one of the primary aims of the Education Inspection Framework when it was launched in 2019 was to discourage the narrowing of the curriculum.[8]

Inspectors are particularly alert to signs of narrowing in the Key Stage 3 curriculum. If a school has shortened Key Stage 3 to two years to allow for

---

5   Donnelly et al., *An Unequal Playing Field*, p. 4.
6   Donnelly et al., *An Unequal Playing Field*, p. 4.
7   See https://educationendowmentfoundation.org.uk/education-evidence/teaching-learning-toolkit/arts-participation.
8   See https://www.gov.uk/government/publications/education-inspection-framework.

a longer GCSE, inspectors will look to see that the school has made provision to ensure that students still have the opportunity to study a broad range of subjects in Years 7 to 9. Extra-curricular activities can clearly help here.

If extra-curricular activities are used to provide a broad and balanced offer, then it is important that all students engage with those activities. If not, then schools will be in danger of perpetuating gaps in students' knowledge and cultural capital or of denying some students the breadth of curriculum content – knowledge, skills and understanding – they need to be fully prepared for the next stage of their lives.

THE CHALLENGES

Whether we use extra-curricular activities to build cultural capital or to ensure that students are afforded opportunities to gain new skills for learning's sake, it is important that schools evaluate the impact of their extra-curricular provision to ensure it is providing quality and value for money.

So, how can we measure the effectiveness of extra-curricular activities? Participation rates can be a helpful indicator, but case studies of students who take part are also a useful way to showcase their commitment to those activities, as well as demonstrating the development of skills such as resilience and, ultimately, the academic impact of extra-curricular provision.

Before we look at how your school provides extra-curricular activities, let's first consider the logistics of running them because, while no one would argue against the merits of offering students the chance to experience a wider curriculum and to participate in enjoyable and enriching activities, the problem for schools is often one of resources.

Extra-curricular activities need to be staffed and resourced. They may involve keeping the school open for longer, thereby incurring additional costs, especially in the current energy crisis. Many activities also require specialist equipment, involve heavy transport costs when taking students out of school or payments to external agencies; the costs soon add up.

A further hurdle for schools is when to run activities in a way that doesn't unduly inconvenience staff or students, including the site staff who may have to open the school early or keep it open later. Furthermore, the timing of activities mustn't exclude some students because of transport issues or other commitments outside of school.

So, how can schools overcome these challenges and offer a rich programme of extra-curricular activities to which all students – including working-class students who may live in poverty – have access?

STAFFING

The first question to ask is: who should run extra-curricular activities? Should it be teachers or support staff? Should it be staff employed by the school at all or perhaps local volunteers or external organisations? Should adults run activities or is it sometimes feasible, and indeed advisable, for older students or school alumni with a penchant for a particular skill to offer peer-taught sessions?

The answer to these questions will obviously be different for every school. What is important is that school leaders try to enable as many extra-curricular activities as possible. Working with school council representatives to assess which type of activities are in demand from students would make sense, as would finding out which teaching and support staff would be willing to run something.

The second question is: should the individuals running the activities do so voluntarily or should they be paid? If they are to be paid, should the payment be monetary, or in the form of time in lieu, or something altogether more abstract such as goodwill?

Paid or voluntary can be a tricky issue. They key point is that the school should be transparent about who is getting paid. In our experience, there will be a number of staff willing to run clubs and groups on a voluntary basis, whereas external providers must be paid.

SCHEDULING

Once we have solved the problem of who, we need to consider the when: when is the best time to run activities? Extra-curricular activities tend to work best straight after school, with regular days for set activities, but a flexible approach is sometimes needed to suit the needs of staff and students. Some schools offer Saturday morning activities which can also be popular.

Whatever part of the day we use, sessions tend to work best when they are weekly and on the same day, so the students can build them into their routines. However, when a school doesn't have a culture of many students attending after-school activities, some will need to be scheduled within school time.

RESOURCING

When we know the who and the when, we need to turn our attention to the what, in the form of resources.

If an activity requires specialist resources, who pays for this: the school or parents/carers? If students are expected to foot the bill, is money made available for those who cannot afford to pay and thus would otherwise be excluded from participating – typically the working classes? If so, where will the money come from, and how will its impact be measured and reported? How can schools identify those students who want to engage with activities but don't express an interest because they know they won't be able to afford to take part? And how can schools ensure that those students who are helped financially aren't singled out by their peers?

Financing is a big challenge, but some programmes can be supported financially through pupil premium funding, while others can attract exter-nal funding. The pupil premium grant can be used to pay for extra-curricular activities, whether this is targeted at those in receipt of the funding or not.

It can be used flexibly – including on provision for those not eligible – so long as its impact can be demonstrated by a closing of the attainment gap for those in receipt. The Department for Education suggests three tiers of strategies that schools can implement using the pupil premium: high-quality teaching, targeted academic support and wider strategies. Under 'wider strategies', it cites 'Extra-curricular activities, including sport, outdoor activities, arts and culture … and school trips' and 'Extended school time, including for summer schools'.[9]

SPONSORSHIP AND PHILANTHROPY

Some schools can pay for extra-curricular activities through sponsorship or donations. While visiting one school in London a few years ago, Andy met a head teacher who had allocated the duty of fundraising to one of his office team. There are many creative ways to do this. In our experience, schools are more likely to receive donations if sponsors are given specific details about the programme/project/club for which funding is being sought and about the intended benefits to participants. This might involve using platforms such as GoFundMe or seeking support from local or national businesses.

---

9   Department for Education, *Using Pupil Premium: Guidance for School Leaders* (March 2023), p. 8. Available at: https://www.gov.uk/government/publications/pupil-premium.

THE PROCESS – PLAN, DO, REVIEW

As experienced trip-takers, we would like to share some thoughts on what to do before and after a trip. We will offer ideas on how best to prepare students for the experience and suggest ways of maximising the potential learning. Apologies if some of these seem too obvious; however, if you and your team consistently follow the mantra of plan, do, review for every experience, they are much more likely to be successful.

PLAN

- **Start with why.** Give students the heads-up as to where they will be going and the purpose of the trip. During the trip, we should ask them: 'Why are we here?' Give the students pocket-sized notebooks for recording their own thoughts about the trip.

- **Expectations and manners.** Remind the students of the importance of good manners during an experience; when off-site, students represent their school. Poor behaviour can sour relationships with outside organisations, especially when they have gone out of their way to accommodate a trip. Reinforce some do's and don'ts, and be clear about the sanctions that will be imposed.

- **Read ahead.** Asking students to pre-read information about an organisation or place they are about to visit can be a good idea. Perhaps specify an article or summary to give them some useful background knowledge for the trip.

- **Prepare three good questions.** Getting students into the routine of creating and asking questions can prime them before a trip. This can also apply to visiting speakers. When this becomes habitual, they can use their notebooks to record questions and then be tasked with getting the answers to them.

DO

To maximise the possibility of sparking interest, it is important that staff play an active role during the experience. As well as monitoring behaviour, they should be encouraging the students to ask questions and pay attention to what is around them. Off-site experiences are a good opportunity to gain more rapport with students by getting to know them better. Staff should try to have conversations with students at every opportunity, asking them questions and listening to what they have to say.

For museum and gallery visits, it is wise to create a quiz so the students are active in seeking information. Most have education teams who will have quizzes available. Alternatively, create your own by doing a pre-visit to wherever you are going.

REVIEW

Finally, it is important to debrief every experience. Debriefs don't have to be particularly long or formal and can even happen on the coach or train on the way home from a trip. Again, giving students some reflective questions to consider either in their notebooks or in discussion with peers can be a simple way of drawing out the main lessons from the experience. Here are some suggestions:

- What did you learn from [today's] experience?

- Has anything from [today's] experience changed your thinking?

- Have you got any unanswered or new questions based on [today's] experience?

REFLECTIVE QUESTIONS

- What is your current extra-curricular offer? Which clubs are best attended?

- What other extra-curricular activities would you like to offer?

- What barriers exist to prevent those offers being made?

- What extra-curricular provision do other schools provide?

- Which local organisations support extra-curricular provision?

OTHER STORIES: HAVELOCK ACADEMY

One school that has made a success of their extra-curricular provision is Havelock Academy in Grimsby, Lincolnshire. Here, Havelock's principal Emma Marshall explains her school's approach.

Extra-curricular activities complement and enhance everything that we do at school, supporting the curriculum and the social development of the children. Our school is in an area of high deprivation, with over half of students in receipt of pupil premium funding, and so it is important to provide high-quality extra-curricular activities because many students simply would not get these opportunities elsewhere.

Sports and the arts are the two most dominant strands in our extra-curricular programme, but there are other activities – including the student librarian scheme, reading for pleasure groups and cooking club – that don't fall as neatly into these categories.

Being part of a multi-academy trust that puts a great deal of emphasis on enrichment, including having centralised support for sport and music, is a great help. Our trust-wide All-Stars programme provides high-quality coaching across different sports as well as for singers and instrumentalists.

Having a sports enrichment officer (SEO) and a musician in residence in most schools adds staffing capacity. But having our own staff who are passionate and committed to providing extra-curricular opportunities in school is also key and accounts for many of our successes over the years.

Most of our activities take place after school, although we also run a breakfast club which is open to all and includes reading materials that kick-start the day. After-school sports clubs run throughout the year, although some are seasonal and change.

As well as the competitive teams, which enjoy fixtures against local and trust schools, we run open-access clubs to encourage participation and fitness. Most sports clubs are staffed by the PE team, made up of six teachers, a sports apprentice and our SEO, but other staff from across the school also support voluntarily.

In the arts, we have after-school clubs for dance, drama and musical theatre, as well as a range of music groups including a rock band and a choir. Students have access to the music suite during lunchtimes for practice and to access support from music staff.

As is the case with sport, most of the arts activities are staffed by the arts teaching team, but volunteers from across the school also support, particularly for our youth theatre, which is a huge team effort, producing a large-scale musical each summer.

All our activities encourage commitment and students are rewarded for regular attendance, be that through further opportunities, trips and visits, house colours awards and other prizes. Teaching the importance of commitment is one of the best things we can do as it serves the children well for life.

Participation in activities also provides invaluable opportunities to build relationships with other children and staff, while exposing the students to a world wider than the taught curriculum and opportunities they may otherwise never be able to access.

Building in external visits, access to professional sports people, musicians, performers and others from the creative industries, and providing the resources to be able to pursue activities beyond school is essential – often providing inspiration and raising aspirations, showing the children that anything is possible.

We provide all regular activities for free and provide the resources needed. This is possible due to the commitment of our staff, who give their time generously, as well as careful use of funding from a range of sources. We are able to use some of the pupil premium grant to ensure all children can access our enrichment offer, and we are very good at fundraising. Ticket sales from performances fund future performances, and we reuse and recycle when it comes to things like scenery, costumes and props.

As an Artsmark school, we are lucky to have a very talented staff team, who in turn ensure that our children are well trained to be able to support their own enrichment programmes. We also invest in youth coaching training in sport, so we are able to create role models in older students who support the younger students with their training.

Where we do have to charge for some experiences, such as school enrichment trips, we have a discretionary hardship fund to avoid children missing out. We keep costs as low as possible for our families, carefully choosing the experiences we offer and calendaring things well in advance, so they are spread out throughout the year, with time to save as needed.

Keeping all of the in-school activities, including the early morning breakfast club, completely free does mean that cost will never be a barrier to any of our families. We accept that many families cannot afford external coaching, lessons or classes, so we make sure that we provide these things.

The long-term impact is clear in our wider school culture. We have nine staff working at the academy, including teachers in maths, computing, music, history, science and more, who came to Havelock themselves as children. Every single one of them was involved in our extra-curricular programmes in some form or other, from leading ladies in our school productions, to sports captains and student council members. It is great having them back with us, inspiring the next generation – and they are all involved in our extra-curricular programmes in some way as they know only too well the value of such activities first-hand.

Similarly, our Havelock Heroes alumni programme sees former students returning for a range of opportunities and events, sharing their journeys with our children, with extra-curricular stories often featuring heavily in their shared memories.

In part due to its extra-curricular provision, Havelock recently improved its inspection rating from requires improvement to good across the board. The Ofsted report said: 'The programme for after-school activities is varied. Most pupils take advantage of this.' As a result, pupils 'appreciate the community in which they live' and 'build strong relationships', and they 'access the important knowledge they need to be healthy and active citizens'.[10]

SPARKING

One of the purposes of extra-curricular activities is to spark students' interests. We first came across the term 'sparking' in Kaz Stuart and Lucy Maynard's excellent book, *Promoting Young People's Empowerment and Agency: A Critical Framework for Practice*.[11] The term refers to a course designer's deliberate attempt to provide an experience which elicits the feeling of 'I want to do that' or 'I'd like to be that'.

10 Ofsted, Inspection of Havelock Academy (11–12 January 2023), pp. 2–3. Available at: https://reports.ofsted.gov.uk/provider/23/135294.
11 K. Stuart and L. Maynard, *Promoting Young People's Empowerment and Agency: A Critical Framework for Practice* (Abingdon and New York: Routledge, 2017).

Andy's experience of sparking occurred in 1984 when he saw his first play, *Hamlet*, at the Barbican in London. Robert Lindsay played Hamlet. He came away thinking: I want to go to the theatre more.

Matt's experience isn't dissimilar. In 1994, he went to Stratford-upon-Avon to see Robert Stephens in the title role of a Royal Shakespeare Company performance of *King Lear*. Stephens's beguiling performance – along with captivating turns from an impressive supporting cast which included Simon Russell Beale as Edgar, David Bradley as Gloucester, David Calder as Kent and Owen Teale as Edmund – was truly enchanting and opened Matt's eyes to the power of the theatre. Before this, his only experience of live performance was the Christmas panto and Punch and Judy at the seaside. Like many, Matt felt that serious theatre – and particularly Shakespeare – was not for the likes of him. But, after seeing Stephens at Stratford, his love of theatre was sparked, and he has been a regular in the stalls ever since.

Both of us have since taken countless students on school trips to the theatre, as well as to art galleries, museums and other cultural experiences, and we have seen first-hand the power of sparking. Matt was particularly moved when he took a class to Stratford to see *Hamlet* and saw reflected in their faces the emotions he had first experienced back in 1994.

Sparking is crucial when designing curriculum journeys. Children from more socially disadvantaged backgrounds are less likely to have had experiences in a range of settings that are normal for the more affluent. Andy remembers two experiences when taking students on a trip that stuck with him.

During a recent trip to the FACT cinema in Liverpool, Andy was talking with a Year 7 student as they were walking from where the coach had dropped them off to the cinema. During this conversation, it came to light that this was the boy's first visit to the city centre. Kirkby is eight miles from Liverpool.

Matt remembers taking an A level English literature class to Haworth to see the Brontë Parsonage Museum and to walk across the moors to Top Withens, which is thought to be the inspiration for Emily Brontë's *Wuthering Heights*. The students were excited not only to see the ruins that brought to life the text they were studying in class but were equally enthralled by the landscape – large expanses of wild moorland, dry-stone walls, streams and waterfalls, free-roaming cattle and birds of prey swooping down from above. These students lived in Halifax, which is just a few miles from Haworth, but had never left the concrete jungle of their hometown.

As Stuart and Maynard make clear, sparking itself isn't enough. Once sparked, students need to be supported to sustain their interest. Later in this section, we will explore what that support might look like. First, let's look at some ideas for trips, and then we will go on to outline how to ensure they run smoothly. We will also share some handy checklists and useful questions to consider.

Below is a list of experiences that may give you some ideas to incorporate into your own curriculum enhancement. Of course, they will have to link with the knowledge, attitudes, skills and habits (KASH) you are trying to build, and some may not be suitable for your context, but hopefully they may be of use.

- Visits to:
  - Museums
  - Universities
  - Art galleries
  - Landmarks
  - Businesses
  - Charities and third-sector organisations
  - Cinemas
  - Theatres
  - Outward Bound activities
  - Hiking
  - Walking tours
  - The seaside
  - The countryside
  - Big cities
  - Libraries
- Visits from:
  - Inspirational speakers such as successful businesspeople[12]
  - Drama groups
  - Ex-students
  - Employers
  - Writers and poets

---

12 See Speakers for Schools, for example, which was founded by political journalist Robert Peston: https://www.speakersforschools.org.

- Artists
- Inventors
- Professionals (nurses, doctors, lawyers, etc.)

■ Virtual tours

■ Zoom interviews with employers/high achievers

 **TEMPLATE**

You may find this template useful when planning your extra-curricular programme. We have examples of pre-populated templates on our website at www.theworkingclassroom.co.uk.

Step 1: Identify the opportunities

Ask: What extra and different could students learn and experience that will give them improved cultural capital alongside deeper subject expertise?

Step 2: Set the success criteria

Ask: What will success look like at the end? How will we know we have been successful? What data will we use to assess this (both qualitative and quantitative)?

Step 3: Choose and justify the extra-curricular experiences

Ask: What will we do? Where will we go?

Step 4: Monitoring and evaluating

Ask: What data will be used throughout (monitoring) and at the end (evaluation) of the curriculum journey to ascertain whether success has been achieved?

Step 5: Logistics and costings

Ask: What are the staffing implications for this extra-curricular activity? What resources will be required? What financial costs will be incurred?

2. Equity for lower-attaining students through adaptive teaching and interventions

Do more for those who start with less through adaptive teaching approaches and additional interventions including, for some, an alternative curriculum.

CHAPTER 6

EQUITY THROUGH ADAPTIVE TEACHING APPROACHES AND CURRICULUM INTERVENTIONS

 KEY QUESTIONS

In this chapter we will answer the following questions:

- How can we ensure equity for working-class students by doing more for those who start with less through adaptive teaching approaches?

- How can we move learning beyond labels and convert the causes of class disadvantage into their tangible classroom consequences, and then overcome them?

- How can we design interventions to help disadvantaged students to access the core curriculum with more confidence?

The second action on our three-point plan of equality, equity and extension is to achieve equity through adaptive teaching approaches and curriculum intervention strategies. We will look at each of these elements in turn, starting with adaptive teaching approaches.

ADAPTIVE TEACHING APPROACHES: DO MORE FOR THOSE WHO START WITH LESS

Once we have designed an ambitious curriculum which is broad and balanced, planned and sequenced, and offered it – with equality – to all students, we need to ensure that all students can access that curriculum and achieve.

It starts with equality. Equality is about giving all young people – irrespective of their backgrounds, starting points, and additional and different needs – access to the same curriculum. To do otherwise is to deepen existing differences and disadvantages. In practice, equality means not dumbing down or reducing the curriculum for some students.

But equality isn't enough. Not all students start from the same point, and thus to offer the same diet to all is to perpetuate existing differences. So, we start with equality but then we ensure equity. We achieve equity by doing more for those who start with less. We support those students who struggle to access our curriculum by using adaptive teaching approaches and additional intervention strategies.

The crucial point to remember here, though, is that the adaptations we make should not be open-ended; to continue to adapt the curriculum and our teaching throughout a student's schooling is to perpetuate learned helplessness and to prevent students from becoming independent and competing fairly with their peers. Rather, adaptations should be reduced over time and students should be helped to become more independent.

The sixth and final step of designing our core curriculum is to diminish disadvantage because we have to accept that not all students start from the same point, and that some will require more support and more time to reach their destination. We diminish disadvantage by closing the gap between disadvantaged students and their peers.

This can be achieved, in part, by identifying the academic barriers that each student faces, then choosing appropriate strategies to support them to overcome those barriers. Intervention strategies work best when they are short term, intensive, focused and tailored. What is more, there is no substitute for high-quality teaching, and so improving teacher and teaching quality must always take precedence. We will come back to this later in the chapter.

We can also help to diminish disadvantage by better understanding the effects of disadvantage. One such effect, though by no means the only one, is a lack of knowledge and cultural capital. One of the most tangible forms that cultural capital takes in practice is vocabulary, and so our curriculum should be a means of explicitly teaching vocabulary – what we might call the language *of* and *for* learning – to equip students with the tools they need to access the curriculum and achieve.

One effective way of ensuring equity – of helping all students to access the same ambitious curriculum – is adaptive teaching. In order to explain what we mean by this, permit us an illustration.

OTHER STORIES: JOHN

One of Matt's former students (we will call him John) contacted him recently. He wanted to update Matt on what he had been doing since he last taught him nearly a decade ago.

John was in a class that Matt regularly cites on training courses (Matt made the mistake of mentioning this to him once and now John thinks he is owed royalties!). If you have heard Matt talk about teaching English to 'bottom-set boys on a Friday afternoon', then John was one of those boys.

When Matt reminisces about this class, he usually thinks of the time he tried to teach them poetry during the last lesson of the week when it was windy and there was a dog loose on the field outside the class-room window. Yes, this sounds like hyperbole, as if he is gilding the lily, but it really happened, that perfect storm.

All the boys in that class (it was a co-educational comprehensive school; it just so happened that all the students with the lowest target grades were, as is often the case in English, boys) were predicted Es and Fs. They were what you might euphemistically call 'a lively bunch' – farmers' sons who loved the rough and tumble of the rugby field more than reciting poetry.

And yet, spoiler alert, they all came out with Cs and above. As a result, many went on to study A levels in the school sixth form and then to university, despite having been written off by the system.

The secret – and we accept it is one hidden in plain sight – to helping those boys secure their gateway qualifications was adaptive teaching. Of course, Matt didn't call it 'adaptive teaching' at the time, simply 'teaching'. But his approach was akin to one that is now given that moniker.

So, taking a lead from John's story, what is adaptive teaching?

We define adaptive teaching as short-term alterations made to the way we teach the core curriculum – extra or different things – to allow all students to access that curriculum. We call these alterations 'scaffolds' because they are temporary support structures, much like the scaffolding that enables construction workers to reach high places, that we construct to help students get a foothold.

Scaffolding aims to provide students with temporary supports that are gradually removed or faded out as they become increasingly independent. It is a common component of guided practice – sometimes referred to as 'first, now, next' – building the bigger picture and making connections for learning.

Scaffolds might be visual, such as giving a student a task planner, a list of small steps to complete a task, model examples of work or images that support vocabulary learning. Scaffolds might be verbal, such as explaining a task in more explicit terms and in smaller steps, repeating an instruction, reteaching a difficult concept or using questioning to address misconceptions. Finally, scaffolds might be written, such as a word bank, writing frame or sentence starters.

The trick to using scaffolds effectively is to anticipate and assess students' barriers to learning – which may be different levels of prior knowledge, vocabulary gaps, their ability to decode text, limited working memory capacity, gaps in cultural experiences, common misconceptions and a lack of metacognitive knowledge – and then make plans to address the specific barrier – which may be to read a text in advance, supply background knowledge, use images to contextualise information or explicitly teach vocabulary. We then use ongoing assessment to ascertain whether the scaffolds are working; we might use questioning, tests, tasks, talk, hinge questions, exit tickets or 'show me' mini-whiteboard activities. As a result of these assessments, we make further adaptations on the fly, such as adjusting the level of difficulty, changing our language, using analogy or peer teaching.

In short, whereas traditional differentiation focuses on individual students or small groups of students, adaptive teaching focuses on the whole class. Whereas traditional differentiation often takes the form of differentiating by task or outcome – giving different students different work to do and then assessing them differently and expecting different results – adaptive teaching works by giving all students the same tasks, assessing them in the same way and having the same high expectations for all – but accepting that some students, some of the time, will need additional short-term support to get started.

In effect, it is the difference between teaching up to thirty different lessons at once, matching the pace and pitch to each individual student, and providing different tasks and resources to different students, and teaching the same lesson to all thirty students, and doing so by 'teaching to the top', while providing scaffolds to those who need additional initial support in order to access the same ambitious curriculum and meet our high expectations. Crucially, as we have said, additional support offered in the guise of scaffolding should be reduced over time so that all students can become increasingly independent.

The problem with the former approach – teaching up to thirty different lessons – is that, as well as being hugely time-consuming for the teacher, it can translate in practice as expecting less of some students than we do of others.

There is another problem with differentiated teaching. When a teacher is attending to the individual needs of one student in a class of, say, thirty, the other twenty-nine aren't receiving the teacher's attention. Unlike traditional forms of differentiation, which can perpetuate attainment gaps by capping opportunities and aspirations, adaptive teaching promotes high achievement for all. In fact, according to the 2015 PISA results, adaptive instruction in science is one of the approaches most positively correlated with student performance.[1] In fact, it is second only to ensuring students are from wealthy backgrounds.

Put simply, if we dumb down or reduce the curriculum for some students, we only serve to double their existing disadvantages rather than help them to overcome those challenges to achieve in line with their peers. Adaptive teaching, unlike differentiation, helps to tackle social justice issues and thus helps to promote social mobility.

In Matt's bottom-set boys' class, then, he ignored the target grades his students had been given, and he told his students to ignore them too. To convince them, Matt explained how the targets had been calculated and tore apart the logic. He said there was nothing to prevent them from achieving the very top grades if they worked hard enough. Matt linked those grades to their future life chances, selling the benefits of good qualifications.

He set the bar high. He used GCSE grade descriptors to determine the standard of work he expected from his students, explaining in tangible terms the difference between, say, a grade D and a grade C piece of work. The language of the grade descriptors became the starting point for all his teacher explanations and modelling.

Matt made sure he modelled the very best work, but in doing so, he deconstructed examples of excellence 'live' in front of the students, so

---

1   Organisation for Economic Co-operation and Development, *PISA 2015 Results (Volume II): Policies and Practices for Successful Schools* (Paris: OECD Publishing, 2016), p. 68. Available at: https://doi.org/10.1787/9789264267510-en.

they could see how to get from where they were to where they needed to be, rather than presenting them with 'here's one I made earlier'. In other words, he made his subject expertise visible through thinking aloud. He also explicitly taught frameworks and memory aids (such as mnemonics) to remember key information. He made sure the development of study skills, such as self-quizzing and revision, was also planned and explicitly taught, first in a domain-specific way and then as transferable skills.

Next, he made sure all his feedback was specific and challenging, and that every time feedback was given, the students were afforded lesson time to process it, question it and act upon it. Their progress, however incremental, was then celebrated and made visible. His comments never compared individual students with others in the class, but rather they compared each student with their earlier selves. Matt's feedback made clear where they were now, how far they had come and what their next steps should be.

Most importantly, Matt made sure that every student in the class completed the same task; he didn't differentiate tasks according to ability and nor did he produce differentiated resources. He didn't differentiate the questions he asked either; he made sure that every student was required to answer questions that demanded critical thinking. Each student worked towards the same goal – and, crucially, that goal was the same as he had set for his top set class. Indeed, there was little difference in his teaching between the two classes: expectations were high and the work was challenging.

In setting the same ambitious goals for all students, Matt also provided differing levels of support depending on his students' starting points and additional and different needs. For example, although they all answered the same essay question and were assessed against the same criteria, he provided additional cues to some students to help them get started or he gave some students stem sentences to kick-start their thinking. All these scaffolds fell away over time, though – independence was always the aim.

A further strategy Matt deployed was to better understand his students' lived experiences, which is to say that he got to know his students so he could ensure that he built new abstract knowledge on their existing concrete knowledge. He did this, in part, through structured conversations.

By understanding what they already knew and could do, Matt was able to make connections and teach new information through the lens of what was familiar, and he could ensure that his analogies 'landed'. By understanding prior learning, he was also able to identify the gaps in his students' existing knowledge, as well as any misconceptions or misunderstandings they brought to the classroom, which could then be unpacked.

So, what happened to John after he left school with his C in English? He messaged Matt recently to tell him that he had just embarked on a PhD, having successfully completed his master's, and before that he had graduated with first-class honours.

Self-indulgently, we will give the last word on this subject to John who wrote: 'You are the first person I thought I should tell because you were the one who put the effort in with us all at school. I still see most of the boys from that class and you often crop up in conversation. We are all still grateful you stuck with us – you won't believe how much having that C helped us all – so thank you.'

In sum, adaptive teaching is an approach by which teachers consistently use the following eight elements:

1	Ignore target grades	Link grades to students' future life chances, selling the benefits of good qualifications.
2	Set the bar high	Use the language of grade descriptors as the starting point for teacher explanations and modelling.
3	Model excellence	Deconstruct examples of excellence 'live'; make subject expertise visible through thinking aloud.
4	Explicitly teach frameworks and mnemonics	Use memory aids such as mnemonics to help students remember key information; make sure the development of study skills is planned and explicitly taught in domain-specific ways.
5	Make feedback specific and challenging	Every time feedback is given, afford students lesson time to process it, question it and act upon it; celebrate progress, however incremental.
6	Make sure every student completes the same task	Don't differentiate tasks according to ability or produce differentiated resources, and don't differentiate questions. Make sure every student is required to answer questions that demand critical thinking.

7	Provide differing levels of support depending on students' starting points	Provide additional cues to some students to help them get started or give some students stem sentences to kick-start their thinking – but ensure all these scaffolds fall away over time.
8	Better understand – and talk to – students' lived experiences	Get to know the students to ensure new abstract knowledge is built upon existing concrete knowledge; make connections and teach new information through the lens of what is familiar and ensure that analogies 'land'.

REFLECTIVE QUESTIONS

- How, in your classroom practice, do you do more for those who start with less?

- How do you make use of adaptive teaching approaches as opposed to traditional forms of differentiation?

- What have you done to better appreciate your students' lived experiences, especially those who come from households experiencing poverty?

CURRICULUM INTERVENTION STRATEGIES

The second element of our approach to achieving equity, after adaptive teaching, is the use of curriculum intervention strategies.

WHY DO WE NEED INTERVENTIONS?

Even with the most ambitious, broad and balanced, planned and sequenced curriculum to which all students have equal access, even with the most effective quality first teaching and even with the most carefully planned adaptive teaching strategies, sometimes some students will require more.

Since the National Strategies were launched in the late-1990s, it has been common practice to talk of three waves of intervention. The three-wave model is often expressed as a pyramid similar to Bloom's taxonomy, where Wave 1 sits at the bottom and thus provides the foundation on which all other forms of support are built.

According to the National Strategies, Wave 1 is 'quality inclusive teaching which takes into account the learning needs of all the children in the class-room'.[2] As such, if we don't provide students with quality classroom teaching first, then no amount of additional intervention and support will help them to catch up.

But even with the provision of quality first teaching, some students will require more – and more tailored – support in the guise of Wave 2 in-class differentiations and Wave 3 additional interventions, which take place outside the classroom and off the taught timetable.

Such intervention strategies may take the form of one-to-one support from a teaching assistant or other adult, small group targeted teaching or support from external agencies. In most cases, the aim of additional support is for it to become redundant over time – that is, we want students to become increasingly independent and for the scaffolds to fall away. Indeed, this is the stated aim of most education health and care plans: over time, discrete funding should be reduced as its impact is felt and students require less and less support.

---

2   The National Strategies are now archived but this webpage from Islington Council provides an overview: https://directory.islington.gov.uk/kb5/islington/directory/advice.page?id=j2Rg2OWo71Q.

With this aim in mind, it is important to ensure that all strategic interventions are monitored while they are happening and are:

- Brief (20–50 mins).
- Regular (three to five times per week).
- Sustained (running for 8–20 weeks).
- Carefully timetabled.
- Staffed by well-trained teaching assistants (5–30 hours of training per intervention).
- Well-planned with structured resources and clear objectives.
- Assessed to identify appropriate students, guide areas for focus and track progress.
- Linked to classroom teaching.

We will look at how best to plan interventions in a moment, but first a word of caution.

LEARNING BEYOND LABELS

We think that labels can be problematic. Whether they pertain to socio-economic deprivation (such as 'free school meals' or 'pupil premium') or to social status (such as 'white working-class boys'), they can be tricky.

We aren't suggesting that labels have no place in education. They can be a useful shorthand and so assist us in reporting on generic attainment gaps at a whole-school and national level. They can help us to identify trends and to tackle endemic discrimination. In the case of medical diagnoses such as dyslexia or autism, they can explain why a child finds some aspects of school life more challenging than their peers do. They can also open doors to specialist support and, not least, to the money with which to buy that specialist support.

Labels have a place in our system, certainly, but the problem arises when schools and teachers use them to determine expectations for what a child can achieve – or, more likely, cannot achieve – and to ascertain what additional support will be provided.

A further problem with labels is when they are used to describe a cohort of students and thus stereotype children. Labels can mask significant individual differences within a cohort. There is no such thing, for example, as a typical 'pupil premium child' or a typical 'white working-class child'. The mere notion is ridiculous. Every student is a human being, and every human being is different from every other human being in myriad ways. There may be some shared characteristics, of course, but labels lack nuance and lead us to assume that the problems faced by each child with the same label are exactly the same and that, as such, the solutions must also be the same.

Put simply, there is a difference between *causes* and *consequences*. The cause is the label – or, rather, the label tells us the cause of a student's disadvantage or difficulty. The consequence is what this means in practical terms for each student in each situation. Let us explain … The fact that a student is eligible for the pupil premium, and is therefore labelled 'pupil premium child', might tell you a little about their context. Perhaps they are eligible for free school meals and, in this way, you may know they are categorised as living in poverty. But that, in and of itself, tells you little about what, if anything, they may find difficult at school and what you can do to support them.

To help the student in school, we need to convert the cause, the label, into a consequence to better understand what the label means in practice. And the first point to make loud and clear is that it might mean absolutely nothing! Just because a student is eligible for free school meals doesn't mean they are in any way academically disadvantaged at school. Likewise, just because a student isn't eligible for free school meals doesn't mean that they aren't academically disadvantaged.

Furthermore, a label doesn't mean that a student will be uniformly disadvantaged at school. Which is to say that, while a student may find some aspects of school more difficult than some of their peers do, they are unlikely to find every aspect of school difficult and may even find some aspects easier than most of their peers do.

Labelling students leads to lazy decisions. It was common a few years ago – and still happens in some schools today – to demand that teachers label students eligible for the pupil premium on their registers, to design 'strategic seating plans' and to provide evidence of what they do differently for these children. Why? Such a practice only serves to discriminate against these students and to define them – and publicly brand them – as being 'poor' and thus 'less able' and in need of help.

CONVERTING THE CAUSES OF DISADVANTAGE INTO TANGIBLE CLASSROOM CONSEQUENCES

So, what can we do to convert the causes of disadvantage into tangible classroom consequences and thereby move learning beyond labels for working-class students?

Matt has worked extensively with schools on their use of the pupil premium. Along the way, he has developed a three-point plan, which is as follows:

Let's take a closer look at this plan.

I. IDENTIFY THE BARRIERS

Before you can put in place intervention strategies aimed at supporting working-class students, you must first understand why a gap exists between the attainment of working-class students and their more affluent, privileged peers.

In short, you need to ask yourself: what are the consequences of class disadvantage faced by my students? What barriers might their class disadvantage pose in class? How does their class disadvantage translate itself, if at all, in terms of their ability to access the ambitious curriculum I am teaching and to achieve in line with their peers?

This may sound obvious, but it is a step often missed out by schools who assume that all students eligible for disadvantage funding or who have a label such as special educational needs and disabilities (SEND) must be academically disadvantaged, and similarly so. However, as we say above, when identifying the barriers to learning in your school, it is important to remember that not all the students who are socio-economically disadvantaged will face all, or even some, of the barriers to learning that we will set out shortly, and that there is no such thing as a typical disadvantaged student. Rather, each student must be treated on an individual basis and the support given must be tailored to meet their needs, not the needs of a homogenous group.

As such, schools should identify, on a case-by-case basis, what, if any, consequences students face when it comes to accessing and achieving within an ambitious curriculum.

When seeking to identify the consequences that disadvantage has on a student's schooling, here are some possible signs to look out for:

- Limited vocabulary.
- Low reading age.
- Poor attendance and punctuality.
- Issues caused by a student moving between schools.
- Medical issues, sometimes undiagnosed.
- A lack of sleep or poor nutrition.
- A lack of concentration.
- A lack of family engagement with learning.
- Education not being valued within the local community.
- A lack of role models, especially male role models.
- A lack of self-confidence and self-esteem.

2. SET THE SUCCESS CRITERIA

Once you have identified the barriers to learning faced by your disadvantaged students, you need to be clear about what success will look like. Ask yourself: what do I expect to see as an outcome? What is my aim? For example, is it to:

- Raise attainment.
- Expedite progress.
- Increase reading ages.
- Improve in-class concentration.
- Improve attendance.
- Improve behaviour.
- Reduce exclusions.
- Improve parental engagement.
- Expand on the number of opportunities afforded to disadvantaged students.

In terms of ensuring you meet your success criteria, it is crucial that any intervention strategy is monitored as it is happening and not just evaluated once it is finished. The monitoring may involve more anecdotal data, such as student and teacher feedback, but evidence must be gathered throughout the lifespan of the intervention in order to ensure it is working – or working as well as it could – so that timely decisions can be taken to stop or tweak an intervention if it isn't having the desired effect on student progress. Waiting until the intervention has finished to evaluate its success is too late; if it didn't work, or didn't work as well as it could have done, then time and money have been wasted.

To measure the impact of an academic intervention strategy, both qualitative and quantitative data can be used. The table below includes some examples of each.

Qualitative data	Quantitative data
Student feedback: Conduct surveys or interviews with students who have participated in the academic intervention strategy to gather their opinions and experiences.	Pre- and post-assessment results: Collect and analyse data on student performance on pre- and post-assessments to determine the impact of the intervention strategy on learning outcomes.
Teacher observations: Collect feedback from teachers who have implemented the intervention strategy, such as their reflections on student engagement, behaviour and performance.	Attendance rates: Analyse attendance data to determine if the intervention strategy has had an impact on student attendance rates.
Focus groups: Organise focus groups with students, parents and teachers to discuss the strengths and weaknesses of the intervention strategy and its impact on learning outcomes.	Attainment: Analyse the attainment of students who have participated in the intervention strategy compared to similar students who have not to determine the effectiveness of the strategy.

By using both qualitative and quantitative data, we can acquire a more comprehensive understanding of the impact of the academic intervention strategy. Qualitative data can provide insights into the experiences and opinions of students, teachers and parents, while quantitative data can provide more concrete evidence of the impact of the intervention strategy on learning outcomes.

When setting the success criteria, it is important to consider the best individual approach. For example, evidence suggests that interventions work best when they are short term, intensive, focused and tailored.

- **Short term.** The best interventions help students to become increasingly independent over time; that is, the scaffolds slowly fall away. Interventions should be planned to run for a finite amount of time, therefore, ideally less than a term. Of course, if the evidence shows the intervention is working but that further improvement is needed, then it can be extended, but to slate an intervention for a year, say, is often misguided.

- **Intensive.** Interventions should be intensive, with three or more sessions a week rather than just one. Those sessions should also be intensive in the sense of being short – perhaps twenty to fifty minutes in length rather than an hour or more.

- **Focused.** Interventions should be focused on a student's areas of development rather than being generic. For example, rather than setting a goal of 'improving a student's literacy skills', an intervention strategy should be focused on a specific aspect of literacy, such as their knowledge of the plot of a particular novel or their ability to use embedded quotations in an essay.

- **Tailored.** Interventions need to be tailored to meet the needs of the students accessing them. They must be as personalised as any classroom learning and not off-the-peg programmes. Assessment data should be used to inform the intervention and to ensure it is being pitched appropriately to fill gaps in the student's knowledge.

3. DESIGN AND DELIVER THE INTERVENTIONS

Once we have identified the barriers that each student faces, we must decide what action we can take to help them overcome those barriers and afford each student an equal chance of success at school.

There are some great organisations offering curriculum interventions to schools. Some are regionally based, while others have a national scope. We have already mentioned White Water Writers (in Chapter 4). We have listed below others we have come across and the issues they address.

- Dramatic Recovery is an award-winning Liverpool-based organisation which specialises in creating drama interventions to support students with mental health issues such as anxiety, self-esteem and anger management. Through the medium of drama, young people work towards a performance or the creation of a piece of verbatim theatre where they can demonstrate their learning. To declare an interest here, Andy and his daughter, Anna Griffith, are directors of the company, alongside Megan Peet.

https://www.dramaticrecovery.co.uk

■ Arts Emergency is an award-winning mentoring charity and support network. They work with young people in London, Brighton, Greater Manchester and Merseyside. Their network offers gateways into hard-to-crack industries such as TV, publishing and architecture.

https://www.arts-emergency.org

■ Commando Joe's is a nationwide organisation set up by a former member of the armed forces, Michael Hamilton OBE. They specialise in running interventions for students at risk of exclusion or who have become severely disaffected in school. They offer programmes that work directly with young people as well as parents and teachers.

https://commandojoes.co.uk

There are hundreds of other organisations that schools can employ to run specific interventions or train school staff to do so. It is important to get good endorsements from other schools before bringing them in because quality assurance is vital. Where the school identifies that interventions may be helpful, it is often wise to look outward for support specialists.

Many social issues within the community, such as knife crime or grooming, can be addressed either in-house or through working alongside partner organisations. Schools will always need to make a judgement as to what the most appropriate interventions will be, who will be involved as a cohort and what might be the best method to deliver it. The template in this section and the reflective questions will help you to make the right choices.

Whether you engage external organisations or run interventions in-house, there are some common principles we need to consider when deciding which strategies to use:

1   We should ensure that our strategies promote an ethos of attainment for all students rather than stereotyping working-class students as a group with less potential to succeed.

2   We should take an individualised approach to addressing barriers to learning and emotional support and do so at an early stage rather than providing access to generic support as students near their end-of-key-stage assessments.

3   We should focus on outcomes for individual students rather than providing generic strategies for whole cohorts.

4 We should deploy our best staff to support students in the most need, perhaps developing existing teachers' and teaching assistants' skills rather than using additional staff who don't know the students well. If you use an external provider, ensure they are quality assured and supported by school staff.

5 We should make decisions based on frequent assessment data, responding to changing evidence rather than using a one-off decision point.

6 We should focus on high-quality teaching first rather than on bolt-on strategies and activities outside school hours and outside the classroom.

OTHER STORIES: GEORGIA

Georgia had always had an interest in how filmmakers created prosthetics and used make-up. She happened to mention this in a careers interview in Year 9. The school Georgia attends has an excellent career education team and organises Zoom interviews for students with people working in the industry they are interested in joining. These interviews take place on an evening when a member of staff, the student, a parent or carer and the industry expert can meet virtually.

Ahead of her interview, Georgia prepared questions about the interviewer's career and how they had secured their current post. The industry expert was Reza Karim who has worked on films including *Labyrinth* (where he applied Davie Bowie's make-up) and *Jurassic World: Dominion*.

Not only did Reza provide useful insider information, but he also sent Georgia an expensive book about film make-up and prosthetics. The experience thoroughly invigorated Georgia. She was much more driven afterwards and has since secured work experience on a film set due to her dogged letter and email writing.

Over time, the school has created a database of contacts who are happy to take part in either face-to-face or virtual interviews with students. These people are friends and family members of the staff, and even friends of friends.

REFLECTIVE QUESTIONS

■ How do you convert the causes of class disadvantage into their tangible classroom consequences? What more can you do? Do you follow a process similar to the three-step sequence advocated in this chapter, and if not, might it be helpful to do so? How do you support students to overcome these consequences? What more can be done?

■ How do you currently design curriculum interventions to help working-class students to access the core curriculum with more confidence? What more can you do? How do you ensure interventions are short term, intensive, tailored and focused?

■ How do you ensure that you select the right students for interventions, decide what types of intervention are best and when an intervention should be triggered? What more can you do?

■ How do you make interventions work within the school timetable without adversely impacting on staff workload? What further action can you take to address the workload implications?

PLANNING TEMPLATE:
CURRICULUM INTERVENTIONS

Here is a template you may find useful when planning intervention strategies in your school. You will find some pre-populated examples at www.theworkingclassroom.co.uk.

STEP 1: IDENTIFY THE BARRIERS

Ask: What is inhibiting students' ability to access the ambitious curriculum we are teaching and to achieve in line with their peers? How many students are facing this barrier? To what extent are there common barriers (identify causes and consequences)? What are the key differences among the cohort that may need to be addressed?

STEP 2: SET THE SUCCESS CRITERIA

Ask: What type of intervention will we create? What will success look like at the end? How will we know that we have been successful? What data will we use to assess this (both qualitative and quantitative)? Will success look the same for all students? What follow-up actions may be needed to ensure success is sustained?

STEP 3: CHOOSE AND JUSTIFY THE DELIVERY MODEL

Ask: How would the delivery model for the intervention be described? Who will deliver it? When will it be delivered? Where will it be delivered? How often will it be delivered? What are the main advantages of this model? What is the research base for this model? What other intervention models have we considered and rejected? What are the reasons for this?

STEP 4: MONITORING AND EVALUATING

Ask: What data will be used throughout (monitoring) and at the end (evaluation) of the intervention? How can the data be disaggregated to understand outliers and the reasons behind this? How will the data be used to ensure continued refinement of the curriculum intervention?

STEP 5: LOGISTICS AND COSTINGS

Ask: What are the staffing implications for this intervention? How, and how often, will the leaders of the intervention communicate with classroom teachers? How, and how often, will the leaders of the intervention communicate with parents and carers? What financial costs will be incurred?

THE ALTERNATIVE CURRICULUM

One other form of intervention that we might deploy for lower attaining working-class students who are struggling to engage with the traditional academic curriculum is the alternative or flexible curriculum.

For various reasons, and in limited circumstances, some students are unable to cope with the full curriculum, so the school may decide, in consultation with parents or carers, that it is in a student's best interests to follow a reduced timetable, to be educated off site or to have a flexible timetable.

Home education isn't generally considered suitable for alternative provision, but there are some local authorities that operate an 'educated other than at school' system. This may involve a model whereby schools use an authorised package that provides quality assured and safeguarded virtual learning through an online tutoring programme. This is generally a time-limited and restricted package which serves the purpose of re-engaging students in more face-to-face learning. Such programmes can complement bespoke hands-on learning that is of real interest to the student.

Alternative provision must be formalised and regarded with the same level of seriousness and scrutiny as the mainstream curriculum if it is to be impactful rather than regarded as a youth club or a way of keeping students busy. Alternative provision is also relational; it is important that those providing the alternative curriculum build rapport with their students to engage them and win their trust. It is important, too, that those providing the alternative curriculum are teachers, not tutors, and have the requisite skills for the job.

WHY DO SOME STUDENTS NEED AN ALTERNATIVE CURRICULUM?

We wrote about the 'forgotten third' in Chapter 2. Most schools have some students who, according to the current assessment system, don't perform well. These students typically go on to receive GCSE grades 1 or 2 or find themselves on a crash course with repeat exclusions and even permanent exclusion. For some schools, especially in socially disadvantaged areas, this can represent a double-digit percentage of each year group.

In 2019, a briefing from the Children's Commissioner entitled 'The Children Leaving School with Nothing' found that almost 100,000 students a year leave school without basic qualifications.[3]

Since the pandemic, there have been challenges in getting students back into school. Lee Elliot Major, professor of social mobility at the University of Exeter, has described this situation as a 'national persistent truancy crisis' in England.[4]

The best schools don't just work to reduce the percentage of students who don't access education. Instead, they proactively and creatively help those students in other ways, including:

- Considering the need for long-term or short-term quality alternative provision.

- Tailoring the curriculum offer to give students experiences and placements through which they gain key employability skills beyond the two-week work experience placement in Key Stage 4.

- Finding suitable in-house alternative qualification pathways that better suit their students – indeed, some schools have created their

3   Children's Commissioner, Briefing: The Children Leaving School with Nothing (20 September 2019). Available at: https://assets.childrenscommissioner.gov.uk/wpuploads/2019/09/cco-briefing-children-leaving-school-with-nothing.pdf.
4   Quoted in S. Weale, Texting Parents May Help Schools Tackle 'Truancy Crisis' in England, Say Experts, The Guardian (20 February 2023). Available at: https://www.theguardian.com/education/2023/feb/20/texting-parents-may-help-schools-tackle-truancy-crisis-in-england-say-experts.

own vocational and interest-based qualifications to cater for their students' needs, such as equine studies and e-sports.

- Brokering suitable alternative pathways with external providers to offer a wider range of qualifications for their students, including courses in hair and beauty, construction, automotive mechanics and so on. These courses often involve a hybrid delivery model whereby students are in school for two or three days a week and with the external provider for the remainder of the time.

- Sourcing suitable off-site pathways that require a five-day-a-week placement where the provider offers a vocational educational experience and a more tailored delivery of national curriculum requirements like English, maths and science.

- Sourcing suitable full-time external provision, which may not lead to qualifications but will ensure that a student's social and emotional needs are met, that they remain engaged in education and don't become isolated or alienated, and that they don't become at risk of becoming NEET.

 STORY

We are going to share some examples of schools that have changed their curriculum in creative ways to ensure their students stay in education for as long as possible. Hopefully, these stories and the reflective questions that follow will help you to critique what your school does with similar students. As with some of the other stories in this book, we have changed some of the names.

OTHER STORIES: ELLIE

Ellie went through all manner of in-house interventions aimed at keeping her actively engaged in mainstream education. But it didn't work.

Ellie then worked her way through several providers until finally finding a setting where emotional and mental well-being took priority over academic outcomes. Ellie had had several visits to A&E due to mental ill-health breakdowns.

Ellie's school was aware of some of her issues when she first entered Year 7. Ellie lived with her grandparents and was subject to a special guardianship order. She was involved in several behaviour incidents, including one where she injured staff members during a fight.

Since Ellie received alternative provision, her engagement in education has improved and so has her self-esteem. There have been no violent incidents. The school put this down to Ellie being more engaged with the content of the new curriculum from the alternative provider.

Some schools may have permanently excluded Ellie, either when she injured staff or when her first placement broke down. However, through perseverance and a commitment to work with the student and her family, the school got her to the end of her formal education – albeit with fewer qualifications than had been projected in Year 6. But, in the place of qualifications, she now has a promising future and is working towards an apprenticeship in youth work.

OTHER STORIES: JAMES

James's attendance was below 60% and he showed persistently low engagement in lessons. He suffered from severe anxiety which prevented him from travelling to and being in a school setting. A recent house move contributed to his problems.

The family had requested elective home education. However, through discussion with the school, it was decided that this would not be in his best interests. As a result, appropriate alternative provision was sought. James's family were fully involved in this process. He went through two different providers before finishing his formal education.

James achieved some GCSEs and received higher grades than he would have achieved through home schooling. He transferred to a sixth-form college to continue studies that will allow him to access valuable employment.

We are sure that your school could proffer comparable stories of students who don't fit into the one-size-fits-all system. What schools do about this makes an enormous difference to the lives of these young people. Dogged determination to find suitable alternative provision, in whatever form, impacts on the life chances of the young person themselves but also their family and the wider community.

Get it right, and a higher percentage of these students will become more active citizens who go on to gain employability skills which ultimately lead to successful careers. Get it wrong, and these young people will become another NEET statistic. Their life journey could be one of criminality, unemployment or low income, stuck in insecure employment.

The best schools go through several stages before they decide to create an alternative or flexible curriculum for a student. Evidence must be gathered and questions must be asked, such as:

- Have we monitored the student through report cards or similar? Does this show any trends?

- Have we diagnosed any SEND?

- Have we changed teaching sets for the student?

- Have we reduced the number of subjects the student studies?

- Have we reduced the number of teaching staff with whom the student interacts?

- Have we allocated a member of staff to work intensively with the student's family

- Have we established clear and regular contact with home?

- Have we provided internal support in school through one-to-one or small group provision?

- Have we provided an in-house intervention first?

- Have we brought in an external provider to support/lead a school-based intervention?

If, despite making the changes above, the student is still highly disengaged (i.e. attendance remains low or sporadic, or behaviour is still poor), alternative provision may be the best option. As we outlined earlier, there are various models for this. From our research, we have found that best practice in this area involves persistence. If the first alternative provision model breaks down, the school – in liaison with the provider – analyses the reasons and tries to get the student back on track or to find a different placement. The key is perseverance and commitment – to continually work with the student and their family to find the best fit.

Below is a template for alternative or flexible curriculum planning. Like the other templates in this book, it can be adapted to suit your context. If you live in part of the country that has good access to a skills centre, further education college or suitable workplace provider, we are sure that many of the questions will be helpful to you. Alternatively, you can adapt the template and create your own set of questions to make decisions about the why, who, what and how of alternative or flexible curriculum planning.

PLANNING TEMPLATE: ALTERNATIVE CURRICULUM

Here is a template you may find helpful when planning your alternative curriculum. You will find pre-populated examples at www.theworking-classroom.co.uk.

STEP 1: IDENTIFY THE BARRIERS

Ask: What is inhibiting students' ability or desire to access the ambitious in-house curriculum we are teaching and to achieve in line with their peers? How many students are facing this barrier? To what extent are there common barriers (identify causes and consequences)? What are the key differences among the cohort that may need to be addressed?

STEP 2: SET THE SUCCESS CRITERIA

Ask: What curriculum offer will we create? What will success look like at the end? How will we know that we have been successful? What data will we use to assess this (both qualitative and quantitative)? Will success look the same for all students? What follow-up actions may be needed to ensure success is sustained?

STEP 3: CHOOSE AND JUSTIFY THE DELIVERY MODEL

Ask: How would the delivery model for this alternative curriculum offer be described? Who will deliver each element of it? When will it be delivered? Where will it be delivered? How often will it be delivered? Will it definitely meet the legal thresholds for delivery requirements? What are the main advantages of this model? What is the research base for this model? What other intervention models have we considered and rejected? What are the reasons for this?

STEP 4: MONITORING AND EVALUATING

Ask: What data will be used throughout? How will the data be used to ensure continued refinement of the alternative curriculum?

STEP 5: LOGISTICS AND COSTINGS

Ask: What are the wider implications for this curriculum offer? How, and how often, will the alternative curriculum provider communicate with the host school? How, and how often, will the alternative curriculum provider communicate with parents or carers? What financial costs will be incurred?

CHAPTER 7

EXTENSION THROUGH CURRICULUM ENHANCEMENTS

 KEY QUESTIONS

In this chapter we will answer the following questions:

- What are the reasons for enhancing the curriculum for some students by providing extra opportunities?

- How can we most effectively design curriculum enhancements to reduce the impact of economic disadvantage?

- How can we ensure that students and their parents or carers engage with the extra and the different that the school has provided?

3. Extension for higher-attaining students through curriculum enhancements

Use enhancements to build knowledge and cultural capital. and equip working-class students with the secret knowledge they need to compete at school and university, in work and in life.

In this chapter, we will focus on designing and delivering curriculum enhancements. Let's start by explaining why these curriculum enhancements are so important.

WHY DO WE NEED CURRICULUM ENHANCEMENTS?

The primary aim of curriculum enhancements is to counteract the structural bias in our society that is opposed to working-class children achieving success in their adult lives. Many children unconsciously absorb messages that tell them they aren't as worthy of success as those from more affluent backgrounds. Some will come from families who face poverty. Poverty isn't just about money, though. Another form of impoverishment is *knowledge poverty*, whereby some students have knowledge gaps compared to their more affluent peers.

The Malit Scholars' Programme (so named after Andy's company Malit[1]), which forms the main case study in this chapter, aims to provide the 'secret' knowledge to which the middle and upper classes are usually privy but which is often denied to the working classes. The programme targets working-class students who have the potential to achieve a university degree or higher-level apprenticeship. Many will achieve this without curriculum enhancement, but many will not unless something extra and different is offered to them throughout their secondary school years.

PLANNING CURRICULUM ENHANCEMENTS

Curriculum enhancements have much in common with the curriculum interventions we covered in the previous chapter. Of course, their purposes are different – interventions are designed to help lower-attaining students catch up with their peers, while curriculum enhancements are targeted at higher-attaining working-class students to provide access to 'secret knowledge' – but the logistics are similar. For example, how we determine when, where and how often these activities take place is comparable, as are the means and methods we use to select students; likewise, how we staff the activities. Also similar is the importance of identifying the success criteria before instigating the activities.

---

1 See http://www.malit.org.uk.

While the extra-curricular activities we explored in Chapter 5 are open to all students and are voluntary, we may identify certain students who would particularly benefit from access and then provide funding for those who would otherwise miss out. Curriculum enhancements are targeted at high-performing working-class students and focused on providing access to the secret knowledge that would otherwise be denied to them because of their social status.

AN EXAMPLE ENHANCEMENT: THE MALIT SCHOLARS' PROGRAMME

In 2016, Andy was set a learning design challenge by Tony McGuinness, the head teacher at All Saints Catholic High School. He wanted an in-school programme to:

- Support the improvement in attainment for all students across the school.

- Improve the popularity of the school within the community.

- Increase the percentage of students who aspire to study at university.

- Engage more parents in the work of the school.

- Improve the career prospects and employability of course participants.

Working to this success criteria, Andy set out to create a programme. Here are his thoughts on how to design such a course.

CURRICULUM ENHANCEMENT DESIGN CONSIDERATIONS

It is essential that, once you are aware of the remit or need, you plan backwards from a successful outcome. This means you will need to have clarity about what you are trying to achieve and how you intend to go about it. So, the first step is to plan backwards.

Planning backwards, or reverse engineering, is something Andy has written about before. In his 2019 book, *The Learning Imperative*, he said it was:

> a process that starts with the learning goal very clearly in mind. This learning process can be represented quite simply as a gap – a gap between the desired destination (KASH) and the starting points of the learners. For anyone designing a learning programme and hoping to ensure high impact, the challenge is to narrow this disparity.[2]

Too often, passionate and well-meaning professionals rush into creating enhancements, learning programmes and even whole curriculums without being clear about what they are trying to achieve. We prefer to design a road map for success rather than an imprecise set of vague hopes.

The main benefits of backward planning are:

- The programme/enhancement is more likely to succeed because the delivery team has clearly defined goals and a carefully considered road map for getting to this destination.

- Clarity on the KASH destination makes it much more likely that all the planning steps and learning processes will be aligned.

- The programme can be replicated or used for research purposes because the designers have carefully documented their planned processes.

- The programme can be adjusted as it unfolds as evidence of the participants' progress and non-progress is gathered.

---

2   Burns and Griffith, *The Learning Imperative*, p. 157.

CLARITY ON THE DESIRED KASH DESTINATION

As we have mentioned, the acronym KASH stands for knowledge, attitudes, skills and habits. Knowing what an ideal or excellent KASH outcome would be is the most important first step in planning any enhancement, programme or project. To meet the remit he was given, Andy created the KASH grid below.

Knowledge	Attitudes
▪ Academic ▪ Cultural ▪ Personal ▪ Social	▪ An ever-growing positive attitude towards the Scholars' Programme and to high attainment. ▪ An ever-growing attitude to applying for a future degree course or higher-level apprenticeship.
Skills	**Habits**
▪ Note-taking, revision and memory. ▪ Confidence in a range of fields or settings. ▪ Communicating with adults in a variety of formats.	▪ Efficient time management. ▪ Reading for pleasure and purpose. ▪ Adopting taught strategies when in fish-out-of-water situations.

The programme deliberately built academic, personal, social and cultural knowledge; all the lessons in Part III are taught as part of the programme. Alongside this, other experiences were designed to develop the desired KASH and to cultivate study skills, communication skills and student confidence, especially in new and unfamiliar situations. It also intended to turn the knowledge, attitudes and skills that were acquired into habits, especially around managing more time for study, reading and being more prepared for feeling-like-a-fish-out-of-water situations that might arise in students' future lives.

LESSONS FROM KASH

It is tempting to produce a long list of hopes or desirables for any programme, but experience has taught us to be concise about what we are trying to achieve. This enables the delivery team to maintain a more consistent focus; plus, fewer, tighter KASH criteria are easier to communicate to participants and other stakeholders.

One way of doing this is to play 'Winner stays on'. Create a thorough list of hopes from the programme in each of the KASH areas, and then – through discussion, elimination and conflation – get the list down to the most important two or three. In creating tight KASH criteria, we are more likely to keep our focus and not drift from our core purpose.

First, let's consider who may be delivering the curriculum enhancement, who will go on it and when it will be delivered.

WHO WILL BE THE ADULTS INVOLVED?

Before we launch any programme that falls outside the normal timetable, we need to ensure that we have the adults available to deliver it. They can come from the staff body or from outside the school, but they will need to show they have the capacity to deliver the proposed curriculum enhancement. Ideally, those delivering it will have been involved in the planning process.

As each curriculum enhancement is likely to have different aims and methodologies, there is no generic set of criteria for a delivery person or team. However, if we were drawing up a person specification, we would suggest these 'desirables':

■ Passion – they should hold a genuine interest in the problem that the enhancement is attempting to address.

■ Capable – they should have strong competency in the type of KASH-building required for the enhancement. They will need to inspire trust from those involved. A good track record of achieving high grades with previous classes or success with previous extra-curricular programmes would be a good source of confidence.

■ Commitment – they should be prepared to put some of their own time into the planning, delivery and evaluation of the programme. This will involve preparing content, coordinating experiences and organising the logistics of getting students off their normal timetable so everything runs smoothly. It also helps if the personnel involved with the programme are consistent because this builds trust with all stakeholders, so ideally the staff selected will commit to do so for a few years.

■ Team-building and networking mentality – even if there is just one person delivering the bulk of the programme, there should be a team of people working in the background. This has several advantages. Firstly, members of the team can cover each other in case of absence, ensuring that planned sessions go ahead and momentum is maintained. Secondly, a team approach leads to more ideas coming forward at both the planning stage and throughout its delivery. Finally, they should be looking to widen the network of staff and outside bodies that are available to support young people. In doing so, a constant flow of people who can help with elements of the programme will always be available.

DELIVERY TEAM

For any curriculum enhancement to work there must be a team with clear responsibilities. As Peter Block says in his book *Community*, 'the small group is the unit of transformation'.[3] The team will need to work well together to build the desired KASH for the group. Among other things they might need to:

■ Deliver in-school sessions.

■ Monitor students' participation in reading challenges between sessions.

■ Encourage participation and stimulate enthusiasm for the programme.

■ Arrange experiences.

■ Accompany students on trips.

■ Organise careers research.

■ Build networks of employers for careers experiences such as work experience and interviews.

■ Organise parent sessions.

■ Facilitate sessions with parents.

■ Populate social media.

3   P. Block, *Community: The Structure of Belonging* (San Francisco, CA: Berrett-Koehler Publishers, 2009), p. 99.

No one person can achieve all this, so it is crucial to have clarity around roles and responsibilities. To aid in this, the team should be able to meet formally on a regular basis.

WHO WILL BE THE YOUNG PEOPLE INVOLVED?

Cohort selection can be a tricky issue, especially when students are being selected for an enhancement that has a finite number of participants. Getting it wrong can lead to parental complaints about why their child wasn't chosen. There are other ways that we can get it wrong too.

Remember, the main purpose of curriculum enhancements is to make up for gaps that working-class students may have in their knowledge or experience through no fault of their own. Therefore, we must challenge ourselves to pick a cohort that isn't simply made up of students who are already rich in the KASH that the programme will be building.

The Malit Scholars' Programme has learned from the criticisms of many similar programmes that used to be described as gifted and talented (G&T) – for example, that they are elitist, divisive and gimmicky – and has incorporated this wisdom into the selection criteria for inclusion. For this reason, we carefully consider ways to design effective curriculum enhancements that do make a difference, aren't divisive and don't support the already advantaged.

The Malit Scholars' Programme takes 25% of each year group as a cohort. That represents about fifty students who are divided into two groups of twenty-five. Head teacher Tony McGuinness was keen to involve students who would not have met the old-fashioned G&T criteria, so the cohort is heavily loaded with pupil premium students, higher-performing SEND students and boys. Bigger cohorts have a larger effect on outcomes as an increase in their results acts as a multiplier effect on the school's overall attainment data.

WHAT ABOUT THOSE WHO AREN'T INVOLVED?

Just as we must choose a suitable cohort for a curriculum intervention, we have the same challenges when choosing which students are going to benefit from a curriculum enhancement. In this book, we have explained that enhancements are designed for higher-attaining students whereas interventions are for lower-attaining students, but not being chosen for an enhancement doesn't mean that a student is low-attaining or that we don't see potential in them. We therefore need to handle selection – and communicating non-selection – sensitively.

The reasons why a student isn't selected will usually relate to their suitability for the pathway – in this case, for higher education or a higher-level apprenticeship. Some students won't go on to get the requisite grades for these pathways or make it clear that they don't intend to take that route. Other students will miss out on selection due to poor behaviour, especially when it is felt that this could negatively affect others in the cohort or damage the school's reputation when taking trips and undertaking work placements, both of which are a key part of the programme.

There will have to be a limit on the size of the cohort too. Having said this, students might be able to join the programme midway through as others leave. Parents or carers can therefore lobby for a student's inclusion, as can teachers.

To avoid confusion or distress, we encourage schools to develop a set of clear selection criteria and to be resolute in their justification of the starting cohort. We also encourage schools to go beyond the obvious and target those who are most marginalised. It must be stressed that those not selected are in no way less worthy, it is merely that they are on a different pathway.

WHEN DOES THE ENHANCEMENT TAKE PLACE?

Just as most teachers have become averse to participating in training in after-school sessions called 'twilights', the students we want to help might baulk at being asked to be part of a programme that takes place after school hours. We have stressed how important it is that schools have a strong extra-curricular provision, but if your school only tries to extend the curriculum with after-school clubs then they are missing an opportunity to help the most in need. Some students simply cannot stay after school due to caring responsibilities or because they need to do part-time work. Or they won't stay after the last lesson of the day because doing so may run counter to the norms of their friendship group, which frowns on studying hard or aspiring to do well in exams.

To be blunt, running activities after school won't have the same impact as a fully developed curriculum enhancement programme for students on the margins – the ones who fall into the categories you particularly want to help. It is always great to see lots of students staying after school, participating in clubs and doing homework or extra work, but to really make a difference we need to challenge ourselves to have a big cohort and to allocate time during the school day.

REFLECTIVE QUESTIONS

- How will you choose the cohort who will benefit from the curriculum enhancement?
- How will you ensure the cohort isn't too safe?
- What characteristics will be needed from the person(s) who will lead the curriculum enhancement?
- What roles will members of the team take?

CURRICULUM ENHANCEMENT MODELS

Below are some suggested models for curriculum enhancements within school time.

MODEL I

A calendared programme between Year 7 (January) to Year 11 (September) which focuses on the development of the KASH associated with the programme. This is the current model being used for the Malit Scholars' Programme. In-house sessions are delivered in the school library.

- 1 x two-hour session delivered each half-term = twelve hours per year.
- 1 x 'experience' each half-term to build knowledge and spark interest = six per year.
- 1 x book each term that students are urged to read = three per year.
- 1 x work placement of one week in Year 10.
- 1 x evening session with parents to inform them of the course content and how to further support students each term = three per year.

The programme culminates in term 1 of Year 11 with student presentations and awards. At the end of the programme the students will have received:

- Thirty hours of in-school lessons on some of the topics we have covered in this book, such as motivation, memory, revision, class discrimination, habitus and so on.
- Twenty-four experiences that students have prepared for and been debriefed on.
- Twelve books that they will own for life.
- A one-week work placement.

The table on page 148 is an example of the structure of the Malit Scholars' Programme.

Advantages of this model:

- Minimal disruption to subject teachers.
- Has strong quantitative and qualitative data behind it.
- Spacing out sessions and experiences enables reflection between sessions.
- Students look forward to the sessions and experiences, thereby building engagement and motivation.

Disadvantages of this model:

- Group size doesn't enable the course leader to get to know all the students.
- Students' work isn't monitored and there is no wider reading between sessions.
- The delivery team isn't very broad.
- Students need to be taken out of lessons.

Year 10 – Preparing for future exams and career

TERM 1A	TERM 1B	TERM 2A	TERM 2B	TERM 3A	TERM 3B
Student session 1: Stoic philosophy and its application	Student session 2: History of classism and struggle	Student session 3: Preparation for Year 10 work experience (part 1)	Student session 4: Revision and exam methods (part 1)	Student session 5: Revision and exam methods (part 2)	Student session 6: Preparation for Year 10 work experience (part 2)
Experience: Business visit	Experience: FACT cinema	Experience: Carmel College	Experience: Keele University	Experience: Edgehill University London	
Parent/carer session: Year 11 presentations		Parent/carer session: Helping your child to prepare for exams and work experience			Parent/carer session: Preparing your child for Year 11
The Obstacle is the Way: The Timeless Art of Turning Trials into Triumph by Ryan Holiday			Eat That Frog! Get More of the Important Things Done Today by Brian Tracy		Book voucher for each student to buy a book to read over their summer holiday

MODEL 2

One weekly session delivered after school at Key Stage 4 with some experiences built into the programme.

This could entail:

- Fifty-plus hours of after-school lessons on the four knowledge domains over Years 10 and 11.
- An additional range of experiences, such as university and business visits, built in alongside the lessons.
- Elements of individual project work or portfolio building which can be ongoing.
- Half-termly focus on a particular element of the desired KASH.

Advantages of this model:

- More regular contact means that the course leader gets to know the students better.
- More time can be allocated to learning about the knowledge domains.
- Students don't need to be taken out of lessons.
- Students take more interest in the study skill elements when in the GCSE years.

Disadvantages of this model:

- Only motivated students will attend sessions; others who feel forced to attend might become resentful and not engage with the programme.
- By not starting in Key Stage 3, the students have less time to build good study habits.
- It can feel like just another lesson and lose its specialness.
- Lots of content must be created by the delivery team.

MODEL 3

An intensive two-week course, possibly at the end of Year 9 or 10, or two one-week courses.

This could entail:

- Fifty-plus hours of learning about the desired KASH.
- Can be a residential setting such as a university.
- Book and film studies.
- Whole days can be allocated to building the desired KASH, such as how to present or create an argument for a debate.

Advantages of this model:

- Builds a team mentality among the cohort.
- Concentrating the programme into a dedicated block of time makes it a more intense and memorable experience for the students.
- Staffing costs are lower if delivered after Year 11 leave school.
- More time to go into greater depth in KASH-building.

Disadvantages of this model:

- Less time between sessions stifles reflection.
- There is less opportunity for the students to build good habits.
- Some students won't enjoy having to work away from their friends for a prolonged period.
- A lot more organisation is required from the school.

Note: we have not discussed the costs of each model, which will have to be factored in too, but we hope that by sharing the pros and cons you can consider what is right for your context.

REFLECTIVE QUESTIONS

■ Which of the suggested models, if any, works for your timetable and calendar?

■ What other delivery models could you use?

■ How will you ensure that the sessions and experiences align with the KASH you are trying to build?

■ Once you have chosen a model, how will you ensure that the delivery team create a high-quality programme that engages the students?

■ What plans do you have to spark interest in the programme?

THE LAUNCH

Whichever model you adopt for the enhancement, it will need a carefully planned launch. This should introduce the reasons for the course, outline the journey ahead and specify any rules or contracts that students (and sometimes parents and carers) are required to sign up to. It is also a good idea for course leaders to share their backstories, expertise and passion for the issue being addressed.

Senior leaders and course leaders should ideally be present to signify the importance of the programme. The parents and carers of the students who have been chosen should attend, as should the students themselves. This will take place at an evening event.

The launch should get everyone talking and thinking. Parents and carers should go away thinking that it will be worthwhile for their child to be a part of the programme, and the students should also see the benefits and opportunities that might arise and be excited, or at least intrigued, by the journey ahead.

REFLECTIVE QUESTIONS

- Which experiences will be most suitable for the curriculum enhancement you are planning?

- How do you intend to build a list of potential experiences for your students? How can other staff help with this?

- How will you ensure the students are prepared for each experience?

- How will you brief staff on expected behaviours during the experience?

LEARNING FROM EVALUATION

If you intend the curriculum enhancement to run for a long time, you will want to ensure that there is year-on-year improvement. Curriculum enhancements should be evaluated in two ways: quantitatively and qualitatively.

You will want enhancements to contribute to improved attainment as measured by examination results (quantitative) and also judged to be worthwhile or even popular (qualitative). It is difficult to isolate the quantitative impact of extra-curricular activities and curriculum enhancements, so it is important to collect a raft of qualitative data over time from surveys, interviews and questionnaires.

Here are some suggestions of how this can be achieved:

- **Pupil voice:** Some of the students sampled each year through pupil voice surveys can be members of the cohort going through the curriculum enhancement.

- **Student evaluations:** Students can complete evaluations at different points of the year.

- **Parent/carer surveys:** Parents and carers can be surveyed about their opinion of the impact of the programme on their child.

- **End-of-year reviews:** The delivery team can review the sessions and experiences with a view to how well they went and how they can be improved for the following year.

- **Open forums:** A range of stakeholders can be invited to a real or virtual open forum where they can express their opinions on the effectiveness of various aspects of the enhancement.

Evaluation is crucial if you want the impact of curriculum extras and enhancements to grow from year to year. Developing a suite of easy-to-administer qualitative tools will enable you and your team to judge where there has been impact. Some of the reflection questions below can also be incorporated into the forms of qualitative analysis that you intend to use.

OTHER STORIES: JAMIE

Being elected head boy by teachers and his peers was a significant achievement for Jamie – certainly the biggest of his life to date. The election happened at the end of Year 10, and he would take up the post immediately after the Year 11s had finished their exams.

Jamie was one of the best students in the school. Committed and motivated, his predicted grades at GCSE were 8s and 9s. Yet, back in Year 7, he was often getting into trouble and was frequently disengaged in lessons. However, in the January of Year 7 when teachers and heads of year decided who should be selected for the Malit Scholars' Programme, Jamie was put forward. Despite his poor behaviour, he clearly had academic potential.

Steadily, over Year 7 and 8, his behaviour improved. By Year 10, he had become an exemplary student. Jamie explains that the reason for his transformation was in large part due to the Scholars' Programme. Some of the sessions on motivation and story particularly resonated with him. He learned to take more control of his inner dialogue. The experiences of visiting universities also fostered his determination to get a degree in law. Experiences such as a work placement in a solicitors' office and a Zoom interview with a barrister strengthened this even further.

REFLECTIVE QUESTIONS

- What qualitative tools do you intend to use to measure the impact of the curriculum enhancement?

- What times of year will you use them?

- How will you process the results?

- With whom will these results be shared?

- Which sessions seem to have had the most impact? Why do you think this is?

- Which experiences have had the most impact? Why do you think this is?

- Has the structure of the curriculum enhancement provided enough time to build the desired KASH? If not, how might it be changed next year?

PLANNING TEMPLATE:
CURRICULUM ENHANCEMENTS

Here is a template you may find helpful when planning curriculum enhancements in your school. As ever, you will find pre-populated examples at www.theworkingclassroom.co.uk.

STEP 1: IDENTIFY THE OPPORTUNITY

Ask: What extra and different can students be given the opportunity to learn and experience that will provide greater equity for them compared to their more affluent peers? What criteria will be used for selection? How many students can be given this opportunity? What barriers do they commonly face (identify causes and consequences)? What are the key differences among the cohort that may need to be addressed?

STEP 2: SET THE SUCCESS CRITERIA

Ask: What type of enhancement will we create? What will success look like at the end? How will we know we have been successful? What data will we use to assess this (both qualitative and quantitative)? Will success look the same for all students? What follow-up actions may be needed to ensure success is sustained?

STEP 3: CHOOSE AND JUSTIFY THE DELIVERY MODEL

Ask: How would the delivery model for the enhancement be described? Who will deliver it? When will it be delivered? Where will it be delivered? How often will it be delivered? What are the main advantages of this model? What is the theory of action behind this model? What is the research base for this model? What other enhancement models have we considered and rejected? What are the reasons for this?

STEP 4: MONITORING AND EVALUATING

Ask: What data will be used throughout (monitoring) and at the end (evaluation) of the enhancement, and how will this data be gathered? How can the data be disaggregated to understand outliers and the reasons for this? How will the data be used to ensure continued refinement of the curriculum enhancement?

STEP 5: LOGISTICS AND COSTINGS

Ask: What are the staffing implications for this enhancement? What resources will be required? What financial costs will be incurred?

CHAPTER 8

HOW CAN WE ENGAGE PARENTS AND CARERS AS PARTNERS IN THE PROCESS?

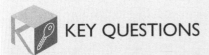

KEY QUESTIONS

In this chapter, we will answer the following questions:

- Why is the engagement of working-class parents and carers so important?

- What are the optimal home–school communication methods?

- How can we best build relational trust between home and school?

Having both worked in multiple schools in different socio-economic circumstances, we both recognise that it is harder to engage some parents and carers in a conversation about how best to support their child as they journey through secondary school. The reasons for this will be unpicked shortly, but one of the chief causes relates to the core message of this book: some parents find secondary schools unwelcoming. Added to this are some of the insecurities that working-class parents often feel in what can seem like a pretty middle-class world.

One of the problems working-class students face is that they are denied the home advantage. While we may have to offer some compensatory parenting – or, put another way, step in to help students when their parents don't – the best solution is to engage parents as partners in education. Indeed, when schools work effectively with parents and carers, students benefit from higher academic achievement, good attendance and punctuality, and better behaviours and attitudes to learning. Improving parental engagement can lead to an increased level of interest among students in their work.

OTHER STORIES

JANE (PARENT OF A YEAR 11 STUDENT)

I hate parents' evenings. I've been to a few, but I just come away feeling flat and that I'm a shit parent. You get five minutes with each teacher and although some are nice, most tend to look at me like they feel sorry for me or something. I'm constantly hassled by the school with texts, and the sooner Amber leaves that place the better.

GED (PARENT OF A YEAR 10 STUDENT)

I've been to a few school parents' evenings but don't enjoy them. There's just loads of people with suits and ties talking about stuff I don't understand. My son's going to be a lorry driver like me. School thinks he lacks aspiration or something, but I'm earning twice as much as anybody in a school, except the head teacher probably, and I like what I do. That tells me quite a few teachers are snobs.

BARBARA (PARENT OF A YEAR 9 STUDENT)

I'm really impressed by the way that school is communicating with us. I've downloaded the Arbor app and can see what progress my daughter is making. The school seems efficient and the teachers committed. I would just like a bit more face-to-face with teachers. I work most evenings so couldn't attend the last parents' evening. I'm on my own now so no one else can go in my place. This made me feel bad. My daughter has a lot of anxiety issues, and I'm not sure what to do a lot of the time. I don't want to contact school as they all seem so busy.

No two working-class parents are the same. But the quotes from real parents we have interviewed for this book are very revealing. Of course, all schools work hard on parental engagement, but could some – perhaps yours – work smarter?

WHY PARENTAL ENGAGEMENT MATTERS

Parental engagement has never been more crucial. Secondary schools that are successful in going beyond mere engagement with their students' parents and carers – and ensure that they are *involved* in, not just *informed* about, school life – are more likely to be successful across a range of outcomes.

It is in a school's best interests to ensure that staff make regular contact with parents, because when students' families become partners in the education process, they are more likely to support the school when times get tough, as well as stand shoulder to shoulder with teachers in celebrating the good times. Put simply, if schools and parents work as a team for the benefit of young people, life is easier for everyone and students' life chances are enhanced.

And parental engagement is even more crucial for students who arrive at school at a disadvantage – such as those from a working-class background. The old adage tells us that it takes a village to raise a child, and that is certainly true of education. Schools alone cannot tackle the inequalities in society; they must work in partnership with parents, families, external agencies and communities. And yet the parents of working-class students are sometimes the hardest to reach because they don't feel comfortable talking to teachers in educational settings and because they struggle to find the time to attend school events.

So, what can schools do to ensure they fully engage with the parents and carers of working-class students? In this chapter, we will explain why parental engagement matters and outline some optimal methods for communicating with them. We will also explore the role that technology can play in this process. We will recommend investing heavily in building strong relational trust with parents and carers within your school community. Many working-class parents need this a lot more than you might think. Finally, we will explore possible training or information sessions that can be run with parents and carers that will help them to help their child. Done in the right way, these sessions can be game changers in building positive home–school relationships.

FOUR STARTING PRINCIPLES FOR BETTER PARENTAL ENGAGEMENT

Before we delve into some specifics, let's consider a few principles that you may wish to bear in mind.

1   **Parental communication needs to start early and continue throughout a student's journey through school.** The parents of children moving from primary to secondary won't want to receive information halfway through the summer holiday, at which point it will be deemed too late. Schools need to engage with parents early and clearly set out their expectations and requirements.

2   **Parental communication needs to be a two-way process.** As well as the school staying in touch with parents, parents also need a means of staying connected with the school. One way to do this is to create a frequently asked questions page, as well as a Q&A facility and a parents' forum on the school's website. This will need to be monitored carefully, of course, or perhaps have comments vetted by a gatekeeper before they are made live. For this to be viewed as worthwhile, the school will also need to communicate its response to parental comments and suggestions, perhaps through a 'You said, we did' page.

3   **Parental communications need to be appropriately timed, relevant and useful.** One way to do this is to use the experience and expertise of students and their parents. For example, the parents of current Year 7 students will be able to share their thoughts on what information they needed when they went through the transition process with their child not so long ago, as well as when they needed it most. Meanwhile, current Year 7 students will be able to offer their advice about how to prepare for secondary school – for example, by providing a reading list for the summer and sharing their tips on how to get ready for the first day of school.

4   **Parental communications should take many forms and embrace new and emerging technologies.** The use of digital technologies such as email, texting, websites, videos, webinars, electronic portfolios and online assessment and reporting tools can make communication between parents and teachers more timely, efficient, productive and satisfying.

Of course, doing all of this well takes time, so it is important to balance the needs of parents and carers with those of hard-working teachers. We don't want the unintended consequence of adding to teachers' workloads. How can we ensure that we remain mindful of workload concerns while meeting the needs of parents? What special considerations do we need to make for working-class parents and carers?

WHAT BETTER PARENTAL ENGAGEMENT LOOKS LIKE IN PRACTICE

Here is some advice based on the best schools with whom we have worked.

BEING MINDFUL OF STAFF WORKLOAD

There is a growing trend for parents to be given teachers' direct email addresses and for teachers to make a set number of phone calls to parents each week. While it is undoubtedly helpful for parents to have easy access to their child's teacher, and regular contact between the school and home is a good thing for students, it is important to consider the impact of this approach, particularly on a teacher's workload and well-being. The last thing your school needs is to lose a great teacher because they are burnt out.

Of course, we want parents to work in partnership with us; for them to be involved in – not just informed about – our schools. School leaders need to remember that they are the gatekeepers for communication flow. Staff need to be protected from over-zealous and needy parents who want to send hourly emails. Staff also need to be shielded from angry and belligerent parents. Simple protocols and systems can mitigate these problems.

ENSURING PARENTS AND CARERS FEEL INVOLVED AND INFORMED

A welcoming and straightforward parental engagement policy can solve a lot of the issues we have raised. Such a policy should do two things: firstly, set out clearly what parents and carers can expect from the school and, secondly, set out what the school expects from parents and carers.

Always start with what parents and carers can expect from the school. First and foremost, schools must show how they will make working-class parents feel comfortable. Remember those stories at the beginning of this chapter. It is far more likely that a working-class parent will feel alienated by the experience of interacting with school staff. In our busy working lives, we can easily lose sight of this. Here are a few suggestions for how best to achieve this. For example, parents and carers can expect:

- To receive clear and timely communication about their child's progress.

- Parents' evenings and meetings are high-quality interactions.

- Documentation can be easily understood.

- The school will treat their child fairly.

- Behaviour rules are clearly explained and enforced, which enables the school to work as a well-functioning community.

Documentation will also need to be unambiguous around what behaviours the school would like to see from parents. We might want to encourage parents and carers to:

- Be supportive.

- Maintain a direct involvement in their child's progress.

- Understand what the school is trying to achieve for their child.

- Take a positive position – for example, contribute to initiatives like home visits and information-gathering events such as parents' consultation evenings.

- Visit school and stay informed about issues and initiatives.

- Support events that promote the school's efforts.

- Be aware of and support any home–school agreements.

A parental engagement policy should also outline how your school intends to communicate with parents and how it will consult with them on key decisions. It may be useful to start with a statement of intent such as: 'Our school, to be effective, must acknowledge, appreciate and respond to the views of parents. It needs to take informed decisions following consultation.'

The school will need a clear strategy for communicating effectively and expediently with parents in each of the following ways:

- Parents' consultation evenings.

- Open evenings.

- Information meetings.

- Parents' workshops and discussion forums.

- Parents' associations or committees.
- Formal questionnaires and market research products.
- Regular newsletters.
- School website.
- Online reporting and parents' portal.
- Text messaging.
- Email.

As well as writing letters (your school should have a policy that dictates your house style, and letters should be checked and formatted by the admin team), it is likely that you will use email and text messages to communicate with parents. Before relying on electronic messaging to impart important information, it is vital that you understand access arrangements: do all parents have internet and mobile phone coverage, and do all parents have the financial means to utilise it? Will you disadvantage some parents if you rely solely on email and texts? You may need to adopt a belt and braces approach to communication by sending a text and/or email to indicate that a letter is on its way.

And what of the school website? Your school should have a policy explaining how it will use its website to aid communication. It is likely that it will be used for publishing news articles, celebrating school successes and reproducing the school calendar. It may also – and to be an outstanding school that extends the boundaries of learning, it should – be used for setting work and providing help and advice to students. The website may provide an overview of each course and syllabus taught in school and may have links to homework and extension tasks should students and parents wish to do extra work to secure the learning or revise.

As well as having a policy for how your school communicates with parents, you will also need a policy on how staff use these means of communication to ensure accuracy, timeliness and appropriateness.

Two-way communication involves parents hearing their voices reflected back; they need to feel included and represented. We need more working-class voices in education to help working-class parents feel they belong and are welcome in school. Some of these mechanisms might include:

- Parent conferences or forums.
- Open/information evenings.
- Workshops, videos or webinars.
- Parent–teacher associations or school community councils.

- Sending home portfolios of student work every week/month for parents to review and comment.
- Phone calls from teachers and school leaders.
- Emails or updates via the school website.
- Text messages.
- Home visits by a member of staff.

To be effective, parental communications need to be:

- **Clear:** Information should be given in plain English and avoid room for confusion or misunderstanding.
- **Timely:** Information should be given at appropriate times when action is needed and not too far in the future.
- **Consistent:** Information should be logical and in line with the school's policies and should reflect the school's values and attitudes. Ideally, it should emanate from a single source or be passed through the school office to avoid giving contradictory messages.
- **Acted upon:** Information requests should be followed up and all promises kept. This might mean being more realistic about what can be achieved within set timescales rather than promising parents the earth to appease them.

Parental communication can be improved by making a habit of positive praise – for example, weekly 'good news' telephone calls to parents by teachers and leaders can help to build rapport and establish a strong partnership. When a phone call from school conveys good news – rather than always being about poor behaviour, attendance or progress – the relationship between school and home will improve.

However, particularly for new teachers, it can be difficult to make that first phone call to a parent or carer. Preparing for the call will make it easier and rehearsing the opening lines can alleviate some of the anxiety.

Here are some guidelines to help teachers prepare for a phone call:

- Introduce yourself – what is your name, what is your role in school and what is your relationship to the student?
- Tell the parents what their child is studying in class – what is the current topic and how does it fit into the wider curriculum?
- Comment on their child's progress to date – in what ways have they improved over time? What do you predict of their achievements this term or year?

- Comment on their child's behaviour and attitude to learning – are they attentive, keen, industrious, polite, helpful towards others and so on?

- Inform them of their child's achievements – have they won any awards or received any house points?

- Inform them of their child's main strengths or share an anecdote about their performance in class.

- Ensure the parent knows they can contact you to discuss their child at any time in the future and remind them of the ways they can stay in touch with the school.

STRIKING THE RIGHT TONE

Some schools are also offering advice to parents in the form of in-house sessions, online sessions, videos, webinars and written documents such as flyers. This is very much an extra for a school to take on, but where it has the capacity, schools can inform parents on topics that have a direct effect on their parenting.

We welcome that the education profession has become more research informed. It is heart-warming to see how many teachers and leaders take an active part in learning about the latest research on neuroscience, pedagogy, psychology and more. Many educators use this new-found knowledge to communicate with parents because, by sharing it, they can open up a dialogue around how home can support what is happening in school. This has certainly been an opportunity that Andy has embraced on the Malit Scholars' Programme. Each term, he leads a discussion around themes that parents tell him they are interested in learning about. These are delivered in short forty-five to sixty-minute sessions and are a mixture of in-person and online delivery.

Parents and carers won't engage in these sessions if they feel talked down to, not listened to, or are prevented from asking questions and making contributions. The tone needs to be professional but also informal and friendly. It is always worth stressing that parenting is hard; no one teaches us how to be a parent and there is no one way to tackle an issue or barrier to learning faced by a child. However, as the teaching profession becomes more informed about research, staff can offer suggestions to parents about strategies they may not have tried or have not yet persisted with.

It is helpful, but not essential, that the person delivering the session is a parent themselves as this creates greater empathy. All sessions should be quality assured by a senior member of staff; having them in attendance at the session (for both in-person and online events) enables parents to give some feedback afterwards and emphasises the importance of the sessions.

ENGAGING HARD-TO-REACH PARENTS

We all know that there are some parents and carers within the school community who are much harder to reach. Every school, no matter the socio-demographic context, will have these challenges, but schools in socially deprived areas will face significantly more challenges. We have no firm data to back this up, but it is our experience of working in schools in socially deprived areas.

For these parents and carers, some of the reasons are likely to be:

- Poor experience of education themselves.
- Lack of transport to get to school events.
- Shift-working patterns.
- Lack of childcare for younger children.
- Feeling unwelcome or labelled by the school.
- Health issues.
- Poor literacy and numeracy skills.
- Linking school with authority figures.

It is vital to be conscious of these physical, emotional and psychological barriers. There will also be parents and carers with complex personal problems.

Best practice with these families would involve:

- **Building positive relationships from day one of secondary school or before.** Secondary schools will receive intelligence from primary feeder schools on parents who are hard to engage with. This knowledge can help new schools to forge more positive relationships built on trust. One way of doing this is for Year 7 pastoral leaders to progress through to Year 11 with the year group. This enables long-term relationships to be developed and, ultimately, more trust.

- **Never giving up.** If normal channels of communication aren't working, then some creativity, proactivity and persistence will be required. This can involve home visits and flexible attendance times for school meetings and conversations. Some schools combat this by employing learning mentors and non-teaching assistant progress leaders. As well as creating long-term relationships, each of these members of staff has a mobile phone provided by the school to communicate with parents (sometimes in the evening or pre-school) and where they can leave messages.

- **Being positive and welcoming.** Try to avoid threats of fines or sanctions when talking with parents who are difficult or recalcitrant. Remember, it is a five-year-plus journey so carefully play every positive card at your disposal. As we mentioned earlier, make sure parents feel welcomed. Greeting adults at parents' evenings and asking about their experience is good customer service. Use data from parental surveys, letters (both the praise and the complaints kind) and conversations with parents to continually improve the issues they are concerned and care about.

OTHER STORIES: PETER

Peter is a sixth-form college principal. Taking over the leadership of a large institution which serves a socially deprived area meant that almost the whole of Peter's summer holiday was spent on site getting ready for September. The college was rated as requires improvement by Ofsted and results were consistently poor. In this new post, he soon realised the scale of the challenge when the A level results came through that summer – they were dire. Certainly, some students would not get the university places they had hoped for.

On A level results day, Peter cleared his diary and arranged office space to take meetings with parents who would come in to complain. He also readied himself for the many phone complaints that would come through. In his previous role as the assistant principal of a college in a more affluent area, he often had to deal with numerous parental grievances. He was ready for a long day.

As the students filed in to pick up their results, Peter noticed that they and their parents, although disappointed and sometimes upset, left the college and went home. On that day, not one parent contacted him, nor anyone else at the college, to express their dissatisfaction or anger. Not one.

Peter learned a lot from this experience. He realised that he and his leadership team would need to be more like the sharp-elbowed, middle-class parents who were prevalent in his previous college. The teaching staff would need to take being *in loco parentis* more seriously.

He realised that day that, for many working-class parents, complaining was regarded as fruitless because they wouldn't be listened to, or else they didn't know what standard they should expect. Their lack of confidence and secret knowledge was something that his new leadership would need to address.

REFLECTIVE QUESTIONS

- What does your school do well in terms of parental engagement?

- What does it not do so well?

- What efforts does your school make to boost attendance levels at parents' evenings and other sessions provided by the school? What responses have been forthcoming from this work?

- How does your school ensure that parents and carers feel welcome?

- How does your school balance two-way communication with home alongside managing staff workload?

- What role is technology playing in improving the efficiency of home–school–home communication?

- What parenting sessions could you provide within your school community that aren't currently being offered? How can you make these happen?

- How well does your school work with the most difficult to engage families? What other approaches could you use?

PART III

SEVEN LESSONS TO TEACH WORKING-CLASS STUDENTS

In this part of the book, we would like to share seven lessons that you can teach to your students to help equip them with the knowledge and skills they will need to tackle the classism evident in their own lives.

Why? Because aspirations aren't enough; we need tangible action. We want to do more than talk about working-class students developing a positive mental attitude or growing in confidence. We actually want to *do* more to build their concrete knowledge and skills.

A report by the House of Commons Education Committee published in June 2014 said it well: 'if low aspirations were found to exist, a correlation between this and low performance did not mean that *raising* aspirations would be sufficient'.[1] Stephen Gorard, the professor of education and public policy at Durham University, also quoted in the report, described attitudes and aspirations as 'a red herring'. Gorard said:

> I do not think we have enough evidence that [raising aspirations] cashes out into improvements in attainment [...] What you have are high correlations [...] It does not seem that raising aspiration in itself makes a difference. You need to raise competence in order to make an actual difference to attainment, and if you raise the competence then the attitudes go with it.[2]

We hope these lessons help you to help your students raise their competence and, with it, their attitudes. Each lesson will take about two hours to teach; they can be taught in any order or in isolation. We have shared more lessons like this at www.theworkingclassroom.co.uk.

1   House of Commons Education Committee, *Underachievement in Education by White Working Class Children. First Report of Session 2014–15*. HC 142 (11 June 2014), p. 28 (original emphasis). Available at: https://publications.parliament.uk/pa/cm201415/cmselect/cmeduc/142/142.pdf.
2   House of Commons Education Committee, *Underachievement in Education by White Working Class Children*, p. 28.

WHAT IS CLASSISM?

WHY TEACH ABOUT CLASS AND CLASSISM?

Raising awareness of class and classism is important for several reasons. Firstly, it provides an understanding of how society's policies and practices are often designed to favour the more affluent. In a single lesson, you won't be able to go too deeply into the concept of classism. Nevertheless, we think the lesson will prompt some thinking and provoke discussion, research or further reading.

Secondly, understanding classism will help the students to develop greater self-awareness and empathy for people of all social classes. For working-class students, the knowledge gained in this lesson will enable them to better appreciate the added challenges they face now and are likely to face in the future, compared to their more affluent peers. Other (non-working-class) students can consider the extent to which they hold classist attitudes and whether it affects their behaviours.

Talking and teaching about issues such as class discrimination and poverty need to be carefully handled. In our research, we came across an exercise from the American Psychological Association where students were asked to stand in a line and take a step forward if they had experienced certain things during their childhood. For example: 'If you ever had to skip a meal or were hungry because there was not enough money to buy food when you were growing up, take one step back' or 'If your parents brought you to art galleries or plays, take one step forward.'[1] Activities such as these have the potential to shame participants. There is a separate session on class shaming (Lesson 2) which would be an ideal follow-up to this lesson.

---

1   See https://www.apa.org/pi/ses/resources/publications/privilege-exercise-kahn.pdf.

WHAT IS THE CLASS DIMENSION TO THIS TOPIC?

Sadly, the demise of subjects like sociology at GCSE mean that students rarely, if ever, come across terms such as social class, class structure, social hierarchy, social identity or class discrimination. We think that students should leave school with a decent understanding of class and class relationships. This is especially important in the UK and the United States, where class appears to be a much bigger issue than in other countries.

This lesson will refer to the term 'classism' a lot, so it is important that teachers clearly define it. Unlike other forms of bigotry, such as racism and sexism, class prejudice isn't outlawed. Nevertheless, there are many of us who are calling for class to become a protected characteristic under the law and added to the Equality Act 2010.

This lesson explores the notion of classism and how its effects can be pernicious. Classism involves the delegitimisation of others. It occurs when a person is judged negatively on factors such as their postcode, income, occupation, accent, dress and even their name.

HOW DOES THIS LESSON WORK?

We suggest that to best handle the topic of class and classism, you provide information and plenty of space for questions and discussion. We suggest the following lesson format:

Aim: To help students understand the causes of classism and its effects

Age group: 14–18 years

Time: One to two hours (depending on the use of documentary clips)

Activities: Notetaking, Q&A, discussion, quiz analysis, reading

Resources: Computer and screen, magazine article, mini whiteboards (optional)

TO START THE LESSON

There are different ways to explain the notion of class hierarchy, but one way we have found that engages students is through computer game design. Many have characters with different social statuses, and their position within the hierarchy often limits them to playing certain roles.

A common hierarchy looks like this:

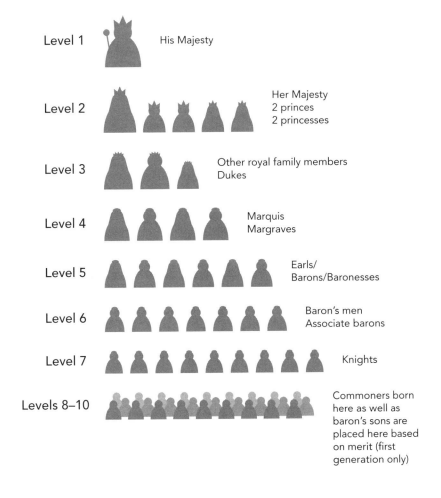

Level 1	His Majesty
Level 2	Her Majesty 2 princes 2 princesses
Level 3	Other royal family members Dukes
Level 4	Marquis Margraves
Level 5	Earls/ Barons/Baronesses
Level 6	Baron's men Associate barons
Level 7	Knights
Levels 8–10	Commoners born here as well as baron's sons are placed here based on merit (first generation only)

Explain that hierarchy exists in all societies. Think of it like a ladder with each rung representing a particular class or caste. Students will probably have studied either the Egyptians or Romans, or perhaps both, in primary school. In these societies, there was a clear hierarchy with strict rules for each class. These civilisations can be revisited by way of explanation.

Ask the students to start to take some notes under the heading of 'classism'. Inform them that classism is a type of prejudice that stems from the belief that people from certain social classes are superior to others.

Explain the tripartite system of class – upper, middle and working class, as well as the A to E social grade system that is favoured by sociologists. Then use either or both schemas to explain the notion of *downward classism*, which is when people in higher social groups discriminate against or marginalise people whom they perceive are in lower social groups. Ask the students to record this term.

Share the following quotation from David Cannadine's *The Rise and Fall of Class in Britain*:

A Briton's place in this class hierarchy is also determined by such considerations as ancestry, accent, education, deportment, mode of dress, patterns of recreation, type of housing, and style of life. All these signs and signals help determine how any one individual regards him- (or her-) self, and how he (or she) is regarded and categorized by others.[2]

Take each of the eight points or 'markers' raised by Cannadine in turn and see where downward classism may be at play. You can place each of these eight points on a slide, so the students can continue to take notes. Visuals for each one would obviously help to create some distinctions.

1   Ancestry – the belief that the 'stock' you come from should convey your place in society. For example, if you are born into a family from the aristocracy – that is, you have a title that will be passed on within the family – then you are superior to someone born into a middle- or lower-class family.

2   Accent – the belief that someone with a posh accent is superior to someone who has a regional accent. In *The Shortest History of England*, James Hawes says: 'Since the 1870s, the accent which became known as received pronunciation, or RP, was the sole permissible one.'[3] Speaking with an RP accent has been a signifier of the elite ever since.

3   Education – the belief that the type or status of the school, and possibly university, you went to should determine your place within society. Hence the phrase 'old school tie'.

2   D. Cannadine, *The Rise and Fall of Class in Britain* (New York: Columbia University Press, 1999), p. 23.
3   J. Hawes, *The Shortest History of England* (Exeter: Old Street Publishing, 2020), p. 172.

4   Deportment – the belief that your manners, posture and body language indicate your suitability for certain roles in society, especially those of leadership.

5   Mode of dress – the belief that how you dress and the clothes you wear make you superior/inferior to others and indicate your suitability for certain roles in society. Again, this goes back hundreds of years. What a person wears or adorns themselves with is a sign of class standing. Although this has receded in many aspects of British life, such as in office culture, the suit and tie are still regarded (for males) as appropriate or formal dress.

6   Patterns of recreation – the belief that the way you spend your leisure time, and with whom you mix while doing so, is a strong indicator of your class origin.

7   Type of housing – the belief that the cost of a person's property, its postcode or its type should determine your status within society.

8   Style of life – the belief that how you live your life and how you spend your money shows your taste for certain things that might be considered either 'cultured' or 'vulgar'. Those who are cultured are superior to the rest of us.

Explain that the notion of hierarchy and class is based on the idea that some people are the social betters of others.

Now address the concept of *internalised classism*. This is the acceptance and justification of classism by working-class people themselves. They have internalised the belief that those 'above' them in the hierarchy are better than them. Examples include feeling inferior around higher-class people, deference to the values that higher-class people hold or feeling shame about your family background or heritage.

RESOURCES

There is an interesting BBC series on class called *How to Crack the Class Ceiling*, written and presented by Amol Rajan.[4] It consists of two episodes, both an hour long. It is a sequel to *How to Break into the Elite* (2019). If your school has a BBC iPlayer account, some episodes or scenes from the series can be shown to the students. The series follows several working-class people who are trying to make their way in the world.

---

4   See https://www.bbc.co.uk/programmes/m001fygr.

One of the central themes of the programme is whether to change the system or to change yourself to fit in with it and thereby get on. This is sometimes referred to as 'code-switching' or 'posh-washing', which is when working-class people try to hide aspects of their working classness to progress within a company or profession. Talking of which, should working-class people try to become more middle class?[5]

Alternatively, or additionally, you could get the students to discuss the idea of posh-washing and ask them questions like:

- In what situations that you currently face do you feel that you have to act differently?

- In what future social situations do you fear you might not fit in?

After exploring the notion of class signifiers, and possibly looking at another clip from *How to Crack the Class Ceiling*, pose some questions and facilitate some discussion. For example:

- What methods of allocating by class had you heard of previously?

- Are you personally aware of any examples of classism or class prejudice? Give some examples.

- Do you think the superiority of some in society is earned or unearned? Explain your views.

- Where do you think beliefs in the superiority of some humans over others has come from?

Now go deeper into the term 'class ceiling'. Ask the students if they are aware of the term 'glass ceiling'. It usually refers to women in the workplace and how challenging it is for them to get promoted. According to 2022 data from the polling company YouGov, 68% of young people think their life chances are 'broadly determined' by their parents' socioeconomic backgrounds.[6]

Ask the students whether they agree with this statement or not by a show of hands and see if the percentage in the class is close to that from the survey. Ask the students to share reasons for their own opinions on this matter.

---

5   For an interesting slant on how working-class people can feel obliged to suppress aspects of identity, such as accent and appearance, see G. Tonic, Wearing Masks: How to Navigate Your Career as a Working-Class Person, *Dazed* (13 May 2022). Available at: https://www.dazeddigital.com/life-culture/article/56090/1/wearing-masks-how-to-navigate-your-career-as-a-working-class-person.

6   See https://yougov.co.uk/topics/politics/trackers/do-people-growing-up-in-the-uk-today-all-have-equal-opportunities.

CLASS STATISTICS QUIZ AND DISCUSSION

The next part of the session will explore some statistics from various professions. You can display this information in different ways. A quiz can be an effective way to get across some interesting job/career statistics.

Ask the students to write 1–10 in their margins and answer the following questions, either individually or in pairs/small groups. The first five questions relate to wealth and income inequality in the UK and the second five relate to careers and occupations. Go through the answers once the students have completed all ten questions.

1   **What percentage of students go to private (fee-paying) schools in the UK?** Answer – 7%. The remaining 93% go to state schools. (*Source*: https://www.gov.uk/government/news/elitism-in-britain-2019)

2   **What percentage of all private wealth in the UK is owned by the wealthiest 1%?** Answer – 24%. (*Source*: https://policy-practice.oxfam. org/publications/double-trouble-a-review-of-the-relationship- between-uk-poverty-and-economic-ine-620373)

3   **How many times higher is the wealth of the richest 1% of households in the UK compared with the least wealthy 10% of households?** Answer – 230 times higher. The richest 1% of households are worth at least £3.6 million and the least wealthy 10% are worth £15,400 on average. (*Source*: https://www.theguardian. com/money/2022/jan/07/richest-uk-households-worth-at-least- 36m-each)

4   **According to an Oxfam report,** *Survival of the Richest* **(published in January 2023), the richest 1% gained new wealth, created since 2020, worth $42 trillion. What percentage of total wealth created during this period does this represent?**

    Answer – 66%. (*Source*: https://www.oxfam.org/en/press-releases/ richest-1-bag-nearly-twice-much-wealth-rest-world-put-together-over- past-two-years)

5   **The percentage of stocks and shares (financial wealth) held by the wealthiest 1% is greater than what percentage of the population?**

    Answer – the bottom 80%. (*Source*: https://www.ft.com/content/ d52743ca-c669-4c71-941f-8281230a21b5)

6   **What percentage of senior judges in the UK come from private schools?** Answer – 65%. (*Source*: https://www.suttontrust.com/ our-research/elitist-britain-2019)

7   **What percentage of current members of parliament are from private schools?** Answer – 29%. (*Source*: https://www.gov.uk/ government/news/elitism-in-britain-2019)

8   **What percentage of members of the House of Lords are from private schools?** Answer – 57%. (*Source*: https://www.gov.uk/ government/news/elitism-in-britain-2019)

9   **What percentage of award-winning actors are from private schools?** Answer – 44%. (*Source*: https://www.gov.uk/government/news/ elitism-in-britain-2019)

10 **What percentage of medal winners in the 2012, 2016 and 2020 Olympics were from private schools?** Answer – around 33%, averaged across the last three Olympic Games. (*Source*: https://www. schoolmanagementplus.com/sports-and-outdoors/ more-than-a-third-of-tokyo-olympic-medallists-independently-educated)

You can award points to whoever was closest to the correct answer (suggestion: award bonus points for perfect or very close answers). Mini whiteboards may be helpful for students to display their answers.

It would seem from the quiz that people from more privileged backgrounds (the upper classes or social class A) do better than the rest when it comes to earnings and career advancement in certain professions. Try to display all the answers on one slide to aid discussion.

Possible discussion questions:

- Which of the quiz answers seems most surprising or unfair? Explain why.

- What are the reasons for some of these answers? Refer to specific questions from the quiz and speculate why these statistics might exist.

- Consider how privileged or advantaged people could deliberately keep out working-class people from their professions. List some strategies they could use. Note: students may be quite naive about some of these, but any additional research or information you can provide about unadvertised jobs, unpaid internships and so on will help you to tease out possible answers.

Ask the students to add some of the learning from the quizzes and list-making to their individual notes.

At this point, at the risk of being seen as biased, it is important to challenge these statistics as non-problematic and to dispute the notion that people from elite classes are more deserving of these positions. (Note:

Someone in a private school could easily use this quiz as evidence of the innate superiority we are attempting to interrogate.)

FINALLY

This session has informed the students, but it also has the potential to anger or even depress them. There are a few other lessons in *The Working Classroom* that might prove to be a good follow-up to this one, such as Lesson 2 on class shaming and Lesson 4 on motivation. Both lessons address some of the consequences of classism and suggest strategies for dealing with it on a personal level.

FINAL THOUGHTS

- Where in your school's curriculum are students taught about class and classism?
- When does this take place?
- How much time is allocated to it?
- What type of pedagogies are used to teach about these issues and concepts?

SUGGESTED FURTHER READING FOR THIS LESSON

Blandford, S. (2017). *Born to Fail? Social Mobility: A Working Class View* (Woodbridge: John Catt Educational).

Dorling, D. (2014). *Inequality and the 1%* (London: Verso Books).

Friedman, S. and Laurison, D. (2019). *The Class Ceiling: Why It Pays to Be Privileged* (Bristol: Policy Press).

Gilbert, I. (ed.) (2018). *The Working Class: Poverty, Education and Alternative Voices* (Carmarthen: Independent Thinking Press).

Savage, M. (2015). *Social Class in the 21st Century* (London: Pelican).

CLASS SHAMING

WHY TEACH ABOUT CLASS SHAMING?

Class shaming is something all working-class people experience at some point in their lives. Certainly, we have both experienced class shaming, which has motivated us to teach others about it. We have undertaken a lot of primary research for this book by interviewing fellow working-class people; being shamed by more privileged people is a universal experience for them too. In this lesson, we have collated a series of real-life scenarios that we will use to help prepare students for similar situations they are likely to face.

Most working-class adults can identify with being stigmatised and stereotyped. Many of these attitudes are borne out of ignorance or a lack of understanding. The overt classism of television programmes such as *Little Britain* and *Benefits Street* certainly plays into these prejudices.

Our research indicates that shame can be evoked when a privileged person tries to devalue or delegitimise someone whom they perceive to be less important or less entitled than them. Through their words or actions, the privileged can, if successful, contribute to making another person feel unwelcome or unworthy.

Writer Brené Brown defines shame as 'the intensely painful feeling or experience of believing that we are flawed and therefore unworthy of love and belonging – something we've experienced, done, or failed to do makes us unworthy of connection'.[1]

WHAT IS THE CLASS DIMENSION TO THIS TOPIC?

So, building on this definition, shaming occurs when someone tries to provoke those feelings in another person. One form of shaming is class shaming. This happens when someone from a more privileged background

---

1   B. Brown, Shame vs. Guilt (15 January 2013). Available at: https://brenebrown.com/articles/2013/01/15/shame-v-guilt.

tries to demean someone who has less income, wealth, knowledge or life experience than them.

Dealing with shame can be very difficult for adolescents. Teaching about shame – and, more importantly, how to deal with feelings of shame – can have a positive impact on mental health. We can and should teach shame resilience in schools to help young people deal with overwhelming feelings of shame.[2] The common mantra 'forewarned is forearmed' is the salient reason for teaching working-class students about this important issue. It is highly likely that they will experience class shaming at some point in their lives, especially in scenarios where they encounter people from other social classes.

In our conversations with fellow working-class people, many cite experiences from settings such as academia, social situations and the workplace. Therefore, teaching students about how they might be shamed, and how they can best respond to it, can help them to develop vital coping strategies which will enhance their well-being.

Of course, class prejudice and snobbery has been around for centuries, and so too have barriers to entry to various professions and cultural pursuits. Some of those barriers are financial: the cost of studying for certain qualifications, having to self-fund through unpaid internships or moving to a more expensive part of the country to find work. Other barriers are non-financial, such as a lack of access to networks of people who have useful or insightful experience of that area.

In Chapter 2, we explained – through sociologists such as Pierre Bourdieu – how the privileged often rig the rules within certain fields to make it harder for working-class people to thrive within them. One tactic they use is to try to embarrass or humiliate others. When the privileged are successful, working-class people tend to quit and remove themselves from the field, thus leaving the way open for the elites to further dominate that sphere. Our job is to help prepare working-class students so that these attempts at class shaming fail.

The scenarios we share in this lesson have all happened to real working-class people. There will also be space for other issues to be raised and other scenarios to be created by the students attending the session. Despite the seriousness of the topic, there are also a lot of opportunities for fun. The sessions represent real-life rehearsals and, just like rehearsing for a play or film, there will be plenty of mistakes and outtakes along the way. The main message of the lesson is: don't let the buggers win!

---

2   B. Brown, Shame Resilience Theory: A Grounded Theory Study on Women and Shame, *Families in Society: The Journal of Contemporary Social Services*, 87(1) (2006), 43–52. https://doi.org/10.1606/1044-3894.3483

HOW DOES THIS LESSON WORK?

This session uses drama or skillstreaming, which are effective pedagogies for dealing with challenging social situations.[3] If you aren't comfortable using drama as a pedagogy to address class shaming, don't worry, the strategies below can also be taught through discussions. Having said that, we do think some role play helps the students to appreciate different ways to respond. With this in mind, we will suggest a lesson format for addressing class shaming using a drama-based approach.

We suggest the following lesson format:

Aim: To help working-class students build shame resilience

Age group: 14–18 years

Time: One-and-a-half to two hours

Activities: Q&A, drama, discussion

Resources: Flipchart and pad

TO START THE LESSON

Lay out the room so the students can move around and see each other perform later in the lesson. Removing or reducing tables normally creates the space required.

Discuss with the class the need to set some ground rules, including participation, confidentiality and so on to create a safe environment. Prepare to model the strategies you want the class to adopt or use drama students to assist you with the modelling. Note: some young people may be reluctant to get involved. Don't pressure anyone to perform but encourage as much active participation as possible. At the very least, they should all be active observers – meaning they will be expected to contribute ideas and scenarios.

Explain to the students that skillstreaming is a form of role play where skills are practised in a safe environment to prepare participants for potential real-life situations. Inform them that they will be expected to participate in the session in the following ways:

■ Be an active role player – get up and take part in a scene.

---

3   See A. P. Goldstein and E. McGinnis, with R. P. Sprakin, N. J. Gershaw and P. Klein, *Skillstreaming the Adolescent: New Strategies and Perspectives for Teaching Prosocial Skills*, rev. edn (Champaign, IL: Research Press, 1997).

■ Be an active observer – offer feedback and ideas for role players.

Explain that skillstreaming involves four elements:

1   Modelling – where the trainer/teacher demonstrates a particular skill.

2   Role playing – where participants experiment with using the skill.

3   Group performance feedback – where trainers/teachers and observers give feedback and share ideas and opinions.

4   Transfer training – think about how you can use these skills in real-life situations.

Ensure these steps are displayed and explained.

A warm-up/icebreaker is always a good idea when preparing students for this type of session. One icebreaker you could use is called 'double wheel'. Here, the class form two circles of equal numbers, one inside the other. The circles rotate in opposite directions until the teacher says 'Stop'. Then each person introduces themselves and asks whoever is opposite a question, which could be as innocuous as, 'What's your favourite television programme?' Each interaction should last between thirty to forty-five seconds, and the process is repeated three times. Starting the session with a lively activity creates good energy and can be used to generate questions and scenarios.

Repeat the double wheel, but this time ask the students to question their partners as follows: 'How might someone be shamed by others?' or 'How might someone be shamed for being working class?' Again, repeat this three times, then ask them to retake their seats.

At this point, encourage the students to share some responses from the last question. Some of these could be turned into scenarios for role playing later in the lesson. Possible answers might include things such as accent, not knowing certain knowledge, not having the best or most fashionable clothes and so on.

Explain to the students that this lesson is about class shaming. Ask them to speculate how a more privileged person might want to shame someone from a lower social class.

Question: How might someone more affluent try to shame a working-class person?

Possible answers:

■ Ridicule/make fun of their accent.

■ Ridicule/make fun of their clothes.

■ Ridicule/make fun of their lack of knowledge around …

- Ridicule/make fun of their lack of money.
- Ridicule/make fun of their lack of experience.
- Ridicule/make fun of their lack of connections.

You might add: In certain situations, people from a privileged background may try to make you feel uncomfortable or unwelcome. Sometimes this is accidental, but sometimes it is deliberate.

The rest of the lesson could take the students through a series of modelled responses. Explain that the lesson will look at some scenarios in which the students may find themselves in the near future. Indeed, it is worth asking if they have already encountered such situations. Explain that the modelled responses are tactics or tools: you use them when you need them.

The five modelled responses or strategies that can be used across multiple shaming situations are:

1   Being awkward, not feeling awkward.

2   Being stoic in the face of insults.

3   Responding with pride.

4   Responding with information/knowledge.

5   Using humour as a shield.

Note: it is possible that the students might suggest some violent responses to the scenarios. Responding with violence should not be considered as an option, however tempting! Even physicality should not be entertained. Responsible teachers will get the students to consider the possible consequences of any physically aggressive response.

Explain all five strategies before allocating a group to each one. Either in front of the whole class or with each small group, model an example of how this strategy might be used. Explain to each group that their job will be to demonstrate that strategy in an upcoming scenario which will be presented to the class shortly. Now go through each of the strategies in more detail.

STRATEGY I: BEING AWKWARD, NOT FEELING AWKWARD

Write the word 'awkward' on a flipchart pad, whiteboard or screen. Ask the students, 'What do you think when you see this word? What is it to *be* awkward? How is *being* awkward different from *feeling* awkward?'

Explain that awkwardness can be viewed in two ways. It can be something you *feel* or something you *are*. A common insult to working-class people (and others who are oppressed) is that we have 'a chip on our shoulder'. Quite a few people we interviewed certainly play this card when they sense that someone is trying to put them in their place. Having a chip on your shoulder isn't necessarily a bad thing. It is the very epitome of being awkward; it can be used as a tactic to signify that you aren't going to simply take the abuse or insulting behaviour.

Allocate one group of four or five students the challenge of representing 'being awkward, not feeling awkward' in a scenario. This means that the group helps the main actor to be awkward (difficult) in the face of someone trying to shame them, not feel awkward.

STRATEGY 2: BEING STOIC IN THE FACE OF INSULTS

Stoicism is an ancient philosophy that has a lot of modern-day admirers. Indeed, we recommend a few books on Stoicism in the further reading at the end of Lesson 5 on emotional regulation. One of the main Stoic philosophers, Epictetus, wrote, 'we ought not to yearn for the things which are not under our control' (*Discourses*, 3.24).[4] He and other Stoics believed in the importance of undertaking daily thought exercises that can be rehearsed over and over. This rehearsal can happen in your head, through discussions or through journalling.

These daily practices can help to reduce the possible fallout from situations such as when another person tries to shame you. For example, Epictetus counsels that your initial response to something apparently bad or undesirable happening, such as a more privileged person trying to shame you, is to tell yourself that this was not unexpected. Effectively, expect it and shrug it off, just as you would a rainy day. Preparing for

---

4   Epictetus, *The Discourses as Reported by Arrian: The Manual and Fragments*, vol. 2, tr. W. A. Oldfather (Cambridge, MA: Harvard University Press and London: William Heinemann, 1925).

adverse events such as class shaming is known as *premeditatio malorum* by the Stoics. It is like a pre-mortem – preparing for things to go wrong.

In the lesson, the main character can also display stoic body language and be genuinely unbothered by the abuse that is raining down. They could even smile in the face of the insults as they have probably played out most of them in their head already. They have prepared for this moment, and they have responded with quiet, controlled calmness. Stoics train themselves to not be concerned with things outside their control. The behaviour of others falls into that category.

In the drama lesson, the main character can choose to ignore the insults, perhaps imagining the words bouncing off them and into space. Their internal monologue should be: what this person is doing is nothing to me.

Allocate a group to explore and rehearse a stoic response to attempted shaming. One member of the group will need to come forward as the main character who models being stoic in the scenario.

STRATEGY 3: RESPONDING WITH PRIDE

We think there are lots of reasons to be proud of coming from a working-class background. Allocate one group the challenge of preparing the main actor to be shame resilient because they are proud of their background, what they own, what they know and the people that provided this for them.

Many of us use class as part of our identity. Knowledge of where we have come from and the sort of lives led by our parents, grandparents and great-grandparents can help us to appreciate them and their struggles. In recent years, there has been a growth in interest about genealogy and heritage. Television programmes such as the BBC's *Who Do You Think You Are?* attract millions of viewers. Learning about our families, their occupations and the times they lived through can provide insights and be the source of much pride and gratitude at an individual level.

A key strand of this session is celebrating working-class culture and achievements. There are many ways to elicit pride in being from the working classes. We could easily focus on working-class heroes to celebrate and study. Learning about these icons and what they stood/stand for will help to counter many of the negative stereotypes that surround the working classes. Being proud of our roots can galvanise us when encountering those who try to demean or patronise us. Make clear to the students that those who try to demean others are the ones with the problem – just as racism is a white person's problem, not a Black person's problem.

Working-class history is often framed through the lens of struggle. Although many things that we might currently take for granted in society have been achieved through working-class struggle – such as the universal franchise, the welfare state, paid holidays, bank holidays, employment laws and so on – there is much more to the working-class, including creative achievements in fields such as music, literature, the arts, business, sport and so on.

The working classes are people who have historically built things, created things, fixed things and maintained things, so that everyone in society can live their lives more easily. Remind the students that the room they are sitting in, the vehicles they travel in, the streets, drains, shops, sports facilities and so on were all built by working-class people.

Allocate a group to explore and rehearse responding to attempted shaming with pride. Allocate one member of the group to be the main character who models showing pride in being working-class in the face of potential shaming.

STRATEGY 4: RESPONDING WITH INFORMATION/KNOWLEDGE

This is when the person being shamed comes back with information that humiliates the person who is trying to humiliate them. The following clip is from the film *Good Will Hunting*: https://www.youtube.com/watch?v=hIdsjNGCGz4. It illustrates how someone who tries to belittle others can be belittled themselves by someone with a superior intellect. This could be shown to the students at any time within this scenario.

Knowledge not only acts as a shield against fake news and misinformation, but it also acts as a weapon against those who seek to denigrate us because we aren't wearing the right clothes for the occasion, or we have made a faux pas with a fork at the dinner table. That is why, like all educators, we are great advocates of encouraging students to stretch themselves in terms of what they read, listen to and watch.

Allocate a group to explore and rehearse responding to shaming with facts and knowledge. Allocate one member of the group to be the main character who models responding to insults and shaming with facts, knowledge and information that destroys the whole premise of what the shamer is trying to achieve.

STRATEGY 5: USING HUMOUR AS A SHIELD

Humour can be a great coping mechanism. The group using humour can use it in a variety of ways – to belittle, to confuse or to correct the aggressor in their ignorance.

The working classes have a rich history of creating humour. Certainly, many comedy writers are proud to call themselves working class and create comedy about working-class people. We can also use humour to laugh at privilege and deal with stressful or challenging situations. In fact, there is a long tradition of lampooning the upper classes in Britain that you can lean on in this strategy.

Now to the tricky bit – creating a set of rules around how we use humour but not stifling engagement in the process. Any adult will be aware of the huge controversies around the guidelines and boundaries for humour. Here are some rules that you are welcome to take off the peg or adapt to suit your own context:

Rule 1: Have a go at trying to appreciate and create humour.

Rule 2: Don't judge others harshly if they share different views to you about what they find funny.

Rule 3: Don't use humour deliberately to try and put someone else down. For example, avoid material that is racist, misogynistic, classist or designed to deliberately hurt someone. But do use humour as a shield when someone is trying to put you down.

There are several types of humour that students can use: witty wordplay, imitation or even physical comedy.

Allocate a group to explore and rehearse responding to shaming with humour. Allocate one member of the group to be the main character who models humour as a shield. As with the rest of the anti-shaming strategies, the group should help the actor to generate ideas and rehearse them. At the very least, the main actor should show how they can use humour to protect themselves from shame, and even humiliate the shamer.

Now introduce the first scenario to students.

SCENARIO 1: THE FIRST DAY

Remind students of the four steps to skillstreaming, and then introduce them to the scenario. Using the theme of 'the first day', prompt the students to use one of the five strategies within the scenario.

Example: It is your first day at college. You are nervous, and you overhear someone from a more affluent background make a negative comment about you to others. Speculate what you might do in this situation.

Each of the five groups are then set the task of demonstrating how this scene might play out. Characters will need to be chosen to represent the shamer(s) or the teacher can play this role.

The main character should try to model an excellent response to the given scenario (chosen from any on the recommended responses list). At the end of the scene (or throughout), the observers can suggest alternative or improved responses. The main character can freeze the scene at any time, have another attempt or interact with the audience to seek feedback. Once the main character freezes the scene, the co-actors should remain still and silent while the main character (or teacher) thinks through the following skill steps aloud:

1   Stop and identify the decision that needs to be made – for example, what should they say to this? What should they do now? Could they do this better?

2   Invite ideas from the audience.

3   Identify the potential positive and negative consequences of each option.

4   Choose what is agreed as the best response.

5   Start the scene again, using the strategy decided on in step 4 to create a 'better' response.

At any stage in the process, the teacher can stop or review a scene and ask questions. This can be done both when the small groups are performing or when the whole class are together. For example:

■ What are characters A, B, C and D feeling at this stage? What does the scene teach us about the values or intentions of each character?

■ What choices does the main character have at this point – for example, laugh off the insult, come back with a comment, remain silent?

■ What are the implications of each choice (especially for the main character)?

Repeat the strategy and change the actors so that other students get an opportunity to practise it.

Try to rotate the actors as much as possible. It is helpful to get the actors to play both being shamed and doing the shaming. Remember, the primary aim of the lesson is to help the students to become shame resilient.

Another more subtle aim might be to get more affluent students to consider their own behaviours and prejudices.

The final part of any skillstreaming session involves getting the students to transfer what they have learned to real situations. Admittedly, some of these may be way into the future, but it is essential that you find some time for talking about transfer.

Ensure that each of the five groups have performed and then allow a few minutes for a talking or stretching break before the next scenario.

SCENARIO 2: I CAN'T AFFORD TO …

This scenario is about affordability. Others from a more privileged social class say something sneering to the main character, such as:

- 'What do you mean you can't afford a laptop or better laptop?'

- 'Why do you have to have a part-time job at uni?'

- 'Did you get to university on a scholarship? How can someone like you afford it?'

As with scenario 1, the students should help the main character to develop the best response to this situation. What might they come back with? What could they say to the shamer(s) that would potentially shame them in return? Again, use the five modelled strategies, and encourage the groups to swap over and model a different strategy. Again, support each group with advice and feedback before, during and after the performance.

After (or throughout) each performance, the main character may freeze and seek advice or feedback from the audience. This means that no performance must be polished; the groups can simply show what they have produced in the time they have been set.

Finally, transfer. After all the performances, ask the students to once again speculate how they might transfer this skill to real-life situations. Ask the whole class to consider which of the five responses was the best or most suitable. Does working through a different skill change their preferred response from scenario 1, or will they keep to the strategy they indicated that they would be most comfortable with earlier? Allow a few minutes break before the final part of the session.

CLOSING MONOLOGUES

Both scenarios used in this lesson help the students to react to class shaming situations that they may face years in the future. Therefore, there is a good chance the students might have forgotten them if that moment arrives.

In a way, the last part of the lesson is a third scenario. Here, the students work again within their groups and suggest ways of getting others to remember that class shaming isn't the fault of the victim. Ask each group to devise a short monologue on why it is important not to feel shamed, and to remember that the problem lies not with you but with the aggressor.

Once again, the students can perform these monologues and, if time permits, the class can discuss any issues that arise. It is essential to make clear that although certain social spaces can be hostile towards working-class people, the best way to deal with this hostility is to challenge it. We are just as entitled to be in that place or space as more privileged people.

FINALLY

Explain that this lesson has provided the space to rehearse different responses to being shamed. Hopefully, it will build the students' confidence. Many working-class people suffer from imposter syndrome – a feeling of not deserving to be in certain places or to be in receipt of accolades. Nevertheless, emphasise to the students that millions of people around the world fight forms of discrimination such as classism on a daily basis. They do it because it makes the world a better and fairer place. Encourage them to support others, not just friends, who are being shamed because they are different in some way.

There are a few other lessons in *The Working Classroom* that might prove to be a good follow-up to this one: Lesson 3 on the power of story and Lesson 5 on emotional regulation.

FINAL THOUGHTS

- Where in your school's curriculum are the students taught about class shaming?
- When does this take place?

- How much time is allocated to it?
- What types of pedagogies are used to teach about these issues and concepts?

SUGGESTED FURTHER READING FOR THIS LESSON

Brown, B. (2008). *I Thought It Was Just Me (But It Isn't): Telling the Truth About Perfectionism, Inadequacy and Power* (Sheridan, WY: Gotham Books).

Emunah, R. (1994). *Acting for Real: Drama Therapy, Process, Technique and Performance* (Abingdon and New York: Routledge).

Hauck, P. (1991). *Hold Your Head Up High* (London: Hachette UK).

Holiday, R. (2015). *The Obstacle is the Way: The Ancient Art of Turning Adversity to Advantage* (London: Profile Books).

Rutherford, A. (2021). *How to Argue with a Racist: History, Science, Race and Reality* (London: Weidenfeld & Nicolson).

LESSON 3

THE POWER OF STORY

WHY TEACH ABOUT STORY?

Earlier in the book we shared our own stories. When students pass through secondary school, it is crucial that they learn about the power of story. It is something that can be returned to repeatedly to see if someone's story has changed. According to Paul Hannam, author of *Significance: How to Refocus Your Life on What Matters Most*, 'Your life story is an unseen force that greatly influences your daily experience. Moment to moment, you are largely unconscious of its impact.'[1]

So, how does this knowledge help a teenager? Well, in some cases, due to various forms of conditioning and some life experiences, young people tell themselves that they are 'doomed' or that they aren't intelligent or deserving. This can affect children from all social classes, but it is likely to be more pronounced in those who are economically disadvantaged. Private schools teach their students to adopt a self-identity through the stories they tell. In this case, young people are trained to tell themselves that they are 'destined' to be society's leaders and influencers.

Everyone has a story. Listening to stories from those with different experiences to us enables us to empathise with others, and this is vital for human connection. Teaching students about the stories we tell ourselves has many advantages. It seems obvious that one person could experience the same event and interpret it in diverse ways. Learning to slow down and realise that there may be more ways to think about something and to get into the habit of questioning our own perceptions, beliefs and ways of thinking is an important life skill to acquire.

---

1   P. Hannam, *Significance: How to Refocus Your Life on What Matters Most* (Farnham: Bright Future Publishing, 2020), p. 26.

WHAT IS THE CLASS DIMENSION TO THIS TOPIC?

As we have seen, coming from a disadvantaged background can make you feel like a fish out of water. Limited or rarely experienced events – such as eating in a restaurant, going on holiday, visiting the countryside and so on – can lead to the belief that 'those places aren't for me'. Of course, that isn't to say that this is the experience of every young person from a disadvantaged family or that every affluent child is comfortable in every situation, but when it comes to *aspiration*, a word overused by politicians, it can be much harder to achieve for those who don't see themselves as 'the type of person who goes to university' or 'someone who can do a job like that'.

Therefore, teaching about story has class implications. If there are disadvantaged students in your school, they may have internalised certain beliefs about themselves that could hold them back from the life they could have had.

HOW DOES THIS LESSON WORK?

This lesson is about perception: how we perceive ourselves and others. It may also encourage the students to question where their perceptions come from. The lesson starts by examining the concept of our own story and then encompasses others' stories – specifically, stories from those of working-class heritage. Teaching about perception opens the door to exploring optical illusions and more.

We have also included some suggestions for reflective activities that can provoke discussion or some journalling.

We suggest the following lesson format:

Aim: To help working-class students to develop a more empowering self-narrative

Age group: 11–18 years

Time: Up to four hours

Activities: Q&A, discussion, primary and secondary research, creating a biography

Resources: Computer and projector, notebooks

TO START THE LESSON

Start by telling the students that your life story is the most important story you tell yourself. It creates your self-identity. Your story provides you with meaning and direction, explaining where you have come from and where you are headed. The only problem is that the story we tell ourselves isn't real. It is our personal edited version of the thousands of hours we have spent on this planet so far. Our brains love taking shortcuts and looking for simple answers, so we are all unreliable autobiographers.

The samurai Miyamoto Musashi, author of *The Book of the Five Rings* (written during the sixteenth century), talks about the difference between the perceiving eye and the observing eye. Where the perceiving eye is weak and looks for obstacles and problems, the observing eye is strong as it sees events clear of exaggerations and misinterpretations.

Explain to the students that our brains can easily edit out potential opportunities either because we don't see them or because we believe that they aren't for us. Our belief system affects the way we see ourselves now and the aspirations we hold for our future.

Teach the students that we all have the power within us to make our story the best possible version of ourselves. This doesn't mean creating a fake story in which you project yourself in such a way that others like you or are impressed by you. Rather, it is about creating a story that makes us happy and content, one where we live by our values.

Now show the students a series of optical illusions such as the ones below or others that you can find. It is easy to find them on the internet in the form of still images or YouTube clips, such as the 'Monkey Business Illusion' designed by psychologist Daniel Simons.[2]

2   See https://www.youtube.com/watch?v=IGQmdoK_ZfY.

MY PERCEPTION IS …

Explain that illusions distort reality because they are designed to make us see things that aren't there. Ask the students to be honest and say if they have been wrong or had misplaced confidence in an answer that seemed 'right' or 'comfortable'. Say something like: 'The lesson is that our brains often look for easy solutions rather than right solutions or answers. In life, you will encounter the unfamiliar and the uncomfortable sometimes – it's the only way we grow. Try to be open to new ideas and experiences.'

Ask the students to tell you what their perceptions are of a range of experiences or situations. Here are some examples:

- My perception of people who go to university is …

- My perception of people who read for pleasure is …

- My perception of people studying hard for an exam is …

Feel free to add to this list. Our advice is to collect this information on index cards; ensure you note down the students' names and the date so you can learn more about their individual perceptions. This can be important feedback: knowing that a student is very against going to university or is feeling apathetic towards revision is useful knowledge for a teacher. There may be various opportunities to drill into the reasons behind this throughout their time in school. One-to-one reviews are particularly good for this.

WHO DO YOU THINK YOU ARE?

The last part of this lesson on the power of story requires the students to consider their own story – and how to change their story if it isn't working for them. Leave them with an understanding that they, like all of us, have been conditioned through our life experiences to date and our interpretation of these. Ask them to make the following notes:

Optical illusions teach us that things are sometimes not what they seem. It's highly possible that we might not see the potential that lies within us! We might be able to achieve more than we think.

OTHER PEOPLE'S STORIES

So far, the session has been about perception and our own story. For many students, their personal story or self-narrative is working – they have a clear sense of who they are and have agency. For others, their story isn't working. It will take more than one lesson on this subject to turn this around, but hopefully it will plant a seed in a few of the students you teach. By getting them into the habit of adopting some of the exercises in this lesson, their own self-narrative may become healthier and more productive. Before we look at these exercises, let's examine the stories of others. The learning from them may help the students to consider their own.

As the focus of this book is classism, we have especially focused on researching and discovering the stories of working-class people. We believe that learning about their struggles and triumphs can inspire students and counter stereotypes about the working classes.

As well as eliciting pride in traditional working-class values, this lesson can explore the achievements of working-class people. This could include traditional working-class jobs but also working-class people who have become business leaders, musicians, teachers, academics, barristers, solicitors and so on.

Collecting and curating these stories will be important if you want to change the students' beliefs. There are several ways of doing this:

1   Explain social class classification A to E to students and ask them to find and interview someone within their family or community who is working-class (i.e. in social class C2, D or E).

     Get them to conduct an interview and/or collect memorabilia to create a biography of a working-class person. The aim of the interview should be to teach others about their lives.

     Suggested questions:

     ■   What job(s) are you doing/did you do in your lifetime?

     ■   What have you learned from being a working-class person?

     ■   When have you felt discriminated against for being working class?

     ■   How did you deal with this discrimination?

     ■   Why should people be proud to have a working-class heritage?

     Using this new knowledge, the students can display it in various formats, which should be no more than ten minutes long:

     ■   A brief presentation.

- A short film.

- A short podcast.

- A story, biography or tribute.

If you commit to collecting these stories, try to find a way of archiving them and getting written permission from each contributor to show them to the school community. Depending on the time and resources available to you as a teacher, support the students in editing these stories so they are more interesting to watch or hear. Over a few years, you will have a great bank of positive stories from working-class people that can be used across the school.

2 Reach out to the school community and consult colleagues and friends to find working-class adults who have succeeded in non-traditional careers. Can they share their stories, give a talk, take a Zoom call from a group of students or even mentor a current student? Again, with permission, you could record some of these for other students or parents to access.

This seemingly small event can contribute to a snowball effect of more working-class students applying for these professions, emboldened by learning from these interactions. Just as schools rightly recognise Remembrance Day and show gratitude for soldiers, and also rightly celebrate Black History Month, it is important that working-class students appreciate the skills and talents that have emerged from the working classes. One way of doing this is for your school to celebrate May Day, sometimes referred to as International Workers' Day. Alternatively or additionally, sharing positive stories can counteract the many negative stories about the working class in the media. You could even highlight examples of media stories that demean the working class, but place this in the context of media outlets that represent the interests of the more privileged classes. The ownership of newspapers and increasingly influential social media platforms is concentrated in the hands of just a few billionaires and corporations. This knowledge may get some students thinking differently about the veracity of the stories that emanate from these platforms.

3 Encourage your students to become healthy sceptics. This involves building your 'ideological immune system', a phrase that comes from Jay Snelson, who recommends that we build up knowledge of an issue, so we are less likely to be manipulated by others to believe falsehoods.[3] There is certainly a need for that in today's world where

3   J. S. Snelson, Ideological Immune System: Resistance to New Ideas in Science, *Skeptic*, 1(4) (1992), 444–455.

fake news and conspiracy theories proliferate. Becoming a healthy sceptic also helps us to develop questioning strategies and to be slower to come to a judgement about whether the stories we are being told about others are true or not.

Here is some advice we can give to students to help them become healthy sceptics:

- Frequently examine your own beliefs; we all have a bias blind spot. All humans are susceptible to a range of conscious and unconscious biases (which reflect bias without awareness of the bias). Journalling is a good way to do this.

- Don't be too sceptical about everything all the time. Instead, invest your energies into questioning the claims and assumptions you deem the most important.

- Be prepared to change your beliefs and admit when you have been wrong about something.

- Question those in power. Good questions include: why are we doing this? Where is the evidence for this? Who is this helping?

- Keep working on developing your fake news radar. Looking for truth in a post-truth world can be hard but is not impossible. It is in the interests of those in power to suppress the truth. Truth is essential for the survival of humanity. This might sound dramatic, but in the present climate emergency we need to be able to judge who is helping to save the planet and who is lying, greenwashing and blocking to protect their own interests.

FINALLY

All schools talk about developing the potential of all the students in its care. If your school is serious about this, then the students must understand the power of the stories they hold about themselves and others. We believe that more empowering self-narratives can be trained. We also believe that some limiting and damaging self-narratives stem from internalised classism. Therefore, finding space within the curriculum to address the power of story is crucial for any educator who is interested in social justice.

There are a few other lessons in *The Working Classroom* that might prove to be a good follow-up to this one: Lesson 4 on motivation and Lesson 5 on emotional regulation.

FINAL THOUGHTS

- Where in your school's curriculum are the students taught about the power of story?
- When does this take place?
- How much time is allocated to it?
- What types of pedagogies are used to teach about these issues and concepts?

SUGGESTED FURTHER READING FOR THIS LESSON

Grosz, S. (2013). *The Examined Life: How We Lose Friends and Find Ourselves* (London: Vintage).

Hannam, P. (2020). *Significance: How to Refocus Your Life on What Matters Most* (Farnham: Bright Future Publishing).

Robson, D. (2022). *The Expectation Effect: How Your Mindset Can Transform Your Life* (London: Canongate Books).

Rose, J. (2001). *The Intellectual Life of the British Working Classes* (London: Yale University Press).

Smith, J. (2022). *Why Has Nobody Told Me This Before?* (London: Michael Joseph).

MOTIVATION

WHY TEACH ABOUT MOTIVATION?

The word motivation comes from the Latin *movere* meaning 'to move' because we move towards things that interest us. Learning about motivation can be empowering and revelatory. Lack of motivation may be due to physiological reasons, such as a lack of sleep or having the wrong or a poor diet. There are also psychological, environmental and social reasons for demotivation.

Motivation, particularly self-motivation, is a highly valuable soft skill that will enable students to work effectively and independently. Good motivational skills can also help individuals to rebound from setbacks, seek and take up opportunities, and demonstrate commitment towards what they wish to achieve. Teaching students about this topic could help them to attain better self-awareness and adopt some motivational wisdom.

WHAT IS THE CLASS DIMENSION TO THIS TOPIC?

Not everyone from the working classes lives in poverty, but working-class people often face the most financial challenges. Those who are impoverished feel weighed down, sometimes even ashamed.

Most households living in poverty have at least one working member of the family, despite the common myth about unemployment perpetuated in some corners of the media. Bizarrely, hard-working people can feel ashamed because they are bringing in a low income, even when they are key workers. This lack of income doesn't just prevent them from buying healthy or sufficient food or taking their children on days out; it can also affect the way they think about themselves. Some can internalise the belief that they don't deserve to be 'successful', and this can affect other family members' motivation.

In Chapter 2, we quoted from Michael Sandel, who describes the time we live in as the 'age of merit'. Since the late 1970s, in both the United States and the UK, a myth has arisen that success is solely down to effort rather than what individuals inherit from their families. Sandel says, 'those who land at the top come to believe they deserve their success. And, if opportunities are truly equal, it means that those who are left behind deserve their fate as well.'[1]

Sandel also writes about how an increasing number of his Harvard students are convinced that their success is the result of their own effort, despite two-thirds of them coming from the top fifth of the income scale. There are similar parallels in the UK.

Classism and perceived class position can certainly affect motivation. Many working-class families realise that the idea of a level playing field is a fiction and so fall into a state of learned helplessness.

HOW DOES THIS LESSON WORK?

This lesson can help the students to realise that there are good reasons for low motivation. It can help those who are demotivated to understand more of the reasons for this, which can begin to help them move away from blaming themselves for their own low motivation.

We believe that some students can become more motivated when encouraged to challenge the culture of individualism and the relentless drive to be personally successful that seems to permeate our culture. By replacing this with the idea of considering how their efforts can contribute to the common good, we can help students of all social classes.

Facilitating a mature discussion with young people about issues around motivation is a core part of this lesson. This will, of course, involve a lot of listening and questioning. Skilfully managed, learning about motivation can provide insights for the teacher as much as for the students themselves.

We suggest the following lesson format:

Aim: To help students understand what can drive and undermine motivation

Age group: 14–18 years

Time: Two hours

Activities: Q&A, discussion

Resources: Computer and projector, notebooks

---

1   Sandel, *The Tyranny of Merit*, p. 4.

TO START THE LESSON

BLIND VOTING

Ask the students some questions and ask them to raise their hands if the issue of motivation is relevant to them. It is sometimes a good idea to use 'blind voting' for this, which is when the students close their eyes when they vote and only the teacher can see what they have voted for. Suggested opening questions might include:

- Who would like to be more self-motivated?
- Who would like to get less pressure from adults, such as parents and teachers?
- Who is struggling to find the energy to do the work that has been set for them?
- Who feels that they should be working harder in their schoolwork but cannot seem to find the motivation?
- Who is unclear about their future goals or, if you have a goal, struggling with finding the motivation to put the work in to achieve it?

Hopefully, these questions will resonate with the students and get some buy-in to the lesson. Blind voting also gives you an indication of the size of the issue. Explain that this lesson will explore issues such as why human beings lose motivation and some ideas to help us to be more motivated more of the time.

Firstly, explain the two different motivational types – extrinsic and intrinsic. Get the students to start making notes.

Motivation falls into two specific types: extrinsic motivation and intrinsic motivation.

Extrinsic motivation comes from outside pressure. Without it, someone wouldn't undertake the challenge that has been set for them. This form of motivation is often summarised as 'carrot and stick': others, such as parents or teachers, use punishments (sticks) to get less of the behaviour they don't want or rewards (carrots) to get more of the behaviour they do want. It might also mean deliberately creating disturbance in someone else's mind, so they see the benefits of doing things differently. This might involve posing questions such as, 'How is what you're doing helping me/you/us?' Questions can encourage a young person to stop and reflect on whether their actions are helping them to move towards a goal or are making life harder or easier for others.

Intrinsic motivation is when someone does something because they want to rather than because they are obliged to. This type of motivation is driven by an interest or enjoyment in the task itself and exists within the individual instead of relying on any external pressure or reward. Intrinsic motivators can be triggered through feeling that a task is relevant, fun, challenging or doable. Intrinsic motivation can also be triggered through a liking for the person who has set the task. Many young people admit to working harder when they have good rapport with a teacher or parent.

Here, you could pose some reflective questions such as:

- When has someone used extrinsic motivation with you that you didn't like at the time but now appreciate? Who was this person? What examples of external motivation did they use?

- Which intrinsic motivational triggers tend to make you keep going with a difficult task?

Use the answers as part of a class discussion. Explain that you will be returning to extrinsic and intrinsic motivation later in the session.

Next, inform the students that they will be exploring motivational deficits. Ask them to continue to make notes under the title 'Motivational deficits' – why people lack motivation. Inform the students that motivation is a complex issue with hundreds of books written on the subject. Ask them if they know why human beings lose motivation. The answers should fall into four categories: physiological, environmental, psychological and social. There can be quite a lot of overlap between these categories.

The students can be given or asked to record the following notes:

Physiological factors refer to how factors affecting our body can affect our mind. The main physiological factors affecting a person's motivation are lack of sleep, lack of food, lack of the right kinds of nutrition and physical illness.

Environmental factors affecting a person's motivation relate to the impact that our surroundings have on us. For example, living in a house that is riddled with mould isn't only likely to create higher rates of asthma for the inhabitants, but it will also create a high degree of mental stress. Similarly, living in a community where there is a lot of crime is bound to influence how we feel.

Psychological factors affecting a person's motivation refer to the mental dispositions they may have acquired. One example is learned helplessness. This kicks in when someone has 'learned' that it isn't worth the effort of trying to complete a particular task or getting better at something, so they stop trying. Their life experience has led them to become pessimistic and disempowered.

Social factors relate to how the society we live in can condition some of us to feel disconnected from others. When people feel that they are socially disconnected or don't belong to a 'tribe', they lose their motivation and become depressed.

Once the students have recorded these notes, get them to read the following quote about the power of connecting with others from Johann Hari's book *Lost Connections*:

What if depression is, in fact, a form of grief – for our own lives not being as they should? What if it is a form of grief for the connections we have lost, yet still need?[2]

For Hari, people moving away from values such as community and solidarity, often synonymous with working-class values, and instead embracing more individualistic values, is the cause of the depression epidemic in the Western world.

Again, you could pose some reflective questions such as:

- Which of the four motivational deficits do you have personal experience of?
- How are each of the four motivational factors interrelated?
- Does anyone identify with learned helplessness? Is there something you are studying that you have decided you won't get much better at?
- Can you speculate how some psychological factors might have been influenced by aspects that stem from a person's social class?
- How does being part of a tribe or group affect your own motivation?

Use the questions to stimulate discussion. Ask small groups or pairs of students to record their thoughts on large pieces of paper to be presented

---

2   J. Hari, *Lost Connections: Why You're Depressed and How to Find Hope* (London: Bloomsbury Publishing, 2018), p. 54.

or displayed. In the case of the latter, the students could evaluate each other's ideas at some point in the lesson.

Explain to the students that there will be more on tribes later in the lesson. You will ask them to share what tribe they are in (from football teams to music taste and more).

Returning to exploring the notions of extrinsic and intrinsic motivation, ask the students to take part in another blind voting challenge and pose the following questions:

- Who is intrinsically motivated to work hard when it comes to homework and revision?

- Who needs someone to push them – or, as we have said today, extrinsically motivate them –when it comes to things such as homework and revising?

- Who knows who that person could be?

- Who wants help with how to approach them for help?

Ask the students to uncover their eyes and, unless everyone has admitted to being intrinsically motivated to study hard, offer the following tips. Ask the students to write them down under the heading of 'Five motivation tips'.

Note: the following suggestions should help the students to become more motivated to study and to study more effectively. We advise spending around ten minutes on each of these strategies. Direct the students to write out the recommended exercises in their notebooks, so they can practise them away from school.

TIP 1: FIND MY EXTRINSIC MOTIVATOR

Encourage the students to record in their notebook or planner the importance of having a conversation with someone today who will hopefully help to extrinsically motivate them. They could use phrases or questions such as the following:

- Mum, make sure I do two hours of revision tonight.

- Dad, here's my phone – don't let me have it until 9 pm.

- Nan, can I work at yours tonight?

- [Friend], please can you help me arrange my notes?

- Uncle, please can you test me later?

- Auntie, please can you set reminders for me for …

Explain that asking someone for support is a sensible thing to do. Some students may have parents and carers who push or encourage them, but this exercise (and any advice the school can give parents on motivation) is to help those who don't.

TIP 2: NEVER COMPETE WITH OTHERS

Explain to the students that lots of things in our society are based on competition, such as business, sport and exams. Competition is good in some contexts but, on a personal level, it can be damaging to your motivation if you focus too much on what others are doing.

There is always going to be someone cleverer than you, faster than you, better looking than you and so on. Equally, there will always be someone less smart than you, slower than you and less attractive than you. So, you will either end up feeling that you are worse than other people or feeling you are better than them. This isn't a great way to live your life – feeling inferior one minute and superior the next.

Studying can be hard at the best of times, but it is even harder when you think you are competing with somebody else. You might start thinking to yourself: 'What's the point of trying? I'll never be as good as them.' Instead, try to set yourself daily or weekly targets to beat your previous personal best (PB). In sport, when an athlete achieves a PB they are delighted. So, encourage students to challenge themselves to set a PB for:

- Length of time reading – read a little more each day.

- Note-building – create some revision notes in an exercise book or on flashcards.

- Summaries – try to summarise an article, a chapter of a book or a section of an exercise book. Can you try to beat the number of summaries you can do in a day?

- Testing your memory – try to test yourself each day on things you have previously studied. See if you can beat yesterday's score!

Ask the students to set themselves a PB challenge linked to any of the above study activities. Suggest that they report back their progress to you in upcoming sessions; their notebooks are ideal places to record these PB challenges. If you have trained the students in time management, as we recommend, they can set themselves the challenge of scheduling more time for studying on a calendar or by using one of the block grids (see Lesson 7 on time management). In this case, an 'add a block a day challenge' could work nicely.

TIP 3: TALK YOURSELF UP

Using daily affirmations is a powerful technique for affecting your behaviour. An affirmation is a statement that you read and repeat to yourself to help you feel more positive about something. They help you to rethink or reframe how you think about things. As your thinking affects your behaviour, it can help to move you to doing more of the things that can increase attainment, such as studying and reading.

Affirmations have three rules, known as the 3Ps – they are *personal*, *positive* and written or spoken in the *present tense*. A classic example of a positive affirmation is: 'Every day, in every way, I'm getting better and better.' As regards studying, students could create affirmations such as:

- Every day, I'm enjoying completing the work I've been set.
- I'm loving being an excellent student now.
- By doing my set work, I'm enjoying doing more exams practice each day.
- I'm enjoying completing my work as it helps me to achieve my future goals.
- I'm loving reading more and more each week.

Ask the students to either adopt one or two of these affirmations or create some of their own. The key point is that they should be repeated frequently. Encourage the students to write them out and display them somewhere prominent, such as their bedroom, as a reminder. With repetition and refinement, this process should have a positive impact on self-motivation because the affirmation works slowly and steadily on helping us to consciously think and act in ways that align with these goals.

Providing students with sticky notes and index cards to stick up at home can also be helpful alongside their notebooks.

TIP 4: PROVE SOMEONE WRONG

Ask the students if there is someone in their life who they would like to prove wrong. Have they encountered someone who has labelled them or wronged them? If this is the case, then this person can become the motivation for succeeding.

Plenty of successful people have turned rejection and hurt into a positive. It has provided them with the drive that has helped them to achieve success. Examples include The Beatles, Bill Gates, J. K. Rowling and many others who have used rejection to motivate them to work even harder.[3]

Classism can also play a part in proving someone wrong. There is a long history of working-class people being told that 'you can't do that, do this instead', especially when it comes to attempting to join professions that are traditionally the preserve of the middle and upper classes. Try to collect any examples of this from working-class colleagues and friends.

Ask the students to privately note whether there is someone out there who they can prove wrong. Get them to use their notebooks to set daily reminders that link working hard and challenging themselves to proving the person who hurt, maligned or rejected them wrong. This could become their main driver in committing to working harder.

TIP 5: CHOOSE MY TRIBE CAREFULLY

Human beings are tribal by nature; we like to belong. We can be part of many tribes, which might link to our preferences for a football team, music, religion or political views. When our tribes are close-knit, it feels good to be around people who support us in a variety of ways.

The dark side to tribalism is that we can be hostile to people who aren't like us, who support a different team, who prefer other music or who have different views and beliefs. Sometimes this hostility can spill over into hatred, and then a defensiveness can set in which closes the mind to anyone who we think might be trying to undermine our beliefs.

Explain this to the students by telling them: 'You're the average of the five people you spend the most time with.' Whether the number five is significant or not, it is certainly true that we are influenced by our close friends. Discussions about what makes a good friend and tribalism can involve questions such as:

- Who are your closest friends? What values and beliefs do you share with them?
- Would a true friend or loved one hold you back from fulfilling an ambition you might have?
- Could you become good friends with someone with different values than you (about football, religion, politics, work ethic, studying hard and so on)?
- How might being in a tight friendship group make you more close-minded?

---

3   There is a list here of some amazing people who used rejection to motivate themselves: https://thoughtcatalog.com/rachel-hodin/2013/10/35-famous-people-who-were-painfully-rejected-before-making-it-big.

■ What do you think these questions are trying to help you explore?

■ What are the motives of the people, like me (the teacher), who have designed this course/session/programme?

Be upfront with the students as to your motivation for running this lesson. It might be worth stating that although you might not be in the same tribe as them, in terms of football, music and so on, there are many values that hopefully you do share with them, such as your views on social injustice.

This notion of tribes can prove to be a useful source of discussion and reflection. Tribalism and social influence are fascinating areas for study. This whole topic can also be studied alongside an analysis of media and manipulation techniques.

FINALLY

This lesson tries to be sympathetic to students who have a low motivation for studying. Lack of attainment for working-class students is a major factor in what holds them back from being more successful. However, the lesson also offers a range of tips to help them. Someone with a low motivation to study hard, especially around exam time, should be supported as much as possible. Discussions around motivation should be frequent throughout a student's journey through secondary school.

Creating space for learning about motivation can throw up other issues that the school can help to address. Some students have difficulty finding a suitable space to study away from school, especially if they are from a working-class background. The demise of local libraries has made this situation worse. Either through blind voting or an anonymised survey, try to find out who has this, or a similar, challenge. Offer support in various forms to overcome this problem, such as creating dedicated after-school study spaces, weekend studying options, providing earplugs or headphones, and working with local organisations to offer evening and weekend space for study.

FINAL THOUGHTS

■ Where in your school's curriculum are students taught about motivation?

■ When does this take place?

- How much time is allocated to it?

- What type of pedagogies are used to teach about these issues and concepts?

SUGGESTED FURTHER READING
FOR THIS LESSON

Gilbert, I. (2012). *Essential Motivation in the Classroom*, 2nd edn (Abingdon and New York: Routledge).

Griffith, A. and Burns, M. (2012). *Engaging Learners* (Outstanding Teaching) (Carmarthen: Crown House Publishing).

Hari, J. (2018). *Lost Connections: Why You're Depressed and How to Find Hope* (London: Bloomsbury Publishing).

Nilsson, N. J. (2014). *Understanding Beliefs* (Cambridge, MA: MIT Press).

Pink, D. (2018). *Drive: The Surprising Truth About What Motivates Us* (London: Canongate Books).

EMOTIONAL REGULATION

WHY TEACH ABOUT EMOTIONAL REGULATION?

This lesson will explore the purpose of our emotions and the benefits of learning to regulate, manage or 'tame' certain emotions that can undermine our potential for a successful life. Learning to manage emotions such as anxiety and anger will help the students to be more patient, improve their levels of concentration and make them better able to operate in social spaces.

Emotions and feelings are a vast and complex field. This lesson mostly focuses on managing the emotion of fear, especially anxiety around tests and exams, which can be crippling for students of all social classes. Many students underperform due to not having practised strategies that can help them to alleviate stress.

WHAT IS THE CLASS DIMENSION TO THIS TOPIC?

Emotional regulation has many class connotations. Working-class people tend to be judged more harshly when we 'lose it'. We are often labelled as 'aggressive' or 'out of control' when expressing ourselves, especially when anger is involved. Learning to understand and manage our emotions better can help us to turn around class stereotypes that others may hold.

We also believe that learning about emotional management techniques will help students to filter out some of the modern-day myths about emotional well-being – namely, that we should all strive for happiness. Instead of striving for personal happiness, a rather narcissistic desire, people should work for the common good and derive their contentment from contributing to this.

It is our contention that the rise in anxiety and unhappiness in countries such as the United States and the UK stem from an overconcentration on individual happiness and success. Barbara Ehrenreich's book *Smile or Die: How Positive Thinking Fooled America and the World* is a great accompaniment to this lesson and can be set as a class reader if you have time to go deeper into this with your class or tutor group.[1]

Note that even the language of 'social mobility' plays into this false narrative: the individual who can 'escape' from the working class into the middle class will feel happier and more successful.

HOW DOES THIS LESSON WORK?

This lesson unashamedly provides a series of tips and exercises for managing emotions that can be honed with practice. We also recommend that you inform parents and carers about this advice, so they can encourage their children to repeat these exercises at home. In combination with advice from other lessons in this book (especially Lesson 4 on motivation and Lesson 7 on time management), emphasise that all these tips are useless if the students only try them once.

We suggest the following lesson format:

Aim: To help students better manage their emotions, especially anxiety

Age group: 14–18 years

Time: Two hours

Activities: Q&A, discussion, taste tests

Resources: Computer and projector, notebooks, food (olives, dates, prunes, etc.)

TO START THE LESSON

Explain that today's lesson will be about the benefits of learning to control our emotions. Ask the students to list the many benefits of being competent at regulating our emotions. Here are some suggestions that they can write down, if you wish, but you may add more:

▪ Improved concentration.

▪ Better friendships and other relationships.

▪ More patience.

---

1   B. Ehrenreich, *Smile or Die: How Positive Thinking Fooled America and the World* (London: Granta, 2021).

- More enjoyment/contentment in life.

- Feeling calmer more of the time.

- Feeling less stressed or overwhelmed.

- Less susceptible to anger and angry thoughts.

After the students have written down (or considered) this list, ask them to speculate as to why being able to manage or control our emotions can be helpful. Then ask, 'How might *not* learning to manage emotions affect someone both now and in the future?' Record their answers on a board or flipchart, if appropriate. Turn this into a whole-class discussion until you have exhausted the ideas the students have generated.

EXERCISE: RANK YOUR EMOTIONAL CONTROL

Ask the students whether they would like to be better at managing their emotions. The following Oscar Wilde quote, from *The Picture of Dorian Gray*, can be used as part of this discussion:

I don't want to be at the mercy of my emotions. I want to use them, to enjoy them, and to dominate them.[2]

Ask the students to rank themselves on a scale of 1–10 in terms of their ability to control three emotions in particular: anger, anxiety/fear and disgust.

Inform them that there are lots of ways to improve emotional regulation and impulse control. Indeed, help them to realise how much progress they have already made from the 'terrible twos' (the toddler years) and through primary school to where they are now. Explain that many of us improve our emotional regulation as we get older, but some people are condemned to always be at the mercy of their emotions unless they learn to train themselves. This lesson explains some exercises that millions of people around the world use to improve their emotional control and be more in charge of their feelings.

Next, inform the students that this lesson will mostly look at anxiety, but first we will explore the emotion of disgust through a taste test exercise.

---

2   O. Wilde, *The Picture of Dorian Gray* (Ware: Wordsworth Editions, 1992 [1890]), p. 46.

THE TASTE TEST

The taste test initially involves using a few student volunteers. Their task is to show no emotion when eating unfamiliar foods such as olives or dates. Get them to come up to the front of the classroom, initially one at a time, to eat a piece of unfamiliar food and not show any emotion. They should try to do this for around ten seconds. Meanwhile, ask the rest of the class to speculate through thumbs-up or thumbs-down gestures whether the person at the front likes what they are eating or finds it disgusting. After repeating this with a few single volunteers, move to bringing up students in batches of three or four. If you manage the time well, you should be able to get through the whole class by the end of the lesson.

Disgust is quite a useful emotion to explore, as is joy. In food terms, what might disgust one person may be a culinary delight for another. Here is a link to the Disgusting Food Museum in Malmo, Sweden that you could show to the students: https://disgustingfoodmuseum.com/most-disgusting-foods-in-the-world.

Some food is disgusting for religious reasons. Other cultures might find eating insects normal, whereas we in the West would mostly baulk at a centipede sandwich.

When a student is successful at not showing emotion for ten seconds, they are exhibiting good emotional regulation. You can award points for the best predictors and the best actors – those showing the most self-control.

How good were the class at reading the facial expressions of the eaters? How good are they at reading other people's emotions in general? Now, ask the students how skilled they are at (1) reading their own emotions and (2) being able to alter their emotional state. A discussion can ensue around sulking, being stuck in a mood and so on. Encourage a discussion about this and ask for some students to volunteer to feed back.

SELF-CONTROL AND DELAYED GRATIFICATION

Explain that those who didn't show their true feelings have exercised strong self-control. Say something like: 'Self-control – or delaying gratification – is an important skill to develop in life. When we get good at it, we can override our initial feelings or desires about something.'

Linking this learning to Lesson 3 on the power of story, explain to the students that our initial reactions may be flawed and based on our conditioning or perceptions. For example, when going on a university visit, someone might look around a campus or lecture theatre and not see themselves as someone who could go to such a place. Make clear that any new setting or situation is bound to make us feel uncomfortable, but we must learn to not necessarily trust that initial feeling.

Ask the students to discuss when they have demonstrated self-control and when they wished they had done so. Discuss the advantages of self-control, such as when it is helpful to hide our emotions, count to ten to delay automatic impulses and so on. One modern-day example is how fast we can sometimes respond to a text or email. Many of us have come to regret firing off a text or email in anger. Pausing for a few minutes, hours or even days can give us time to consider a better and more thought-through response.

Now, explore the following quote from Ryan Holiday on emotional regulation and get the class to unpick its meaning:

> Real strength lies in the control or, as Nassim Taleb puts it, in the domestication of one's emotions, not in pretending they don't exist.[3]

This utilises a metaphor that our emotions are like wild or untrained animals, which is echoed in Professor Steve Peter's book, *The Chimp Paradox*.[4] Our emotions are wild, like a chimp or wild dog, but they are trainable and it is sensible to do so. Indeed, life becomes harder if we don't learn how to do this.

ANXIETY

Next, focus on another emotion: anxiety. Anxiety is all about expectation – the expectation that something in the future will cause us some sort of harm. It is impossible to live without anxiety; in fact, some might even be good for us. The key is learning how to manage it.

Anxiety seems to be the major negative emotion faced by young people today. Our message is that we must learn to live with emotions such as anxiety and not try to avoid them. Through practice and learned strategies, we can all cope better with those unwelcome emotions that come along for the ride on life's journey.

---

3   R. Holiday, *The Obstacle is the Way: The Ancient Art of Turning Adversity to Advantage* (London: Profile Books, 2015), p. 30.
4   S. Peters, *The Chimp Paradox: The Mind Management Programme to Help You Achieve Success, Confidence and Happiness* (London: Vermilion, 2012).

TIPS FOR MANAGING ANXIETY

We would now advise that students take some notes. Inform them that the rest of the lesson will involve looking at tips to manage the emotion of anxiety. Ask them to write down the following heading: 'Five tips for managing anxiety' and then to record each of the five tips in turn, along with the accompanying exercises.

TIP 1: ONLY FOCUS ON WHAT YOU CAN CONTROL

The film *Groundhog Day* is a fantastic way to teach students about what we can and cannot control. The film's main character, Phil Connors, played by Bill Murray, is forced to relive the same day over and over again. Gradually, Phil learns to take better control of his emotions, his habits and his character. He transforms himself by experimenting with different ways of thinking and behaving. He comes to realise that he cannot control being trapped in the same day, but he can control how he reacts.

The following diagram can aid with personal reflection. Here's how it works.

Ask the students to copy down the diagram and then list possible concerns, problems or issues in one of the three circles. (Note: they cannot go in more than one place.) When the students have completed this task, ask them to share some examples with the class.

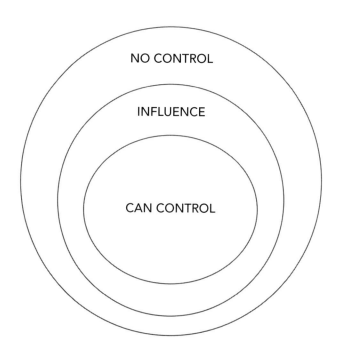

It is important at this stage to correct any student who says something like, 'I have no control over my emotions.' As we get older, and hopefully wiser, we realise through training and using techniques such as those outlined here, that we do have some control over how we react to events and situations.

Understanding that it is within our power to change how we feel about something can help to reduce our anxiety immediately. It can be a useful exercise to write down any events over which we have no control. These might include the past, the future, the weather, what other people think (especially what people think of us), how other people behave and so on. There is an old saying from Scandinavia: 'There's no such thing as bad weather, only bad clothing.' Weather is an event, but just because it rains, it doesn't mean you have to get wet. It is all about how you prepare for the rain.

Explain to the students that, like any other skill, how we respond to events takes practice. In our lives, we learn thousands of skills that we go on to perform automatically. Encourage the students to spend some time each day thinking about how they can best react in certain situations. Role play-ing them in our minds can often help. This practice can give us the power to *choose* a response that will hopefully produce a better outcome.

TIP 2: TRAIN YOUR PERCEPTION TO AVOID GOOD AND BAD

One of the principal Stoic philosophers was Epictetus. He wrote: 'What upsets people is not things themselves but their judgement about these things.'[5]

The Stoics believed that there is no such thing as good or bad, there is only perception. Stuff happens. We then make judgements about what happens. If we judge that something bad *has happened*, then we might get upset, sad or angry, depending on what it is. If we judge that some-thing bad is *going to happen*, then this can also trouble us. All our emotions are the product of the judgements we make.

However, we cannot always judge whether a situation is good or bad at the time it happens. We aren't talking about serious situations, such as someone dying or becoming seriously ill. It is more about those events that might seem big at the time, such as a relationship break-up or receiv-ing a poor test score, but when you look back, you realise that things weren't as bad as you thought they were.

---

5   Epictetus, *The Enchiridion of Epictetus* (n.p.: CreateSpace, 2017), sect. 5, p. 469.

So, when something is causing us some anxiety, we can ask ourselves the following questions:

- Are things making me anxious, or am I making myself anxious?

- Might this problem not seem as bad in a few days, weeks or years?

- When have I had other stressful situations in the past that, on reflection, weren't worthy of that level of anxiety?

Through practice, we can teach our students to use these questions and other exercises to help them realise that it isn't the external event that is causing them the anxiety; it is how they perceive it. What might seem bad at the time might, in fact, be a good thing. As hard as that might be to imagine now, it is important that students learn to get some distance from their emotions, especially those that arise initially.

TIP 3: STRESS INOCULATION TECHNIQUES

Donald Meichenbaum, a pioneer of cognitive behaviour therapy, developed stress inoculation therapy. He argued that in the same way as people can be inoculated against a virus, through an injection that exposes their immune system to a small dose of that virus, we can also be inoculated against stress and become more stress resistant. This process is known as hormesis; by taking small doses of a poison, we can develop more immunity to it.

The message here is to train students to *manage* anxiety, not *avoid* it. Anxiety itself isn't negative. It is just your brain's way of telling you that it believes you are in danger. In those situations, the brain applies the emergency handbrake.

We think it is important to listen to any concerns that students might have about upcoming exams, going on work experience, giving a presentation and so on, so we can help them to prepare as best we can. This should also involve thinking about what might go wrong. Through discussions and/or role play, the students can become better at managing their emotions in these fish-out-of-water situations. Indeed, part of good parenting and good teaching is about encouraging students to grow and develop by challenging their own comfort zones.

TIP 4: LOOK AFTER YOUR PHYSICAL SELF

Are you aware that a lot of people improve their emotional regulation ability through changing their exercise regime, sleep patterns and diet? The very first things that many doctors recommend when dealing with patients who suffer from anxiety is getting them to adopt a regular sleep pattern and consuming a high-protein breakfast. That isn't to say that this will work in all cases where the anxiety is severe, but this advice does help many people.

Similarly, before taking medication or embarking on a psychological intervention, a patient might be urged to try going for long walks or joining a gym. This is immensely sensible, but the obvious is often overlooked by people when they are in a bad place. Lots of exercise, a good protein-heavy diet and plenty of good quality sleep also work well alongside medication and mental strategies. It is worth reminding students of this.

TIP 5: THE ART OF JOURNALLING

Keeping a journal can help students to be clearer on what parts of their day are within their control and what parts aren't. It can encourage them to realise what they have got rather than what they haven't. Journalling can support students to make tomorrow a better day, where they show the world a superior version of themselves.

Journalling has other advantages too, such as generating and refining ideas, organising thoughts and clearing the mind. Encouraging students to write a journal – and explicitly teaching the skills needed to do this – can help them to be at their best more of the time.

EXERCISE: WHAT WOULD MY HERO DO?

The following exercise is a useful way of reconsidering something that may be troubling us. We all have different heroes – people we admire and look up to. We admire them for a reason: they show characteristics that we desire ourselves.

Ask the students to try out this exercise for ten to fifteen minutes. It will require them to divide a page in an exercise book (or use a double page in a notebook or journal) and copy down the headings below:

The problem:	The problem:
How I'm responding:	How my hero would respond:

Invite the students to write down a problem they are currently facing and note down underneath how they are currently dealing with it. Then, using the other column, ask them to record how they think someone they admire would deal with the same problem. It is even better if they know the person because they could talk to them in advance of their journalling.

Thinking *through* someone else can allow us to reconsider our current response. Later in the day or the following day, we can reflect on whether our behaviour has been closer to how our hero or the person we respect would have behaved.

Writing down our thoughts can also help us to acknowledge our worries. Once we have done this, we can ask: what is the belief behind this? When we drill into our belief system, we can start to question whether they are coming from a place of rationality or not. It is useful to notice when we are acting on irrational beliefs. It is also good to know that we can replace our beliefs with ones that work better for us – ones that our heroes or role models would probably hold.

Finally, by keeping a journal, we are learning to talk to ourselves in the right way. How we talk to ourselves deeply affects the direction of our lives. Sometimes we may need to give ourselves a good kick up the backside. This is especially true when we find ourselves repeating patterns of behaviour that don't really work for us. Some tough self-questioning will hopefully create better outcomes. On other occasions, we will need to be gentler with ourselves and recognise that making mistakes is part of learning.

FINALLY

There are many great strategies for emotional regulation that people swear by; we are simply listing a few that we use on a regular basis. The aim of this lesson is to empower and inform. Students, and many adults, fail to realise that we can regulate our emotions with the right tools and strategies. If you agree that emotional regulation is complementary to academic attainment, or even worth learning about as an end in itself, then we hope you find some room for some serious work on this in your school.

Note: we have developed a separate lesson around managing anger and more prompt questions for journalling that can be found in the resources section at www.theworkingclassroom.co.uk. Should you have time at the end of this lesson, ask the students to consider how well they manage anger.

FINAL THOUGHTS

- Where in your school's curriculum are students taught about emotional regulation?
- When does this take place?
- How much time is allocated to it?
- What types of pedagogies are used to teach about these issues and concepts?

SUGGESTED FURTHER READING FOR THIS LESSON

Brown, D. (2017). *Happy: Why More or Less Everything is Absolutely Fine* (London: Corgi).

Ehrenreich, B. (2021). *Smile or Die: How Positive Thinking Fooled America and the World* (London: Granta).

Hammond, C. (2011). *Emotional Rollercoaster: A Journey Through the Science of Feelings* (London: Harper Perennial).

Nussbaum, M. C. (2018). *Anger and Forgiveness: Resentment, Generosity, Justice* (New York: Oxford University Press).

Peters, S. (2012). *The Chimp Paradox: The Mind Management Programme to Help You Achieve Success, Confidence and Happiness* (London: Vermilion).

Pigliucci, M. (2017). *How to be a Stoic: Ancient Wisdom for Modern Living* (London: Rider).

MEMORY AND REVISION

WHY TEACH ABOUT MEMORY AND REVISION?

Solid exam performance has much to do with remembering; therefore, we think it makes sense to teach students explicitly about how their memory works and what can be done to improve it.

It is also much easier to remember things if you understand them in the first place. The best teachers are good at checking for understanding through a repertoire of techniques, such as questioning, retrieval practice and inviting feedback. However, some students may not be so lucky – or have an illness or injury which forces them to learn from home – so this session will arm them with useful techniques they can use away from lessons.

The more a student has the capacity to remember, the higher their attainment will be. Being able to remember well is a trainable skill. By increasing a student's knowledge of how we form memories and the several types of memories that exist, we can help them to realise that their own behaviours and habits affect how much they remember.

WHAT IS THE CLASS DIMENSION TO THIS TOPIC?

At the end of Year 11 and Year 13, exams are crammed into a brief period of time. More affluent parents have the capacity to help their children around exam time in ways that working-class parents often cannot, such as changing home routines to accommodate exam pressures and providing space and time for revision. Middle-class parents are also better placed to help their children with advice and information, or else they are more able to afford a private tutor to do this for them. Teaching memory techniques, alongside the provision of after-school revision clubs and allocating spaces for revision, can really help working-class students.

The key to engaging students when teaching about memory is to build confidence in their own ability to remember things, so this should not be thought of as an isolated one-off lesson. Each subject area should make some time for teaching about how memory works and help the students to use evidence-informed techniques to improve their own ability to recall information. Not doing this can enable certain myths about memory to develop, which advantages the already privileged who are more likely to have a stronger self-concept around being a successful student, especially in terms of examinations.

HOW DOES THIS LESSON WORK?

This lesson informs the students about the best ways to remember and recall information. Like any other skill, improving your memory involves practising certain strategies. This lesson informs students of the best strategies to use, and hopefully many of the teachers they come across will also encourage and endorse them. Some might even set in-class or homework tasks that complement the messages from this lesson.

We suggest the following lesson format:

Aim: To help students improve their memory and revision methods

Age group: 14–18 years

Time: Two hours

Activities: Q&A, discussion

Resources: Computer and projector, notebooks/exercise books, flashcards

TO START THE LESSON

Many students admit to being unsure about how to revise or, indeed, aren't motivated to do so. We have found that the best way to teach students about memory is to take a scientific approach from the outset. This means that the lesson has a bit of a dry start, but we want the students to get the clear message that no one is born with a good memory – which is a belief that some people hold. You can develop and strengthen your memory in a range of ways.

TEACHING ABOUT THE SCIENCE OF MEMORY

Explaining short-term memory, long-term memory and memory loss – and the science behind them – to students can be empowering. We are conscious that we have created some basic definitions of these terms because we want the focus of the lesson to be more about memory improvement. Nevertheless, ask the students to record the following definitions:

Short-term memory (sometimes referred to as working memory) describes the brain's capacity for holding limited amounts of information for a short time (seconds).

Long-term memories are formed by the brain storing memories over an extended period, which can be as long as years.

The following video about the life of 'HM' can help the students to understand the differences between short-term and long-term memory: https://www.youtube.com/watch?v=KkaXNvzE4pk.

The *forgetting curve* was devised by Hermann Ebbinghaus in 1886 to describe the fact that knowledge fades over time.[1] Ebbinghaus's research is still influential today and teaches us some important facts about how memory works. Refer to the diagram below, which demonstrates a steady decline in memory over the period of a month.

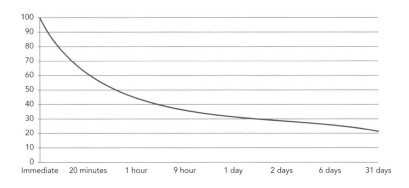

Alternatively, you can use this short video explanation of the forgetting curve: https://www.youtube.com/watch?v=SCsQHe-NpaM.

---

1   H. Ebbinghaus, *Memory: A Contribution to Experimental Psychology*, tr. H. Ruger and C. Bussenius (New York: Teachers College, Columbia University, 1913).

Now, ask the students to list how teachers try to get them to remember what they have been taught. Possible answers might include tests, quizzes, questions, homework, writing tasks and so on. Inform the students that, 'As much as your teachers will try to help you by testing you and staggering all the things you have to learn, you can help yourself too.' Then go on to ask them about the best revision techniques.

WHICH ARE THE MOST EFFECTIVE REVISION TECHNIQUES?

According to Professor John Dunlosky, the best revision techniques that have the most impact on boosting memory are practice testing and distributed practice.[2]

Practice testing involves self-testing. First, advise the students to create a set of notes or flashcards derived from their main notes (found in their exercise books or folders). Then, once completed, they should set aside some time to test themselves on this information.

Distributed practice simply means spreading out your practice over time rather than cramming just before the exam. Dunlosky's research shows that spreading out study time has a more positive impact on what we remember than mass practice (cramming), even when the same amount of time is used for both.

Dunlosky and his team of researchers examined and ranked different methods of revision. Their ranking is based on analysing 1,000 scientific studies and describes practice testing and distributed practice as high utility strategies. In contrast, activities such as rereading, highlighting and summarising are described as low utility.

We would like to think that most secondary teachers will be aware of Ebbinghaus's and Dunlosky's work, but we aren't sure that many students are. We feel it is important to share this knowledge with them.

Ask the students to discuss their revision strategies but be clear what the science shows: practice testing and distributed practice come out as by far the best strategies to use for revision.

---

2   D. Dunlosky, K. A. Rawson, E. J. Marsh, M. J. Nathan and D. T. Willingham, Improving Students' Learning with Effective Learning Techniques: Promising Directions from Cognitive and Educational Psychology, *Psychological Science in the Public Interest*, 14(1) (2013), 4–58. Available at: https://pcl.sitehost.iu.edu/rgoldsto/courses/dunloskyimprovinglearning.pdf.

EXERCISE: TRUE OR FALSE QUIZ

Next, get the students to build more knowledge about memory by completing a quiz. It is always useful to dispel some myths about memory. As we know, the beliefs we hold have a major impact on our behaviour and attitude; therefore, it is vital to challenge students' incorrect beliefs and misconceptions about memory.

Ask the students to list the numbers 1–7 in their notebooks. As you read out or display each question on a screen, ask them to write 'true' or 'false' (or T or F). Reveal the answers at the end and ask them to share their scores.

1   The human brain's storage capacity (long-term memory) is virtually limitless.

   Answer: true.

2   Some people have a photographic memory – they can just look at something like a page of writing and remember it all.

   Answer: false. Nobody can just look at something and remember it. In every case they are applying a memory technique.

3   Some people have a genetic advantage when it comes to memory – they are born with a good memory.

   Answer: false. Nobody is born with a good or bad memory (although some people have brain impairments that affect their capacity to remember things).

4   Memory cannot be improved.

   Answer: false. By applying memory techniques, such as the ones demonstrated in this session, our memory can vastly improve. Memory is very trainable.

5   We remember images more than we remember words.

   Answer: true. This is known as the picture superiority effect. Our ancestors had to remember landscapes and animals long before written language was invented, so our brains remember images to help us survive (the brain's main job).

6   Forgetting is bad.

   Answer: false. On the contrary, forgetting actually helps us to remember. When we find it difficult to retrieve information from long-term memory, the likelihood of recalling this piece of information will increase in the future. This is known as desirable difficulty – the more effort we put into trying to remember, the greater the learning.

7   Memory is like a video.

Answer: false. Our memory isn't like a video or film. Whereas a film is always the same no matter how often we watch it, people remember the same event in different ways and sometimes have a false memory of it. Human beings tend to reinvent, distort and exaggerate memories.

The key message that this lesson needs to convey is that memory is trainable, and it can get better or worse depending on what we do with our time.

To help more disadvantaged students, provide them with some resources to take away from the lessons such as paper, blank exercise books, index cards, coloured pens and so on. We want to remove as many barriers as possible for students. They may not have the space at home, but you can at least give them the techniques and some free revision materials. We believe this should happen all the way through secondary school, not just in Year 11.

TIPS FOR IMPROVING MEMORY

Next, take students through five techniques for developing their memory. Explain that they all take time to master, but spending as little as ten minutes each day on them will start to form habits that will lay the foundation for a good memory. These techniques build on some of the facts from the previous quiz. Get the students to record these tips somewhere so they can revisit them.

TIP 1: TALK UP YOUR MEMORY

Inform the students that how we talk to ourselves affects our beliefs which, in turn, affects our behaviours. It is easy enough to prove this by this simple exercise. Ask the students to pair up and then both stand up. They should allocate themselves either A or B. Direct person A to repeat one of the following mantras to themselves while they imagine they have an upcoming test:

- I've got a terrible memory.

- I forget things easily.

- I'm crap at remembering things.

If there is enough room, ask them to walk around repeating this silently in their heads. At this point, ask person B to simply observe the person's body language and, if walking, their pace and posture. You should also take note of individuals completing this exercise. After a minute or so, ask some B's to comment on their partner's body language or facial expressions; add any of your own observations here too. Ask some A's to share their feelings during this exercise, especially how confident they were feeling in terms of an upcoming test.

Now ask the B's to perform and the A's to observe them. This time, the B's should repeat one of the following more positive mantras about memory:

- I've got a good memory.

- Memory is a skill – with practice it gets stronger.

- I'm good at remembering.

Once again, after a minute or so, ask some A's to comment on their partner's body language or facial expressions. Ask some B's to share their feelings, especially how confident they were feeling in terms of an upcoming test. Now, ask the students to swap over and discuss the differences in their feelings.

Instruct the students to create some positive affirmations in terms of their own memory or discourage them from using negative self-talk around memory.

TIP 2: MAKE EFFECTIVE REVISION NOTES

This part of the lesson introduces students to the art of note-making. Building up a bank of notes is crucial for practice testing.

We particularly recommend giving the students flashcards which can become the basis for their revision. Flashcards are postcard-sized pieces of card; they can easily make some themselves or use index cards. Summarising onto a small piece of card is a good discipline. It is an active way of taking notes and will help the students to retain more information compared to just reading.

Handwriting very small forces us to take shortcuts, such as making abbreviations and creating images. If the students are using lined index cards, explain that it is best to write on every other line. This allows them to add any forgotten information during self-testing.

TIP 3: TEST YOURSELF REGULARLY

Inform students that one of the best things they can do to improve their memory is to review their class notes regularly. As we have already seen in the previous section, writing things down in an organised way enables the students to revisit their notes for self-testing. So, what is the best way to get them into the habit of testing themselves?

- *Get organised.* Without something to review – such as notes, a textbook, an article, a fact sheet or a knowledge organiser – self-testing is impossible. Encourage the students to make their revision notes easily accessible. Keeping each subject separate and in a different box or folder is one way of doing this.

- *Set aside some time for self-testing.* Inform the students: 'You'll need some blank paper or an exercise book. Set yourself the challenge of remembering something you need to learn. This could be the rules for a good answer, a labelled diagram, some facts, formulae or quotes. Whatever it is, write down as much as you can – either in summary form or try to reproduce your notes if you have already made some. Try ten or twenty minutes at the first attempt. As you get closer to major exams, build up this time.'

- *Check how well you've done.* Advise the students: 'Go back to what you're trying to recall. Take particular note of what you've forgotten. Where necessary, amend your revision notes (that's why it's helpful to leave a blank line between each sentence you write on your flashcards). Retest yourself a few days later – hopefully with more success.'

TIP 4: THE POMODORO TECHNIQUE

At the risk of being unoriginal, we must give a shout out to the Pomodoro Technique.[3] Both of us have taught students who have benefited from this revision method. They like it because it minimises revision time and teaches the principle that it is more productive to work in short bursts.

The Pomodoro Technique was developed by Francesco Cirillo, who, when at university in the 1980s, owned a kitchen timer in the shape of a tomato (*pomodoro* in Italian). He set the timer for twenty-five minutes and used this time to complete a single task. Then he would take a short break of three to five minutes. Afterwards, he set the timer again for another twenty-five minutes and tackled a different task. Each of these twenty-five-minute sessions is called a Pomodoro. After completing four Pomodoros, he took a longer break of around thirty minutes; this is called a set.

This technique complements the two most efficient revision methods – practice testing and distributed practice. Firstly, Pomodoros can be used to build some revision notes, such as a set of flashcards. Each twenty-five-

---

3   See https://francescocirillo.com/products/the-pomodoro-technique.

minute session can be allocated to a different subject. Then, once the students have created their revision notes, they can use other Pomodoros for self-testing, focusing on different subjects or topics and trying to recall the notes they have made. Where they have forgotten information or made mistakes, they can insert corrections or create an entirely new flashcard if necessary.

The main reason why students adopt this technique is because they get more things done in less time. It is often a challenge to sell the notion of revision to students, so any strategy that makes it more palatable deserves serious consideration.

TIP 5: GET GOOD QUALITY SLEEP

Perhaps the most famous quote about sleep was popularised by Benjamin Franklin: 'Early to bed and early to rise, makes a man healthy, wealthy, and wise.' Although the following adage might resonate more with many of us: 'The amount of sleep needed by the average person is five minutes more.'

Experts such as Dr Matthew Walker suggest that we use the term 'sleep hygiene' to describe our sleep patterns.[4] This is a useful phrase. We all know that it is unhygienic and therefore dangerous to eat a half-eaten sandwich off the pavement or to share chewing gum with a stranger, but being sleep deprived is just as risky! It is bad for all aspects of our health, and it is especially bad for our brain function.

Inform the students that when we are sleep deprived, the brain's neurons become overconnected and, with so much electrical activity taking place, we cannot save new memories. When we get a good night's sleep, the brain effectively resets and we wake feeling refreshed. The more we improve our sleep hygiene, the better our memory will be.

Here are some tips for the students. Note: if you can get access to parents and carers, try to pass on this information to them as many students will need help with taking this advice. Explain that when it comes to sleep, we are all different.

■ **Quantity of sleep.** The amount they need won't be the same as someone else. Teenagers tend to need more sleep than adults due to their body changing so much – about eight to ten hours on average. If the students are feeling constantly tired throughout the day or cannot function without lots of caffeine, then they either need more sleep or better quality sleep.

---

4   M. Walker, *Why We Sleep: The New Science of Sleep and Dreams* (London: Penguin Random House, 2018).

- **Quality of sleep.** Here is some advice to improve each student's sleep hygiene:

  - Stick to a sleep schedule. It is best to go to bed and wake up at the same time each day. Sleeping in later at weekends won't fully make up for a lack of sleep during the week. A good idea is to set an alarm for bedtime. Often, we set an alarm for when it is time to wake up, but we can also set one for when it is time to go to sleep. According to experts such as Matthew Walker, sticking to a sleep schedule is one of the best things we can do for better quality sleep.

  - Relax before bed. The end of the day should be left for unwinding. Advise the students to get into the habit of doing something relaxing just before sleep, such as reading, meditating, praying or journalling (writing about your day). A hot bath or shower may also help.

  - Have a gadget-free bedroom. Good luck with giving this advice to students who often seem glued to their phones, but parents may be receptive to it. These days, we have access to all sorts of gadgets and electronics. However, when used late in the evening they can overstimulate the brain just when we should be trying to wind down. As hard as it might be for the students to accept this advice, our brains need over an hour to 'come down' from using technology, so young people and their parents or carers should factor this in when thinking about sleep hygiene.

  - Create some bedtime rules. Many students have to share a bedroom with another family member. If they are sharing, they will often need to compromise on issues like when the lights go off and noise levels from the other person. Failing that, buy them some ear plugs and a sleep mask from school capitation!

The Sleep Foundation has some other useful information and tips: https://www.sleepfoundation.org/articles/teens-and-sleep.

FINALLY

Conflicting advice about revision and how to recall information in exams can be confusing for students. We advise that teachers apply Ebbinghaus's and Dunlosky's research in their own teaching practice, but also teach this research to the students so they don't waste time on revision methods such as highlighting and rereading that will have limited impact.

Working-class students often have many more barriers to studying at home. Not being aware of the best revision methods shouldn't be one of them. By providing students with resources, such as flashcards, blank exercise books, coloured pens and even a kitchen timer, we can help them to build a revision kit that they otherwise wouldn't have been able to afford. Demonstrating in lessons how to make revision cards and how to self-test also helps to get students into good revision habits from an early age.

FINAL THOUGHTS

- Where in your school's curriculum are students taught about memory and revision?
- When does this take place?
- How much time is allocated to it?
- What types of pedagogies are used to teach about these issues and concepts?

SUGGESTED FURTHER READING FOR THIS CHAPTER

Eagleman, D. (2016). *The Brain: The Story of You* (London: Canongate Books).

Lorayne, H. and Lucas, J. (1996). *The Memory Book: The Classic Guide to Improving Your Memory at Work, at School and at Play* (New York: Random House).

Morgan, N. (2013). *Blame My Brain: The Amazing Teenage Brain Revealed* (London: Walker Books).

O'Brien, D. (2014). *How to Develop a Brilliant Memory Week by Week: 52 Proven Ways to Enhance Your Memory Skills* (London: Watkins Publishing).

Walker, M. (2018). *Why We Sleep: The New Science of Sleep and Dreams* (London: Penguin Random House).

TIME MANAGEMENT

WHY TEACH ABOUT TIME MANAGEMENT?

Teaching working-class students about time management and helping them to build good time management habits can have a positive impact on their attainment. As students get older, good time management becomes increasingly important. This is why, according to Antonio Valle and colleagues, it is best to practise these skills from an early age, so they are embedded by the time students are expected to engage in independent study.[1]

Common sense also tells us that the more time we put into practising something, the better we get (subject to us practising this task properly). Learning to manage their time well has many advantages for students, perhaps the biggest being that they can take these habits into adulthood.

Those students who possess good time management skills enjoy their leisure activities even more because they are keeping on top of all the other things they need to do and want to do. Good time managers have a quiet confidence that they can deal with current and future pressures on their time. That is a nice feeling for anyone to have.

This session is packed with common-sense strategies and wisdom. Not embracing these ideas condemns people to procrastinating, being less productive and generally having a less fulfilling or imbalanced life.

WHAT IS THE CLASS DIMENSION TO THIS TOPIC?

It is even more important to have good time management skills if you are working class compared to those from more affluent backgrounds. Working-class students often have more care responsibilities, such as picking up younger siblings from school, and more household chores. As

---

1   A. Valle, B. Regueiro, J. C. Núñez, S. Rodríguez, I. Piñeiro and P. Rosário, Academic Goals, Student Homework Engagement, and Academic Achievement in Elementary School, *Frontiers in Psychology*, 7 (2016), 463. https://doi.org/10.3389/fpsyg.2016.00463

they get older, working-class students are also more likely, through necessity, to be holding down a part-time job while studying.

This can particularly affect the amount of study time available to them in further and higher education. There is no guarantee that learning good time management strategies can solve this problem, but it might help. The authors of this book had to work during our university years, and knowing about good time management helped us to manage work alongside studying, sport and socialising.

As working-class students tend to have less available study time than their more affluent peers, this makes it even more important that, during the secondary school years, we explicitly teach working-class students and their parents and carers a series of efficient time management strategies.

HOW DOES THIS LESSON WORK?

This lesson informs the students about the best ways to manage their most precious resource – time. They are taken through a series of tips and reflective questions which they will hopefully start adopting in their own lives.

We suggest the following lesson format:

Aim: To help students improve their time management

Age group: 14–18 years

Time: One to two hours

Activities: Scheduling

Resources: Time grids and schedules, coloured pens

TO START THE LESSON

Start by asking the students to rate their time management skills. This can give teachers some useful insights. Ask them to rank themselves on a scale of 1–10 in terms of how effectively they use their time, especially outside of school. Record this score for each student so they can revisit it later.

Other questions to hook the students could include:

■ Do you ever seem to run out of time to do all the things you want to do?

Do you see other people achieving more with their lives than you do?

Do you ever get into trouble with teachers or parents because of your poor time management?

Do you think you might need to be better at managing your time now and in the future?

Do you want to be able to get homework and revision done and still have lots of free time?

If anyone says yes to any of these questions or has rated their own time management as low (below 5 out of 10), then there is clearly a demand for this knowledge.

Inform the class that you are going to impart some time management secrets that some of the most successful people in the world use. Say something like: 'There is no single system for time management that works for everyone. This session will explore different time management tips. The main reason for some people's poor time management is either that they have a weak system or no system at all. The reason we all need a system is that, as we get older, we have more and more things to do, so it is impossible to keep all these things in our heads. We need some way of recording and displaying the things we must do and want to do.'

Ask the students to share the time management systems that they or their parents use already. Challenge anyone who is 'too good' to have a system and thinks they can manage without one.

Get the students to record the advantages of having an effective time management system. It is important that they are forced to slow down and take notes at this point; the very act of writing will help them to take in the information. The advantages might include:

Achieving more in life.

Better life balance.

More independence.

Less stress.

Greater ability to cope with workload.

Better test and exam results.

Better career prospects.

Better relationships with others.

EXERCISE: HONESTY

Here is a great way to think about how you use your time. It comes from Tim Urban, the creator of a website called www.waitbutwhy.com. His TED Talk on procrastination has had millions of views. Students don't need to watch it, but the link is here should you wish to do so: https://www.youtube.com/watch?v=Rk5C149J9C0.

According to Urban, most people sleep for about eight hours a night. That leaves sixteen waking hours each day or about 1,000 minutes.[2] We can break these minutes down into 100 ten-minute blocks, such as in the diagram below.

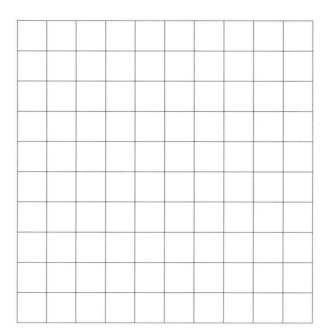

Create and print out a grid for each student. Once you have explained this model to them (i.e. six blocks = one hour), they will need highlighter pens and at least ten or fifteen minutes.

Inform the students that you want them to complete an honesty exercise. Ask them to fill in their personal grids for a recent day – this could be a school day or weekend day. They should try to make it as recent as possible. The students should allocate a different colour or pattern to each

---

2   T. Urban, 100 Blocks a Day, *Wait But Why* (21 October 2016). Available at: https://waitbutwhy.com/2016/10/100-blocks-day.html.

different activity they do – for example, one colour for socialising, one for homework, one for sport, one for watching television and so on – and shade in what they did with their time. Encourage them to be truthful – tell them you aren't going to tell their head of year or parents/carers what you find.

It doesn't matter if the students colour in a typical day or not – the exercise can still garner some interesting results. We have seen many students block off whole afternoons and evenings to TikTok or 'playing out with my mates'. Some grids are stark – school and not school, with no discernible time allocated to homework or studying as soon as they leave the school building.

When the students see their peers' grids, they might start to realise that they could be spending their time in other ways. We will come back to this grid below and explain how it can be used to help the students to change their time management habits.

The rest of this lesson is designed to inform them about time management tips and how they can apply them to their lives.

TIPS FOR EXCELLENT TIME MANAGEMENT

Ensure the students start writing down the five tips and exercises that accompany them. Take some time to explain each of the tips carefully and check that the students find them sensible and logical.

TIP 1: PLAN TIME IN ADVANCE

Every week, we all have the same amount of time: 168 hours. Take off 56 hours for sleeping and our 'awake time' is approximately 112 hours. In this time, we need to do all the things we have to do and want to do. It is important to plan our time in advance because if we don't schedule time for certain things, we might forget to do them. This can have negative consequences for us, such as fines if we forget to get to pay our taxes, arguments if we forget a loved one's birthday or detentions if we forget to do our homework.

Planning isn't just about doing the urgent things; it is also about doing the things that aren't urgent but are important. This includes exercise, studying, socialising and helping our families or others in the community.

So, what is the best way to plan our time in advance? The answer is to create and then stick to a schedule. Explain to the students that later in the session you will help them to make one.

TIP 2: THE ABCDE METHOD

The ABCDE method is more useful than a simple to-do list because it helps us to prioritise. This is how it works:

1   Create a to-do list.

2   Assign the letters A, B, C, D or E to each of the tasks on the list.

Key:

■   A – the most important items on your list. These are tasks that will be the most helpful towards your goals. They need to be done today.

■   B – the items on your to-do list that are important but not as important as your A tasks.

■   C – the tasks that you don't need to get done today. Whether you complete them or not, it doesn't have a lot of impact on your goals, career or happiness. These tasks should only be done if all of your A and B tasks have been accomplished.

■   D – the items you could (and should) delegate to someone else.

■   E – the items that can be eliminated from your list.

Encourage the students to share their to-do lists and suggest other items that should be on it – things that they don't want to do but must do. Most of us tend to forget including activities that aid our well-being, such as exercise, meditation and so on.

TIP 3: EAT YOUR FROGS

Brian Tracy wrote a fantastic time management book with the title *Eat That Frog!* which has sold over 13 million copies worldwide.[3] The premise of the book is this: there are horrible, boring things that we have do in life – these are referred to as 'frogs'. For students at secondary school age, this might include household chores, homework or revision.

Frogs are unpleasant to eat, so if, by law, you had to eat one every day, Tracy poses the question: when would be the best time to eat it? The answer is obvious. Eat that frog first thing in the morning. Get it eaten and out of the way so you can get on with the rest of your day without the dread of eating a frog hanging over you. The message here is clear: don't be a procrastinator, don't let things such as homework, cleaning and so on pile up. If you tackle your frogs as you go along, you won't feel overwhelmed and fall behind.

3   B. Tracy, *Eat That Frog! Get More of the Important Things Done Today* (London: Hodder & Stoughton, 2013).

Tracy argues that 'your ability to select your most important task at each moment, and then to get started on that task and to get it done both quickly and well, will probably have more of an impact on your success than any other quality or skill you can develop'.[4]

It is tempting for us to do things that are fun and easy all the time. For the students, this can include time spent on mobile phones or playing computer games, but doing too much of this will create bad habits. We must all learn to manage some of the less fun, more mundane tasks because this is what builds our knowledge and character. Ask the students to list their personal 'frogs'.

There is a summary of the book and some other time management ideas at: https://www.theexceptionalskills.com/eat-that-frog-summary.

TIP 4: THINK OF TIME IN TEN-MINUTE BLOCKS

Considering blocks of time links back to Tim Urban's 100 blocks method. It is amazing what we can get done in ten minutes or by combining blocks of ten minutes. For example, by getting into the habit of allocating two blocks for reading before sleep each night (which represents twenty minutes) this will mean that, over the course of a year, we would read fifteen more books than we would have done otherwise.[5]

Thinking in ten-minute blocks helps us realise that there is more time available than we may have previously perceived. Say that someone decides to dedicate three blocks (thirty minutes) to exercise each morning. That still leaves them with ninety-seven blocks for other things. When we think about each day as 100 blocks of ten minutes, there is always time for exercise, reading, socialising, play, leisure, helping others and many other activities.

We are all familiar with the phrase 'take five' – taking a five-minute break for yourself – although many of us complain that we haven't got time to take a break. However, when we look at a day through the lens of the 100 square grid, the idea of taking at least five or ten minutes for ourselves seems immensely doable. It is a good idea to advise the students to build in some 'me-time' every day. This can involve some form of mindfulness, meditation, journalling or whatever will help them to unwind.

Ask the students to revisit their grids from the honesty exercise they completed earlier in the lesson and consider whether their day had the right balance. You could say something like: 'Did you spend enough/any time doing things that will help you to be better at school, such as reading, studying or researching? Did you spend enough time doing things that

4   Tracy, *Eat That Frog!*, p. 1.
5   Urban, 100 Blocks a Day.

will make you feel better, such as exercise? Did you spend too much time on your phone, playing computer games or watching YouTube clips? If you don't think you've got the right balance, plan tomorrow better.'

Next, give the students another blank grid, maybe a few, so they can make some changes to an upcoming day. Encourage them to schedule in some frogs, some me-time and some other tasks they might like to fit in.

TIP 5: USE A WEEKLY SCHEDULE

Giving the students a weekly schedule (such as the one on page 249) and teaching them how to plan their time over the space of a week can be helpful. They will need some different coloured pens to do this most effectively.

Here are the suggested steps to share with the students to help them plan their time in advance:

1 **Schedule commitments for the week ahead.** Commitments include tasks that we need to do or want to do. This will include attending school or college, part-time work, going to clubs, practices such as dance or football and social obligations with friends or family. Note: these commitments will need to have different colours associated with them, so the students should create a key.

2 **Think about how to use the remaining white space (unplanned time).** Now, ask the students what they intend to do with the remaining white space on their schedules. It is in these spaces that they may choose to start doing something differently as part of their self-improvement, such as reading or exercising more. They don't have to fill all the white space, but those students who admit to having poor time management habits and/or poor self-control should be especially wary of leaving too much unallocated space.

3 **Schedule frogs that need to be eaten.** Using the weekly schedule, ask the students to say when they will eat their frogs and record this (perhaps with the colour green). Whether it is homework, revision or tidying, encourage them to just eat their frogs. Keeping promises is important in life. Once someone has scheduled to eat a particular frog at a particular time on a particular day, they should keep that promise to themselves. Some say it takes about a month to change a habit, so set a thirty-day challenge to the students to eat their frogs – and ensure you get some feedback, especially from parents and carers, as to whether they have achieved this challenge.

	Priorities						
	Monday	Tuesday	Wednesday	Thursday	Friday	Saturday	Sunday
7 am							
8 am							
9 am							
10 am							
11 am							
12 noon							
1 pm							
2 pm							
3 pm							
4 pm							
5 pm							
6 pm							
7 pm							
8 pm							
9 pm							
10 pm							

FINALLY

When teaching time management, it is only possible to offer guidance to young people. The two key messages that students should hear about time management are that they should *seek balance* and that there is often *more time available than they think*. In terms of striking that balance, a diet analogy might help. There was a recent radio interview on BBC Merseyside with Mona Nemmer, who is head of nutrition at Liverpool Football Club. A listener asked her for one tip on having a balanced, nutritional diet. Her answer: 'Have lots of different colours on your plate.'

The same can be said of managing time and having a good balance between social, mental, spiritual, physical and academic activities: have lots of different colours on your schedule.

Encourage the students to try out these ideas for at least a month. Check in with them on how it is going and encourage them to be kind to themselves if they fall off the time management wagon. If you have taught this session to a particular class or year group, be sure to inform other colleagues via the school bulletin or schedule a reminder assembly on this theme with form tutors present.

FINAL THOUGHTS

- Where in your school's curriculum are students and/or their parents taught about time management?
- When does this take place?
- How much time is allocated to it?
- What types of pedagogies are used to teach about these issues and concepts?

SUGGESTED FURTHER READING FOR THIS LESSON

Clear, J. (2018). *Atomic Habits: An Easy and Proven Way to Build Good Habits and Break Bad Ones* (London: Random House Business).

Culp, S. (2001). *How to Get Organized When You Don't Have the Time* (Toronto, ON: Walking Stick Press).

Duhigg, C. (2013). *The Power of Habit: Why We Do What We Do and How to Change* (London: Random House).

Hannam, P. (2017). *The Wisdom of Groundhog Day: How to Improve Your Life One Day at a Time* (London: Yellow Kite).

Levitin, D. (2015). *The Organized Mind: The Science of Preventing Overload, Increasing Productivity and Restoring Focus* (London: Penguin Random House).

Tracy, B. (2013). *Eat That Frog! Get More of the Important Things Done Today* (London: Hodder & Stoughton).

CONCLUSION

In this book, we have set out to highlight the role that social class plays in school and in life. We think that to deny or underplay the effect of class is, in itself, a form of classism. We don't live in an equal society and meritocracy doesn't exist. Discrimination against working-class people is real, so simply telling them – like Boxer tells himself in George Orwell's *Animal Farm* – to work harder or try harder isn't the solution. Rather, we need to do more; we need to take affirmative action. This is why we have concluded this book with some practical lessons that you can teach to your working-class students, and it is why we have relayed so many stories and shared so many templates. We want you to *do* something, not just *say* something.

As we observed in the Introduction, many of us work in education because we are driven to make a difference by tackling injustices and levelling the playing field. We hope that we have equipped you with the knowledge and tools you need to help play your part and to convince your colleagues to do likewise.

We hope that *The Working Classroom* will inspire you to do something better or do some things differently. This might be taking more of an interest in building social and cultural capital within your subject discipline or designing and delivering a curriculum intervention or enhancement.

We have dedicated a lot of space to showing you that there *is* a class divide and how the education sector might contribute to this, either by accident or design. Our view is that there has never been a better time to tackle classism because now is the time for us to become more prosocial, to care about each other and to act in the common cause. We have seen the devastating effects of individualism and isolationism. We have seen our country ripped apart by the politics of hate and fear. Now is the time for change. Now is the time for *you* to be the change.

In his 1946 play *All My Sons*, Arthur Miller offers a critique of the American Dream and the pursuit of profit above all else. The play tells the story of Joe Keller, a factory owner who shipped faulty aircraft parts to the US Air Force. One of Keller's sons, Larry, is a pilot missing in action. Keller tells himself that his faulty parts couldn't have been responsible for Larry's plane crashing because his factory didn't supply parts for the type of plane Larry flew.

Towards the end of the play, however, it emerges that Larry knew of his father's involvement in shipping out defective parts. What is more, some of Larry's comrades flew the planes affected and they never came back. Keller reads a letter from Larry which makes him realise the truth:

KELLER: [Looking at the letter in his hand] Then what is this if it isn't telling me? Sure, [Larry] was my son. But I think to him [the pilots who were killed] were all my sons. And I guess they were, I guess they were.[1]

Our students are all our sons and all our daughters.

This book has been about what we can control, not what we cannot. We cannot control what happens in the world economy, or even the local economy. We cannot control the forces and policies that have created so many 'left behind' places. But, through voting, lobbying and protesting, we can influence more than we realise, and through tackling the classism that is inherent in our schools, we can help working-class students to get a fair chance and create a more egalitarian and equitable society for their own children to inherit.

Much of this book has been written in anger. We are angered at how unequal our society has become. For the past forty years, the issue of social class has been largely ignored, even among so-called social activists.

Policies driven by a belief in the efficacy of trickle-down economics continue to widen wealth inequalities. These policies have created millions of insecure, low-skill, low-wage jobs that keep families in a constant state of stress. If we could change one thing, it would be the economic system. We would like everyone to have full economic rights, no matter their social background. This means that everyone has a right to a decent income, adequate housing and stable employment – a consensus that was embraced by most political parties in the post-war period who accepted the Beveridge Report.[2]

In the education sector, the working classes and those sympathetic to their plight have a proud history of standing up to injustice, and we should take inspiration from this. Indeed, for us, there is nothing more inspiring than the school leaders and teachers who show passion for the people in their communities. They turn up, day in, day out, and through their everyday actions support families. Many go beyond their job description – lobbying for more funding and resources and informing others about the challenges their communities face. We hope that if you are one of these people, then our book has given you more ammunition for this fight. If you aren't yet at this point, we hope it has stimulated greater interest in the impact of social class on young people's life chances.

---

1   A. Miller, *All My Sons* (London: Penguin, 2000 [1947]), sc. 3, (p. 83).
2   W. Beveridge, *Social Insurance and Allied Services* [Beveridge Report] (London: HMSO, 1942).

We have focused on two types of classism in this book: downward classism and internalised classism. It is the latter that can intensify as a child traverses secondary school, if we don't offer the right antidotes. Many working-class students of secondary-school age internalise feelings of inferiority. Even if we do nothing else, if we challenge these beliefs – with action, not just rhetoric – we can help to foster change. As we have argued, we can challenge these beliefs in the way the curriculum is designed, in the way we assess and define success, and in the opportunities we offer our students to acquire life experiences and world knowledge.

We also think that we need to be upfront with students and their parents about how the game of life is rigged against them. Working-class parents don't need to be told that the world is unfair, of course – they know it only too well. But we do need to prepare students for the challenges they will face, especially if they choose careers in which they will be a minority.

At the same time, we need to be careful that non-working-class students don't feel that they are in some way to blame for this system. Although they aren't responsible, they share some responsibility for what happens next. Following a curriculum and subscribing to beliefs that value, rather than denigrate or ignore, the working class can only help them to become more empathic, prosocial individuals.

What all of us do and don't do has an impact on the world. The young people we teach, whatever their background, need adults around them who can help them to strengthen their knowledge, hone their skills and nurture their talents.

Thank you for reading this book and for caring about others. We hope *The Working Classroom* has inspired you to make more of a difference, more of the time. We also hope this book has armed you with the tools you need to ensure the classroom works more often for the working class. Good luck.

REFERENCES

Aked, J., Marks, N., Cordon, C. and Thompson, S. (2008). *Five Ways to Wellbeing: A Report Presented to the Foresight Project on Communicating the Evidence Base for Improving People's Well-Being* (London: New Economics Foundation). Available at: https://neweconomics.org/uploads/files/five-ways-to-wellbeing-1.pdf.

Arnold, M. (2017 [1869]). *Culture and Anarchy* (New York: Start Publishing).

Association of School and College Leaders (2019). *The Forgotten Third: Final Report of the Commission of Inquiry* (September). Available at: https://www.ascl.org.uk/ASCL/media/ASCL/Our%20view/Campaigns/The-Forgotten-Third_full-report.pdf.

BBC News (2018). 'Most' Internships Unpaid in Retailing and the Arts (21 November). Available at: https://www.bbc.co.uk/news/business-46315035.

Beadle, P. (2020). *The Fascist Painting: What Is Cultural Capital?* (Woodbridge: John Catt Educational).

Beswick, K. (2020). Feeling Working Class: Affective Class Identification and Its Implications for Overcoming Inequality, *Studies in Theatre and Performance*, 40, 265–274. https://doi.org/10.1080/14682761.2020.1807194

Beveridge, W. (1942). *Social Insurance and Allied Services* [Beveridge Report] (London: HMSO).

Blandford, S. (2017). *Born to Fail? Social Mobility: A Working Class View* (Woodbridge: John Catt Educational).

Block, P. (2009). *Community: The Structure of Belonging* (San Francisco, CA: Berrett-Koehler Publishers).

Bourdieu, P. (1977). Cultural Reproduction and Social Reproduction. In J. Karabel and A. H. Halsey (eds), *Power and Ideology in Education* (New York: Oxford University Press), pp. 487–511.

Bourdieu, P. (1986). The Forms of Capital. In J. G. Richardson (ed.), *Handbook of Theory and Research for the Sociology of Education* (Westport, CT: Greenwood), pp. 241–258.

Bourdieu, P. (1990). *In Other Words: Essays Toward a Reflexive Sociology* (Redwood City, CA: Stanford University Press).

Bourdieu, P. (1994). The Field of Cultural Production, or: The Economic World Reversed. In *The Field of Cultural Production: Essays on Art and Literature*, ed. R. Johnson (New York: Columbia University Press), pp. 29–73.

Bourdieu, P. (1996). *The State Nobility: Elite Schools in the Field of Power* (Cambridge: Polity).

Boyle, F. (2020). *The Future of British Politics* (London: Unbound).

Bromley, M. (2019). *School and College Curriculum Design 1: Intent* (Hinckley: Spark Education Books).

Brown, B. (2006). Shame Resilience Theory: A Grounded Theory Study on Women and Shame, *Families in Society: The Journal of Contemporary Social Services*, 87(1), 43–52. https://doi.org/10.1606/1044-3894.3483

Brown, B. (2008). *I Thought It Was Just Me (But It Isn't): Telling the Truth About Perfectionism, Inadequacy and Power* (Sheridan, WY: Gotham Books).

Brown, B. (2013). Shame vs. Guilt (15 January). Available at: https://brenebrown.com/articles/2013/01/15/shame-v-guilt.

Brown, D. (2017). *Happy: Why More or Less Everything is Absolutely Fine* (London: Corgi).

Burns, M. and Griffith, A. (2019). *The Learning Imperative: Raising Performance in Organisations by Improving Learning* (Carmarthen: Crown House Publishing).

Callaghan, J. (1976). A Rational Debate Based on the Facts. Speech delivered at Ruskin College, Oxford, 18 October. Available at: http://www.educationengland.org.uk/documents/speeches/1976ruskin.html.

Cannadine, D. (1999). *The Rise and Fall of Class in Britain* (New York: Columbia University Press).

Chapman, L. and West-Burnham, J. (2008). *Social Justice in Education: Achieving Wellbeing for All* (London: Continuum).

Child Poverty Action Group (2022). *The Cost of the School Day in England: Pupils' Perspectives* (March). Available at: https://cpag.org.uk/policy-and-campaigns/briefing/cost-school-day-england-pupils-perspectives.

Children's Commissioner (2019). Briefing: The Children Leaving School with Nothing (20 September). Available at: www.childrenscommissioner.gov.uk/wp-content/uploads/2019/09/cco-briefing-children-leaving-school-with-nothing.pdf.

Children's Commissioner (2020). Fact Checking Claims About Child Poverty (22 June). Available at: https://www.childrenscommissioner.gov.uk/2020/06/22/fact-checking-claims-about-child-poverty.

Clear, J. (2018). *Atomic Habits: An Easy and Proven Way to Build Good Habits and Break Bad Ones* (London: Random House Business).

Cullinane, C. and Montacute, R. (2018). *Pay As You Go? Internship Pay, Quality and Access in the Graduate Jobs Market* (London: Sutton Trust). Available at: https://www.suttontrust.com/our-research/internships-pay-as-you-go.

Culp, S. (2001). *How to Get Organized When You Don't Have the Time* (Toronto, ON: Walking Stick Press).

CV Library (2020). Brits Believe Class Is an Issue When Securing a New Job (28 January). Available at: https://www.cv-library.co.uk/recruitment-insight/class-issue-securing-new-job.

de Waal, K. (ed.) (2019). *Common People: An Anthology of Working-Class Writers* (London: Unbound).

Department for Education (2011). *The Framework for the National Curriculum: A Report by the Expert Panel for the National Curriculum Review*. Available at: https://www.gov.uk/government/publications/framework-for-the-national-curriculum-a-report-by-the-expert-panel-for-the-national-curriculum-review.

Department for Education (2013a). National Curriculum (14 October; updated 16 July 2014). Available at: https://www.gov.uk/government/collections/national-curriculum.

Department for Education (2013b). *The National Curriculum in England: Key Stages 1 and 2 Framework Document* (September). Available at: https://assets.publishing.service.gov.uk/government/uploads/system/uploads/attachment_data/file/425601/PRIMARY_national_curriculum.pdf.

Department for Education (2014). National Curriculum in England: Framework for Key Stages 1 to 4 (2 December). Available at: https://www.gov.uk/government/publications/national-curriculum-in-england-framework-for-key-stages-1-to-4/the-national-curriculum-in-england-framework-for-key-stages-1-to-4.

Department for Education (2019). *The Independent School Standards: Guidance for Independent Schools* (April). Available at: https://www.gov.uk/government/publications/regulating-independent-schools.

Department for Education (2023). *Using Pupil Premium: Guidance for School Leaders* (March). Available at: https://www.gov.uk/government/publications/pupil-premium.

Donnelly, M., Lažetić, P., Sandoval-Hernandez, A., Kumar, K. and Whewall, S. (2022). *An Unequal Playing Field: Extra-Curricular Activities, Soft Skills and Social Mobility* (London: Social Mobility Commission). Available at: https://assets.publishing.service.gov.uk/government/uploads/system/uploads/attachment_data/file/818679/An_Unequal_Playing_Field_report.pdf.

Dorling, D. (2010). An Introduction to Injustice: Why Social Inequality Still Persists. Available at: https://www.dannydorling.org/books/injustice/injustice-anintroduction.pdf.

Dorling, D. (2012). *Fair Play: A Daniel Dorling Reader on Social Justice* (Bristol: Policy Press).

Dorling, D. (2013). How Social Mobility Got Stuck, *New Statesman* (16 May). Available at: https://www.newstatesman.com/business/economics/2013/05/how-social-mobility-got-stuck.

Dorling, D. (2014). *Inequality and the 1%* (London: Verso Books).

Duhigg, C. (2013). *The Power of Habit: Why We Do What We Do and How to Change* (London: Random House).

Dunlosky, D., Rawson, K. A., Marsh, E. J., Nathan, M. J. and Willingham, D. T. (2013). Improving Students' Learning with Effective Learning

Techniques: Promising Directions from Cognitive and Educational Psychology, *Psychological Science in the Public Interest*, 14(1), 4–58. Available at: https://pcl.sitehost.iu.edu/rgoldsto/courses/dunloskyimprovinglearning.pdf.

Dweck, C. S. (2017). *Mindset: Changing the Way You Think to Fulfil Your Potential*, updated edn (London: Robinson).

Eagleman, D. (2016). *The Brain: The Story of You* (London: Canongate Books).

Ebbinghaus, H. (1913). *Memory: A Contribution to Experimental Psychology*, tr. H. Ruger and C. Bussenius (New York: Teachers College, Columbia University).

Ehrenreich, B. (2021). *Smile or Die: How Positive Thinking Fooled America and the World* (London: Granta).

Emunah, R. (1994). *Acting for Real: Drama Therapy, Process, Technique and Performance* (Abingdon and New York: Routledge).

Epictetus (1925). *The Discourses as Reported by Arrian: The Manual and Fragments*, 2 vols, tr. W. A. Oldfather (Cambridge, MA: Harvard University Press and London: William Heinemann).

Epictetus (2017). *The Enchiridion of Epictetus* (n.p.: CreateSpace).

Farquharson, C., McNally, S. and Tahir, I. (2022). Lack of Progress on Closing Educational Inequalities Disadvantaging Millions Throughout Life, *Institute for Fiscal Studies* [press release] (16 August). Available at: https://ifs.org.uk/inequality/press-release/lack-of-progress-on-closing-educational-inequalities-disadvantaging-millions-throughout-life.

Ferguson, D. (2017). 'Working-Class Children Get Less of Everything in Education – Including Respect' [interview with Diane Reay], *The Guardian* (21 November). Available at: https://www.theguardian.com/education/2017/nov/21/english-class-system-shaped-in-schools.

Fitri, A. (2022). The UK is the Second-Most Unequal G7 Country, *New Statesman* (6 September). Available at: https://www.newstatesman.com/chart-of-the-day/2022/09/uk-second-most-unequal-g7-country.

Freedman, S. (2022). The Truth Is That Schools Do Little to Reduce Inequality, *Financial Times* (22 August). Available at: https://www.ft.com/content/da6ba133-a2ec-40f3-8f81-260c582cb22e.

Friedman, S. and Laurison, D. (2019a). *The Class Ceiling: Why It Pays to Be Privileged* (Bristol: Policy Press).

Friedman, S. and Laurison, D. (2019b). The Class Pay Gap: Why It Pays to Be Privileged, *The Guardian* (7 February). Available at: https://www.theguardian.com/society/2019/feb/07/the-class-pay-gap-why-it-pays-to-be-privileged.

Gilbert, I. (ed.) (2018). *The Working Class: Poverty, Education and Alternative Voices* (Carmarthen: Independent Thinking Press).

Griffith, A. and Burns, M. (2012). *Engaging Learners* (Outstanding Teaching) (Carmarthen: Crown House Publishing).

Griffith, A. and Burns, M. (2014). *Teaching Backwards* (Outstanding Teaching) (Carmarthen: Crown House Publishing).

Goldstein, A. P. and McGinnis, E., with Sprakin, R. P., Gershaw, N. J. and Klein, P. (1997). *Skillstreaming the Adolescent: New Strategies and Perspectives for Teaching Prosocial Skills*, rev. edn (Champaign, IL: Research Press).

Grosz, S. (2013). *The Examined Life: How We Lose Friends and Find Ourselves* (London: Vintage).

Hammond, C. (2011). *Emotional Rollercoaster: A Journey Through the Science of Feelings* (London: Harper Perennial).

Hannam, P. (2017). *The Wisdom of Groundhog Day: How to Improve Your Life One Day at a Time* (London: Yellow Kite).

Hannam, P. (2020). *Significance: How to Refocus Your Life on What Matters Most* (Farnham: Bright Future Publishing).

Hannon, V. and Peterson, A. (2021). *Thrive: The Purpose of Schools in a Changing World* (Cambridge: Cambridge University Press).

Hari, J. (2018). *Lost Connections: Why You're Depressed and How to Find Hope* (London: Bloomsbury Publishing).

Hauck, P. (1991). *Hold Your Head Up High* (London: Hachette UK).

Hawes, J. (2020). *The Shortest History of England* (Exeter: Old Street Publishing).

Heller, A. (2020). Diversity in the Medical Workforce: Are We Making Progress?, *The King's Fund* (3 February). Available at: https://www.kingsfund.org.uk/blog/2020/02/diversity-medical-workforce-progress.

Holiday, R. (2015). *The Obstacle is the Way: The Ancient Art of Turning Adversity to Advantage* (London: Profile Books).

House of Commons Education Committee (2014). *Underachievement in Education by White Working Class Children. First Report of Session 2014–15*. HC 142 (11 June). Available at: https://publications.parliament.uk/pa/cm201415/cmselect/cmeduc/142/142.pdf.

Impetus (2014). *Make NEETs History in 2014* (London: Impetus). Available at: https://www.impetus.org.uk/assets/publications/Report/Make-NEETs-History-Report_ImpetusPEF_January-2014.pdf.

Jackson, P. (1968). *Life in Classrooms* (New York: Teachers College Press).

Jones, C. (2022). Essex School Cannot Afford Textbooks Due to Cost of Living Crisis, *BBC News* (8 September). Available at: https://www.bbc.co.uk/news/uk-england-essex-62828555.

Katz, M. B. (2013 [1989]). *The Undeserving Poor: America's Enduring Confrontation with Poverty* (New York: Oxford University Press).

Kerley, P. (2015). What is Your 21st Century Social Class?, *BBC Magazine* (7 December). Available at: https://www.bbc.co.uk/news/magazine-34766169.

Latham, D. (2002). *How Children Learn to Write: Supporting and Developing Children's Writing in Schools* (London: Paul Chapman).

Levitin, D. (2015). *The Organized Mind: The Science of Preventing Overload, Increasing Productivity and Restoring Focus* (London: Penguin Random House).

Lorayne, H. and Lucas, J. (1996). *The Memory Book: The Classic Guide to Improving Your Memory at Work, at School and at Play* (New York: Random House).

Lough, C. (2022). New Crackdown on GCSE Questions with Middle-Class Bias, *The Independent* (12 May). Available at: https://www.independent.co.uk/news/uk/aqa-maths-england-english-ofqual-b2077543.html.

Lui, W. M. (2011). *Social Class and Classism in the Helping Professions: Research, Theory, and Practice* (Thousand Oaks, CA: SAGE).

Macfarlane, R. (2021). *Obstetrics for Schools: A Guide to Eliminating Failure and Ensuring the Safe Delivery of All Learners* (Carmarthen: Crown House Publishing).

Major, L. E. and Machin, S. (2019). *Social Mobility* (Centre for Economic Performance 2019 Election Analysis Series) (November). Available at: https://cep.lse.ac.uk/pubs/download/ea045.pdf.

Miller, A. (2000 [1947]). *All My Sons* (London: Penguin).

Monroe, J. (2022). Poverty Leaves Scars for Life – I'm Still Scared of Strangers at the Door and Bills Through the Letterbox, *The Guardian* (16 June). Available at: https://www.theguardian.com/commentisfree/2022/jun/16/poverty-scars-life-impact-cost-of-living-crisis-felt-for-years.

Morgan, N. (2013). *Blame My Brain: The Amazing Teenage Brain Revealed* (London: Walker Books).

Myhill, D. and Fisher, S. (2005). *Informing Practice in English* (London: Ofsted). Available at: https://dera.ioe.ac.uk/5475.

Nilsson, N. J. (2014). *Understanding Beliefs* (Cambridge, MA: MIT Press).

Nussbaum, M. C. (2018). *Anger and Forgiveness: Resentment, Generosity, Justice* (New York: Oxford University Press).

O'Brien, D. (2014). *How to Develop a Brilliant Memory Week by Week: 52 Proven Ways to Enhance Your Memory Skills* (London: Watkins Publishing).

O'Brien, D., Laurison, D., Friedman, S. and Miles, A. (2016). Are the Creative Industries Meritocratic? An Analysis of the 2014 British Labour Force Survey, *Cultural Trends*, 25, 116–131.

O'Brien, D. (2019). Class and Publishing: Who Is Missing from the Numbers? In K. de Waal (ed.), *Common People: An Anthology of Working-Class Writers* (London: Unbound), pp. 275–280.

Office for National Statistics (2021). Suicide by Occupation, England: 2011 to 2015 (Data and Analysis from Census 2021). Available at: https://www.ons.gov.uk/peoplepopulationandcommunity/birthsdeathsandmarriages/deaths/articles/suicidebyoccupation/england2011to2015.

Ofsted (2019). School Inspection Handbook (updated 13 September 2023). Available at: https://www.gov.uk/government/publications/school-inspection-handbook-eif.

Ofsted (2023). Inspection of Havelock Academy (11–12 January). Available at: https://reports.ofsted.gov.uk/provider/23/135294.

Organisation for Economic Co-operation and Development (2016). *PISA 2015 Results (Volume II): Policies and Practices for Successful Schools* (Paris: OECD Publishing). Available at: https://doi.org/10.1787/9789264267510-en.

Organisation for Economic Co-operation and Development (2018). *The Future of Education and Skills: Education 2030* (Paris: OECD Publishing). Available at: https://www.oecd.org/education/2030/E2030%20Position%20Paper%20(05.04.2018).pdf.

Oxfam (2023). *Survival of the Richest: How We Must Tax the Super-Rich Now to Fight Inequality*. Available at: https://oxfamilibrary.openrepository.com/bitstream/handle/10546/621477/bp-survival-of-the-richest-160123-en.pdf.

Paine, T. (1792). Letter Addressed to the Addressers, on the Late Proclamation (London: H. D. Symonds and T. C. Rickman). Available at: https://www.gutenberg.org/files/31270/31270-h/31270-h.htm.

Peters, S. (2012). *The Chimp Paradox: The Mind Management Programme to Help You Achieve Success, Confidence and Happiness* (London: Vermilion).

Pigliucci, M. (2017). *How to be a Stoic: Ancient Wisdom for Modern Living* (London: Rider).

Piketty, T. (2017). *Capital in the Twenty-First Century* (Cambridge, MA: Harvard University Press).

Piketty, T. (2020). 'The Current Economic System Is Not Working When It Comes to Solving Inequality', *London School of Economics and Political Science* (21 February). Available at: https://blogs.lse.ac.uk/europpblog/2020/02/21/thomas-piketty-the-current-economic-system-is-not-working-when-it-comes-to-solving-inequality.

Pink, D. (2018). *Drive: The Surprising Truth About What Motivates Us* (London: Canongate Books).

Research Outreach (2021). Classism in Education Still Exists: Here's What to Do About It (5 February). Available at: https://researchoutreach.org/articles/classism-education-exists-heres-what-about.

Robson, D. (2022). *The Expectation Effect: How Your Mindset Can Transform Your Life* (London: Canongate Books).

Rose, J. (2001). *The Intellectual Life of the British Working Classes* (London: Yale University Press).

Rutherford, A. (2021). *How to Argue with a Racist: History, Science, Race and Reality* (London: Weidenfeld & Nicolson).

Sandel, M. (2020). *The Tyranny of Merit: What's Become of the Common Good?* (London: Penguin Random House).

Savage, M. (2015). *Social Class in the 21st Century* (London: Pelican).

Smith, J. (2022). *Why Has Nobody Told Me This Before?* (London: Michael Joseph).

Snelson, J. S. (1992). Ideological Immune System: Resistance to New Ideas in Science, *Skeptic*, 1(4), 444–455.

Social Mobility Commission (2019a). Elitism in Britain, 2019 [press release] (24 June). Available at: https://www.gov.uk/government/news/elitism-in-britain-2019.

Social Mobility Commission (2019b). *Elitist Britain 2019: The Educational Backgrounds of Britain's Leading People* (24 June). Available at: https://www.gov.uk/government/publications/elitist-britain-2019/elitist-britain-2019-the-educational-backgrounds-of-britains-leading-people.

Social Mobility Commission (2020). *Social Mobility Barometer: Public Attitudes to Social Mobility in the UK, 2019 to 2020* (21 January). Available at: https://www.gov.uk/government/publications/social-mobility-barometer-poll-results-2019/social-mobility-barometer-public-attitudes-to-social-mobility-in-the-uk-2019-to-2020.

Southey, R. (1851). *The Complete Poetical Works of Robert Southey* (New York: D. Appleton & Company).

Staufenberg, J. (2016). Private Schools Spend Three Times More on Each Pupil, *Schools Week* (14 October). Available at: https://schoolsweek.co.uk/private-schools-spend-three-times-more-on-each-pupil.

Stiglitz, J. E., Sen, A. and Fitoussi, J-P. (2009). *Report by the Commission for the Measurement of Economic Performance and Social Progress.* Available at: https://ec.europa.eu/eurostat/documents/8131721/8131772/Stiglitz-Sen-Fitoussi-Commission-report.pdf.

Stuart, K. and Maynard, L. (2017). *Promoting Young People's Empowerment and Agency: A Critical Framework for Practice* (Abingdon and New York: Routledge).

Tahir, I. (2022). The UK Education System Preserves Inequality, *Institute for Fiscal Studies* (13 September). Available at: https://ifs.org.uk/inequality/the-uk-education-system-preserves-inequality.

Tassoni, P. (2016). *Reducing Educational Disadvantage: A Strategic Approach in the Early Years* (London: Bloomsbury).

Tonic, G. (2022). Wearing Masks: How to Navigate Your Career as a Working-Class Person, *Dazed* (13 May). Available at: https://www.dazeddigital.com/life-culture/article/56090/1/wearing-masks-how-to-navigate-your-career-as-a-working-class-person.

Tracy, B. (2013). *Eat That Frog! Get More of the Important Things Done Today* (London: Hodder & Stoughton).

Tschannen-Moran, M. and Gareis, C. R. (2015). Principals, Trust, and Cultivating Vibrant Schools, *Societies*, 5, 256–276. Available at: https://

www.researchgate.net/publication/315364994_Principals_Trust_and_Cultivating_Vibrant_Schools.

Tyler, I. (2013). *Revolting Subjects: Social Abjection and Resistance in Neoliberal Britain* (London and New York: Zed Books).

Urban, T. (2016). 100 Blocks a Day, *Wait But Why* (21 October). Available at: https://waitbutwhy.com/2016/10/100-blocks-day.html.

Valle, A., Regueiro, B., Núñez, J. C., Rodríguez, S., Piñeiro, I. and Rosário, P. (2016). Academic Goals, Student Homework Engagement, and Academic Achievement in Elementary School, *Frontiers in Psychology*, 7, 463. https://doi.org/10.3389/fpsyg.2016.00463

Walker, M. (2018). *Why We Sleep: The New Science of Sleep and Dreams* (London: Penguin Random House).

Walton, A. (2021). The Quiet Disappearance of Britain's Public Libraries, *Tribune* (17 January). Available at: https://tribunemag.co.uk/2021/01/the-quiet-disappearance-of-britains-public-libraries.

Weale, S. (2016). Sharp Rise in Children Receiving Private Tuition, *The Guardian* (8 September). Available at: https://www.theguardian.com/education/2016/sep/08/sharp-rise-in-children-receiving-private-tuition.

Weale, S. (2023). Texting Parents May Help Schools Tackle 'Truancy Crisis' in England, Say Experts, *The Guardian* (20 February). Available at: https://www.theguardian.com/education/2023/feb/20/texting-parents-may-help-schools-tackle-truancy-crisis-in-england-say-experts.

Wilde, O. (1992 [1890]). *The Picture of Dorian Gray* (Ware: Wordsworth Editions).

Young, M. (1994 [1958]). *The Rise of the Meritocracy* (New Brunswick, NJ and London: Transaction Publishers).

SQUARE PEGS

INCLUSIVITY, COMPASSION AND FITTING IN – A GUIDE FOR SCHOOLS

FRAN MORGAN WITH ELLIE COSTELLO

ISBN: 9781781354100

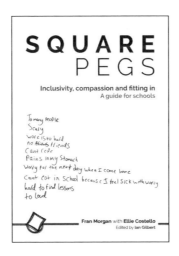

Over the last few years, changes in education have made it increasingly hard for those children who don't 'fit' the system – the square pegs in a rigid system of round holes.

Budget cuts, the loss of support staff, an overly academic curriculum, problems in the special educational needs and disabilities (SEND) system and difficulties accessing mental health support have all compounded pre-existing problems with behaviour and attendance. The 'attendance = attainment' and zero-tolerance narrative is often at odds with the way schools want to work with their communities, and many school leaders don't know which approach to take.

This book will be invaluable in guiding leaders and teaching staff through the most effective ways to address this challenge. It covers a broad spectrum of opportunity, from proven psychological approaches to technological innovations. It tests the boundaries of the current system in terms of curriculum, pedagogy and statutory Department for Education guidance. And it also presents a clear, legalese-free view of education, SEND and human rights law, where leaders have been given responsibility for its implementation but may not always fully understand the legal ramifications of their decisions or may be pressured into unlawful behaviour.

THE LEARNING IMPERATIVE

RAISING PERFORMANCE IN ORGANISATIONS BY IMPROVING LEARNING

MARK BURNS AND ANDY GRIFFITH

ISBN: 9781785832697

In *The Learning Imperative* Mark Burns and Andy Griffith examine the key ingredients that ensure effective learning, and offer leaders step-by-step guidance on how they can achieve it in their own teams and organisations.

Learning is central to the long-term success of any team – and is far too important to dismiss or to relegate to a 'nice to do' list. In *The Learning Imperative*, bestselling authors Burns and Griffith explore the common barriers to effective learning and present a range of practical tools and strategies to help teams bring about – and reap the benefits of – a more positive culture around training and development.

Together they map out the key stages of the learning journey and provide a comprehensive guide for team leaders and managers who want to improve learning in their teams. They also share essential advice on the design and delivery of effective training programmes, and punctuate their instruction with a range of illuminating case studies drawn from real-life contexts across the public, private and third sectors.

OUTSTANDING TEACHING:
TEACHING BACKWARDS

ANDY GRIFFITH AND MARK BURNS

ISBN: 9781845909291

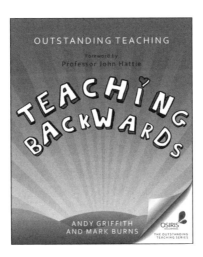

Teaching is a demanding job and one which doesn't afford a lot of spare time to devote to reflecting on practice. Teachers need resources that are clear, concise, and practical. *Teaching Backwards* is just that. It's packed with case studies from primary and secondary teachers, and it's punctuated with reflective questions that invite teachers to slow down and do some thinking about how they currently teach, so that their teaching can have an even more powerful impact on learners. Well-informed by research and with a clear action plan of what to do, and what not to do, *Teaching Backwards* is a guide to ensuring that learners make outstanding progress, lesson by lesson and year on year. Develop learners' knowledge, attitudes, skills and habits (KASH) and help shape the class any teacher would love to inherit. It is not just about results, but building the resilience and mindsets in learners that will enable them to master any challenge they may face, in the classroom and throughout their lives.

Discover the powerful effects of teaching backwards for yourself. Topics covered include: setting high expectations, starting points, defining and demystifying the destination, looking for proof of learning, challenge, feedback.

OUTSTANDING TEACHING: ENGAGING LEARNERS

ANDY GRIFFITH AND MARK BURNS

ISBN: 9781845907976

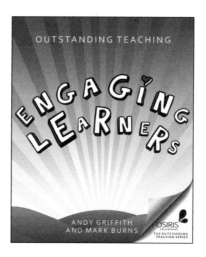

At the end of every week many teachers leave school exhausted. In an era when responsibility for exam results lies with them and not their students it's time to redress the balance so that students take more of the responsibility for their learning and progress. A class can be skilled and motivated to learn without a teacher always having to lead. Engaging learners in this way unpicks intrinsic motivation, the foundation that underpins a productive learning environment and helps to develop independent learning, creativity and improved behaviour management.

Based on five years of intensive research through Osiris Educational's award-winning Outstanding Teaching Intervention programme, during which the authors have trained more than 500 teachers to teach over 1,300 lessons in schools nationwide, this book is packed with proven advice and innovative tools developed in these successful outstanding lessons.

Written in the same humorous, thought-provoking style with which they both teach and train, Andy and Mark aim to challenge all who teach, from NQTs to seasoned professionals, to reflect on their day-to-day practice and set an agenda for sustainable teacher and leadership improvement.